Landels, John G.

Music in ancient Greece &
Rome.

DATE DUE			

DEMCO

MUSIC IN ANCIENT GREECE AND ROME

MUSIC IN ANCIENT GREECE AND ROME

John G. Landels

London and New York

First published 1999
by Routledge
2 Park Square, Milton Park, Abingdon, Oxon, OX14 4RN

Simultaneously published in the USA and Canada
by Routledge
711 Third Avenue, New York, NY 10017
Reprinted 2000

Transferred to Digital Printing 2007

Routledge is an imprint of the Taylor & Francis Group

British Library Cataloguing in Publication Data
A catalogue record for this book is available from the British
Library

Library of Congress Cataloguing in Publication Data
Landels, John G. (John Gray), 1926–
Music in ancient Greece and Rome / John G. Landels.
p. cm.
Includes bibliographical references and index.
1. Music, Greek and Roman–History and criticism. I. Title.
ML169.L24 1999
780′938–dc21 98–3051
CIP
MN r98

ISBN 0–415–16776–0
ISBN 0–415–24843–4

Cover illustration: Group of musicians, Miriamin
3rd century AD, Syria.
Cover design: Leigh Hurlock

Publisher's Note
The publisher has gone to great lengths to ensure the quality of
this reprint but points out that some imperfections in the
original may be apparent

CONTENTS

FIGURES

PREFACE

This book is not intended to be a definitive textbook on the music of the ancient Greeks and Romans; it has a more modest objective – to provide an introduction to the study of an interesting (at times baffling) subject, aimed at the student of Classical civilization, the student of the history of music, and at the general reader with an interest in either or both. It may perhaps be helpful to explain a number of policy decisions which have governed the layout and content.

First, this book concentrates very closely on the sonic and practical aspects of music in the ancient civilizations – the instruments and how they were played, and the sounds, notes and rhythms, in so far as we can re-create them. (To this end, I have experimented in Chapter 4 with English translations which reproduce the rhythms of the Greek words; this is a difficult exercise, and if the results have a certain flavour of William McGonagall, I must ask the reader's indulgence.) It examines the notation the ancients used, and the very small number of musical scores which have survived. I am also very concerned with the role of music in the performance of drama, and in other poetical genres which we do not immediately associate with music. On the intellectual side, the Greek theories about sound, pitch and harmony are treated in some detail, because they yield a lot of information on intonations, scale structures and the sound qualities of various instruments. But on the moral and aesthetic side, the Greek and Roman attitudes towards music, and their suppositions about its possible moral influence, and its role in education and the formation of character, have been copiously discussed by many authors; I feel that, to be honest, I have little to add, and there seems little point in going over such well-trodden ground.

Second, there is the question of the geographical range and the timespan. The great majority of works on Greek music tend to ignore the Roman inheritance of this important tradition, or to pass it over in a few disparaging sentences. It is true, as will be made clear in Chapter 8, that music was of much less importance to the Romans than it had for the Greeks; but that does not mean that the Romans, the ancestors of the nation who would consider themselves the most musical in Europe, were lacking in musical sense or in enthusiasm for music as listeners. Accordingly I have not, as is the fashion, ignored the years after the late Hellenistic period, but have pursued the story of music in comedy right through to Plautus and Terence, and tried to assess the musical culture of the early Empire, and the extent to which the Romans understood Greek acoustical theory.

Third, there is the question of documentation. The majority of Classical scholars have always felt it incumbent upon them to back up every assertion about every subject with a number of references to ancient authors and commentators, and to adduce comparisons or disagreements from the secondary literature. This results in texts with anything up to a hundred or more footnotes per chapter. It is, of course, a fact of life that scholars who are 'upwardly mobile' are forced to do this in order to prove their credentials, and demonstrate the range and depth of their reading; the consideration of whether or not it is helpful to their readers is of secondary importance. But times change, and readers change in their circumstances and needs, and books must change with them. It is probable that only a tiny minority of the potential readers of this book are fortunate enough to be in or near a university which still has a Classics Department and a well-stocked library; for the rest, persistent references to works which are totally inaccessible to them is quite useless, and can be very annoying.

I have therefore reduced the documentation to the absolute minimum, and that has been relegated to the notes at the end of the volume. I have tried to make the text readable and understandable on its own, should the reader prefer to go through it without consulting the notes. I have also deliberately confined the scope of the references. The great majority are either to source material (and comment thereon) in one or other of Andrew Barker's excellent volumes (*Greek Musical Writings*, Vols I and II) or to more extended discussions of various topics in Martin West's excellent, magisterial and extremely full treatment of the entire subject (*Ancient Greek Music*). If my introductory work can encourage and persuade the reader to go on to a deeper study of the subject in these volumes (which are fairly recent and should not be too difficult to access) I shall be well pleased.

My interest in Greek music dates from my student days at Aberdeen University and at Cambridge; over the years since then I have been most fortunate in receiving help from many scholars and friends, some of whom I would like to acknowledge here.

On my first appointment to Hull University, my Head of Department, the late Prof. M.M. Gillies, gave me much encouragement and advice on how to choose, and embark on, my first research project, for which I was most grateful.

There can be no student of Greek music who is not indebted in some degree to the late Prof. R.P. Winnington-Ingram, and my own debt is great. He supervised my research for my doctorate with great kindness, much helpful advice and acute but always good-natured and constructive criticism. It is largely owing to him that I was introduced to Dr Papadimitriou, and allowed to examine the Brauron aulos. I received similar help and encouragement from the other examiner of my thesis, Mrs Isobel Henderson.

I am also grateful to three postgraduate students whose researches on ancient Greek music I supervised – Dr Helen Roberts, Dr Richard Witt and Dr Stelios Psaroudakis. Their fresh ideas, challenging questions and the fruits of their researches have been most stimulating.

Over the years I have persuaded a number of talented musicians to record performances of ancient Greek music, which I have used to illustrate lectures on the subject – David Joyner (baritone), Raymond Foster (horn), Stella Cooke (cor anglais), Tessa Jones (syrinx), Patricia Kerr (mezzo-soprano) and Nigel Burton who, with three baritone colleagues, sang the first Delphic hymn as a *choros*. Each of these performances has been different, and each has added to my understanding and appreciation of the compositions.

The illustrations posed a problem. There are a number of well-known vase-paintings which have appeared in almost every book written about ancient Greek music, and some others which are potentially more interesting, but are imperfect photos of badly damaged vases. I therefore decided to use line-drawings, in which the important details can be picked out and emphasized. I am glad to have been able to call on the services of a skilled archaeological draughtsman, Brian Williams, to draw the 'musical' ones; the technical and scientific ones were drawn by Dr David Sim of Reading University Engineering Department.

More recently, in the preparation of the final version, I have had helpful advice on the bibliography of Greek metre from Dr Laetitia Parker. Miss Stella Cooke (oboist) read Chapter 2(a) in draft, and gave useful advice on the behaviour (and vagaries) of reeds and reed instruments.

The final version of the text was produced on a newly-acquired computer, over which I cannot yet claim complete mastery, and I am very grateful to my expert advisor, Toni Hunter, who guided me through the Windows to Image-in (version 3), and rescued me from the havoc wrought by Winword, a Charybdis-like being who on several occasions corrupted and devoured text files, but unlike Charybdis did not throw them up again after an interval.

Finally, and most importantly, I must thank my wife Jocelyn for her unfailing support over many years, for help in checking, counter-checking and remembering details. To her this book is affectionately dedicated.

Note

The musical letter-notation follows the conventional pattern; middle c and the octave above it are written as c′d′e′f′g′a′b′ and the octave above that as c″d″e″f″g″ etc. The octave below middle c is written cdefgab, and the octave below that as CDEFGAB.

1

MUSIC IN GREEK LIFE, POETRY AND DRAMA

Music played a very important part in almost every aspect of life for the ancient Greeks. It was heard at their public gatherings and at their private dinner-parties, at their ceremonies, both joyful and sad; it was heard at every act of worship, whenever people called upon, or prayed to, or gave thanks to the gods. It was heard in their theatres, whenever tragedies or comedies were staged, and on their sports grounds as the athletes competed. It was heard in their schools, on board their warships, and even on the battlefield. If ever a people had a just claim to be called music-lovers, it was the Greeks.

In reviewing their various musical activities, it will be necessary to make frequent mention of some of the instruments which were in general use. A detailed account of all the important instruments is given in the next chapter, but for the time being it will suffice to describe three of them very briefly:

1) The kithara was a large wooden stringed instrument, played with a plectrum. It was supported by the left arm high in front of the player, who normally played standing. The instrument called *phorminx* by Homer and by some of the later poets was a forerunner of the kithara, similar in sound and function, but a bit smaller.
2) The aulos was a pair of pipes, with vibrating reeds in their mouthpieces, held out in front of the player.
3) The lyre was a smaller stringed instrument, played in the same way as a kithara, but often held lower down – on the player's lap if he was seated.

Music was never far away from the great religious festivals. The two most important Athenian ones, the Panathenaia and the Great Dionysia, were reorganized and expanded in the latter part of the sixth century BC, and in their developed form involved a great deal of music.

The Panathenaia was celebrated by the whole population of Athens and the surrounding district (Attica) in the summer of each year, with a special

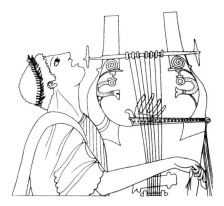

Figure 1.1 Kithara

Figure 1.2 Aulos

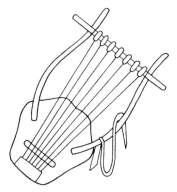

Figure 1.3 Lyre

version, the Great Panathenaia, every fourth year. For that occasion a new robe was woven for the ancient statue of Athena, which was housed in the old temple, the remains of which are still visible on the Acropolis (the Erechtheum overlaps part of its foundations).

The celebrations each year involved a grand singing procession which started near the boundary wall of Athens and wound its way all through the city, across the market-place (*Agora*) and up the slope of the Acropolis, accompanied by musicians and dancers. The musicians in the procession are conventionally represented in vase-paintings by two aulos-players and two kithara-players (there being no room for more figures) and in sculpture by four of each.[1] These probably represent quite a large number of musicians, but it is difficult to be sure about this. There are very few references to large numbers of musicians playing 'in concert' earlier than the third century BC.

The nature of the music which was played and sung can be guessed. There was a type of song called a *paian*, which was most commonly sung in honour of Apollo, but could equally well be addressed to Athena. It is usually a solemn type of composition, expressing hope of deliverance from a dire peril, or as a thank-offering after escape. If it was sung on the occasion of a procession to the shrine of the god, it might be preceded or followed by a type of hymn called a *prosodion*, or processional, in which the god was invoked and praised; this was sometimes written in a different metre from that of the *paian*, but like the *paian* it was usually accompanied by a stringed instrument. The composition of Limenios, which is discussed in detail in Chapter 10, is in the form of a *paian* and *prosodion*.

It was also customary for musicians, usually aulos-players, to play while sacrifices were being offered, or any other solemn ritual was being carried out. As the Panathenaia involved numerous animal sacrifices, and every fourth year the changing of Athena's robe, they must have been fully employed in this capacity. Moreover, apart from the strictly religious part of the festival there were competitive musical contests of all kinds, involving instrumental soloists, solo singers and choral singers and dancers. In fact, throughout most of the festival days the sound of music must have been almost continuous.

The other major Athenian festival, in which music featured even more prominently, was the Great Dionysia, held annually in late March or early April.[2] This was the time of year when the sea became navigable after the winter storms, and things in general 'opened up'.

The festivities occupied several days, and included a number of musical events. The most important ritual involved carrying a very ancient image of the god Dionysos in procession to the boundaries of the ancient Athenian territory and 'welcoming' him once more; this was intended as a gesture of apology for the fact that his original entry had been greeted

3

with less than full enthusiasm. The statue was then carried back to his sanctuary in Athens (which was at the rear of the stage buildings of the theatre) to the accompaniment of ribald songs, reflecting the fact that it was in part a fertility ritual. All this would involve a lot of music.

When the procession returned to the city centre there were a number of musical events – competitions in aulos-playing, kithara-playing and singing; the only entertainment which perhaps did not involve music in the literal sense (though the Greeks would certainly have called it *mousikē*) was the recitation of the poems of Homer by 'rhapsodes' (see p. 10). One which certainly involved a great deal of music was the performance of dithyrambs.

In its very early stages the dithyramb was apparently just a merry song, sung by anybody who was feeling up in the world (usually after a few jars). In the sixth century BC it seems to have become organized into a song for performance by a *choros* of men or boys, accompanied by an aulos-player. At some time early in the fifth century professional aulos-players began to be employed, and they seem to have taken on themselves a more prominent role, putting in 'intermezzi' (*anabolai*) and indulging in elaborate displays of technique. There were calls for them to be put in their place; a poet called Pratinas is quoted[3] as saying: 'Let the *aulos* dance behind, for it is the servant (not the master).'

Dithyrambs were also performed at a number of other Greek festivals, including a number which were not dedicated to Dionysos,[4] but the greatest celebration of this art form was without doubt the Great Dionysia. For certain administrative purposes, all Athenian citizens were assigned to one of ten 'tribes' or clans, and each tribe had to provide two choruses, one of up to fifty men and the other of the same number of boys. Each chorus performed a dithyramb, and there was fierce competition between them for the prizes. Compositions were specially commissioned for the occasion, and the tribes vied with each other to secure the services of the best composers, musicians and chorus-masters. We do not know precisely where they were performed, but it must have been in a wide open space with room for some hundreds of singers and a large audience. The choirs at this festival apparently stood in a circle, and did not dance as part of the performance, as the 'choruses' in the drama did.

From the musical point of view, the drama festival was much the most important part of the Great Dionysia. It involved tragedies, comedies and satyr-plays, which will be dealt with individually later on.

The great games of ancient Greece, which were in themselves religious festivals, involved a lot of musical activity. At the other games (the Olympics, the Isthmians, and the Nemeans) the contests were almost entirely athletic, but at the Pythian games at Delphi (held in honour of Apollo, the divine musician), there were contests for musicians who performed with the same competitive fervour as the athletes. There were a number of different 'events', in which the players could show their special skill. The most prestigious was 'singing to the kithara' (*kitharōdia* in Greek), an art form in which one man (women never competed) was poet, composer, singer and his own accompanist. The compositions they wrote and performed were called 'kithara-singers' *nomoi*; this was the genre in which the most famous innovators made their mark, and to excel in it was their ultimate ambition. There were also contests in kithara-playing on its own, called by the Greeks *psile kitharisis*, a title meaning 'mere' or 'bald' kithara-playing, which may possibly convey a disparaging tone. Perhaps the occasional virtuoso player whose singing voice or poetic skill did not match his playing might compensate by a brilliant display of instrumental technique. The woodwind players were not left out either; they performed solos which were known as 'aulos-players' *nomoi* – extended instrumental pieces with a number of 'movements', some of which seem to have been in the nature of programme music. One famous example told, in five sections, the story of the victory of Apollo over the mythical monster called the Python at Delphi – a very suitable subject for the venue. There were also vocal compositions, intended to be sung to an aulos accompaniment, which of course would require two musicians. This type of duet performance was called *aulōdia*, and figured in the programme at Delphi from a very early date. One ancient writer tells us[5] that some of the typical compositions for *aulōdia* had tragic or funereal associations, and for this reason were eliminated from the programme in about 578 BC, but this is not certain.

Music was by no means confined to the Pythian games, or to the strictly musical contests. There are plenty of vase-paintings from the mid-sixth century BC onwards which show athletes competing in almost every kind of event – running, long-jump, discus, javelin, and others – with an aulos-player standing nearby and obviously playing (Figure 1.4). It is tempting to wonder whether this helped or hindered the athletes.

It is also well known that 'victory odes' (*epinikia* in Greek) were composed in honour of those who won the most important prizes. One of the most successful poet/composers in this genre was Pindar, and a considerable amount of his work survives; unfortunately, we have only the words without the musical notation. He celebrated drivers of chariots (the most wealthy of the competitors, and so the most likely to commission him), boxers, wrestlers, 'long-runners' (who ran a distance of about 2 miles), pentathlon winners, and others. He even wrote an ode celebrating a victory by an aulos-player called Midas who came from Akragas (the modern Agrigento). Luckily, the text of this poem (Pythian 12) survives, and the remarks of some ancient commentators give us some useful evidence on the construction of that instrument. There are some hints in the text of Pindar's odes on the mode of performance, as he writes of himself and his singers in a proud and self-conscious tone. He seems to

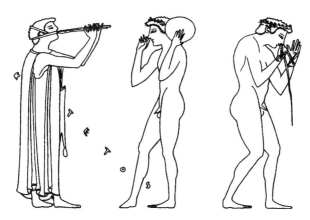

Figure 1.4 Aulos-player with discus-thrower and boxer

have employed a chorus of young men who sang and danced, accompanied by a *kithara* (for which he deliberately uses the old-fashioned word *phorminx*) or an *aulos*, or both.[6] Where he mentions percussion, he is not in fact referring to his own compositions; for example, in two contexts[7] he mentions 'clashing cymbals' and 'beating drums'; but he is describing the worship of Demeter or Rhea, not a victory celebration. Again, on one occasion he calls on someone who happens to bear the same name as the Roman hero, Aineias, to 'urge his comrades on to sing of . . .', though whether Aineias was a soloist, or the chorus-master, we cannot be sure.[8] It appears that the poet himself usually played the *kithara* accompaniment, and directed the performance. There are, however, a number of allusions to 'despatching' an ode to a distant place.[9] This would occur when the performance was to be given in the victor's home town after his return, and the poet, who was based in Thebes, would not necessarily travel there. It seems likely that there would be a number of professional players available to direct performances ('have *kithara*, will travel') who could be coached by Pindar and taught the music orally. It has also been suggested that the dance movements were largely traditional, and could be semi-improvised on the spot.

These were the great public occasions. But in private life too, in the home and among friends, there was a lot of music-making. The most important Greek social institution, the drinking-party (*symposion*) was characterized by witty conversation, music and songs. In the famous dialogue of Plato called the *Symposion* we are told that the host had provided a professional female player of the *aulos* to entertain the guests; when they decide to have an intellectual conversation instead, she is sent out of the room 'to play to the women inside, or to herself'.[10] It should be noted that the women in question would be the host's wife and his daughters, if any, who would take no part in the proceedings, being shut away in a back room to avoid embarrassment (it is not always clear for whom). The women who appear in the party scenes in vase-paintings are prostitutes, many of whom were musicians; they entertained the guests with music in the early part of the evening, transferring later to the other, older aspect of their profession. The characteristic instrument for such players was the aulos, and the connection was so firmly established that the Greek word for a female aulos-player, *aulētris*, was regularly used to mean a high-class prostitute. They were not normally members of the household staff, but were hired for special occasions from an agency.

In his description of a symposium, Xenophon tells of a professional entertainer who comes from Syracuse, and has a girl aulos-player, a girl dancer and a boy who plays the lyre and sings. The girl dancer also performs a juggling act with twelve hoops, and jumps through a frame set with knives. One of the guests attempts to emulate – or parody – these acts.

But the entertainment of the guests at a symposium was not confined to professionals. It was part of an Athenian youth's education to learn to play the lyre (though not the kithara, which was considered more difficult, and appropriate only for professionals) and he might well be expected to contribute his share to an evening's singing. The characteristic piece for such occasions was called a *skolion* in Greek, and a few snatches of these frivolous but very popular drinking-songs have been preserved.

The comedy-writers exploited the comic potential of the symposium situation. In Aristophanes' *Wasps* (produced in 422 BC) there is a scene[11] in which an elderly, vulgar and uncouth man is told what to expect when he dines in elegant, aristocratic surroundings. He must be prepared to 'cap' short snatches of song sung by the other guests, and contribute his own

Figure 1.5 Aulos-players practising their arts

share of challenges. There is no mention made of playing a lyre, but it was commonly assumed that an educated upper-class Athenian would be able to do so. (In an earlier passage of the play, where a dog is on trial for theft of some cheese, his defence counsel asks for leniency, on the grounds that 'he never learnt to play a lyre' – that is, he did not have a proper education.) In fact, when he gets to the party the old scoundrel tells obscene jokes, gets very drunk and runs off with the girl aulos-player, thus depriving the other guests of their accustomed pleasures.

An episode in the *Clouds*, probably written at about the same time,[12] suggests that the practice of guests singing at a party was rather 'old hat' by this time. This episode is a normal meal with father and son at home; when the father asks his son to 'take up the lyre and sing a melody of Simonides' (which would have dated from the early fifth century) the son says that singing songs between drinks is 'old-fashioned stuff' (*archaion*). He then proceeds, much to his father's disgust, to disparage Simonides and Aeschylus, and when pressed to sing something modern, obliges with a bit of Euripides, with a musical style that is 'way-out' and subject matter which is shocking (an incestuous relationship).

Finally, it should be said that even a Greek drinking-party had its more serious moments. All but the most boorish or impious revellers would pause at the end of the meal which preceded the serious drinking and pour three libations of wine on the table or on an altar; if there was an aulos-player in attendance, he or she would play a special 'libation-melody' (in Greek, *spondeion*) while this was being done. Hence the sound of the aulos and the songs became for the Greeks powerful symbols of peacetime and revelry. Both War and Death are deplored as being 'without the aulos' or 'without the lyre'.[13]

However, even in wartime, and on active service, they did not abandon music altogether. We cannot be quite certain whether Greek soldiers normally marched in step; they are certainly shown doing so, led by an aulos-player, on a famous early Corinthian vase of the late seventh century BC (Figure 1.6), but it must be said that other contemporary pictures show synchronised steps in the most unlikely situations – e.g. huntsmen attacking a boar.[14]

A version of the trumpet (see p. 79) was used to give commands on the battlefield, but its notes were almost exclusively connected with war, and it was not considered a truly musical instrument.[15] The warships of the Greek navies were propelled by oarsmen, and the most widely used, the trireme, had a complement of 170 rowers. It was clearly important to keep them strictly in time and, apart from verbal commands given by the boatswain, some percussion instruments, and occasionally an aulos, were used. On one famous occasion, the return of Alkibiades from exile, a well-known virtuoso player performed the office.[16] There could be no more telling illustration of the way in which music sprang to the mind of

Figure 1.6 Soldiers on the march

the Greek at war than the account put into the mouth of a messenger by Aeschylus in his tragedy *The Persians*, based on the historical events which reached a climax in the naval battle of Salamis in 480 BC:

> But when the dawn, borne by her white steeds
> Possessed the whole earth, brilliant to behold,
> First came the sonorous music of the Greek war-chant,
> The prayer for victory, and shrill from island rocks
> The echo cried in answer. Then the foreign foe
> Were gripped with fear, their minds perplexed; the battle hymn
> Was sung by Greeks not in retreat, but surging into battle,
> Their hearts and courage high . . .
>
> (lines 386–394)

The importance of music in Greek life is not a strange phenomenon, nor one which is difficult to understand. But the mention of poetry in the title which I have given to this chapter may cause some puzzlement. We tend to think of poetry in terms of the spoken word, or the printed word on a page. Drama also we receive by means of the spoken word, apart from the particular case of opera, which forms only a tiny minority of our total drama repertoire. But for the Greeks the sung word was almost as commonly heard, and certainly as important, as the spoken word, not only in their drama, but in a number of poetic forms which we do not particularly associate with music. The poet of the Iliad, invoking the Muse in the first line of his epic poem, asks her, not to 'speak' or 'tell' of the wrath of Achilles, but to 'sing' of it. It is difficult to say with certainty what this meant in practice for the epic poet or minstrel. When Homer portrays such artists performing in the 'heroic' world (in the palace of

Alkinoos, king of the Phaeacians, in Book 8 of the Odyssey, and in Odysseus' own house in Book 1 and elsewhere) he regularly describes how they play a few introductory notes on the *phorminx*, and then begin to 'sing' (*a-eidein*), and indeed the word for a minstrel is 'singer' (*a-oidos*). But the performance of a long narrative poem is more likely to have been in the nature of a sing-song chant or recitative than singing as we understand the term. In vase-paintings of two centuries later there are a number of portrayals of 'rhapsodes' – professional reciters who gave performances of excerpts from the Homeric poems and others at the great public festivals. But although the second element of that word carries the connotation 'singers', they are not normally shown carrying a musical instrument, but merely a staff, which seems to have been used as a 'prop' in their semi-dramatic performances (Figure 1.7).

Plato wrote a short dialogue, the Ion, in which Socrates converses with one of these performers, and though there are references to 'singing' other 'poems', the word 'speak' is used in connection with epic, and there is no suggestion of an instrument in their talk. It may be that Homer himself, in the late eighth or early seventh century BC, was keeping up an old tradition of singing which lapsed not long after his time; it is hardly credible that something which appears to be so firmly grounded in folk-memory and in the language of epic should have been pure invention on the poet's part.

Figure 1.7 Rhapsode

Another important genre of literature in which music played a significant part was what the Greeks called lyric poetry. Whatever nuances the words 'lyric' and 'lyrical' may have for us, for them it simply meant a song to be sung to the accompaniment of a lyre-type instrument. From an early date this type of composition divided into two branches, known as the monodic lyric and the choral lyric. Monodic means 'sung solo', and in this type of song we find the earliest attempts to express personal emotion and to make personal comment on life, mankind and the contemporary scene. The two most famous composers of such lyric were Alkaios and Sappho, who both lived on the island of Lesbos in the early sixth century BC. Alkaios wrote songs about contemporary politics and the state of the world, and how a man might best react to it. Sappho, one of the very few women whose poetry has been preserved (though only in brief fragments) wrote highly evocative and atmospheric songs, some of them telling of her passionate feelings towards women. For the Greeks, the proper medium for this type of subject was the song, sung solo by the poet, who accompanied himself (or herself) on a lyre. There is a well-known vase-painting, thought by some[17] to be by the Brygos painter, dating from the early fifth century BC, which shows Sappho and Alkaios, both holding lyre-type instruments (Figure 1.8).

In addition to composing the appropriate music, Alkaios and Sappho each invented a pattern of rhythms for their songs, in the form of a stanza

Figure 1.8 Sappho and Alkaios

which came to be named after them. They did not, however, confine themselves to 'their own' rhythms, but used a range of metres, with lines of various lengths. Though not a single note of their music survives, we may be fairly confident that the distinctions, of what the Greeks later called *ethos*, between music for different moods and for different sentiments began to be drawn from this time onwards; the slow, sad music of Sappho lamenting her parting from a loved one would have had a very different pattern of notes, and a different style of melody, from one of Alkaios' stirring calls to his fellow-citizens to put right their political wrongs.

The other branch of lyric poetry which grew up alongside the monodic was the choral lyric. Indeed, some scholars have suggested[18] that the two forms are exemplified together in a single work, the 'Maiden-song' (Partheneion) of Alkman, a poet who worked in Sparta in the seventh century BC, and that this type of composition was the common origin of both. The conventional view for many years has been that the essential differences lay in the mode of performance and in the subject matter. It used to be accepted that the choral lyric was sung and danced by a *choros*, a group (most commonly of men, but sometimes of women or girls)[19] numbering anything from twelve to fifty, accompanied by an aulos-player or a kithara-player or both. The occasions on which they performed were public, and so the themes and subjects of this type of song were public. This has been called into question in recent times, but most disagreements can be attributed to the obvious fact that there is not always a clear-cut distinction between 'public' and 'private'.

We have already encountered the ode celebrating a victory at the great games, composed by Pindar. Such songs were also composed for religious festivals, and commonly incorporated the narration of a myth from the great Greek repertoire of stories. To what extent the *choros* mimed or acted out the story we do not know, but it seems likely that there was some theatrical element in the performance. Apart from Pindar's works, which date from the fifth century BC, the surviving remains of this type of composition are miserably small, but from a comparison between them and the fragments of solo lyric it is easy to see that the differences in tone and content are very marked. Whereas Alkaios speaks personally to his close friends, and directs his hatred against individuals, the choral lyric speaks to the public at large, and in much more universal terms. It very often deals with religious themes: mankind's dependence on the gods, and the need to observe the divine laws. It must be remembered that for the Greeks this was public business, and the concern of the city, not a matter for a man's individual conscience.

Another early genre of poetry which may have had a musical element is known as elegiac poetry. This is a verse form derived from the metre of epic poetry (see p. 115) with modifications in alternate lines. For a long time it was generally believed that poetry of this type was intended to be sung to the accompaniment of an aulos, but doubt has been cast on this theory. The problem arises from the fact that the main evidence is found in the works of an elegiac poet called Theognis, but it is not clear whether he is referring to a performance of his own work, or more generally to the contemporary musical scene.[20] There is also a further source of confusion in the Greek word *elegeios*, which may simply refer to the rhythmic pattern of the words, while the similar-sounding word *elegos* means a lament or dirge. It is known that this kind of song (which was also called a *thrēnos* in Greek) might be written in the elegiac metre[21] and accompanied by an aulos, but there is plenty of surviving poetry in the same metre which is by no means sad or funereal. In fact, the subject matter tends to be rather similar to that of the monodic lyric: personal reflections on life and love. Over a number of centuries the metre gradually became accepted as the medium for erotic or even obscene poetry – the ancient equivalent of the lewd limerick – of which there are many examples in the Palatine Anthology, a collection of miscellaneous poems in this metre by various authors, dating from the third century BC to the fifth century AD.

But the literary form in which music played the most important part was drama, both tragic and comic, and that strange form of drama which has no modern descendant, the satyr-play. What is more, the Greek practice contrasted strongly with that of almost all later cultures, in that the playwright was expected to compose the music, train the singers and direct the performance of his plays. The sneer aimed at Euripides (who was a very popular composer, his tunes being widely known and much admired) that one of his household slaves had collaborated in some of his compositions,[22] would be completely pointless unless it was the fixed rule that the poet should write all of it.

Aristotle, in his *Poetics*, traced the beginnings of tragic drama from 'the leaders of the dithyramb' meaning, presumably, that in a developed form of the dithyramb there were solo singers who led the dance movements.[23] The Greek word for an actor was *hypokritēs*, which meant the 'answerer' or 'respondent'. This has generally been taken to mean that in the very earliest stages of drama there was one actor who played all the individual parts, and engaged in dialogue with the *choros*. At some stage, he began to speak most of his part instead of singing it. Then (we do not know when) a second actor was brought in. Even then, there was comparatively little dialogue, and a great deal of the story was not acted, but narrated in song by the *choros*.

In the choral songs of Aeschylus, the earliest of the three great tragedians, there is a considerable amount of narrative, usually relating to the events which preceded the action of the play. The most striking examples are the first three choral songs in the *Agamemnon*, the first of which tells of the sacrifice of Iphigeneia at Aulis and the second and third of the elopement of Helen from Sparta and her arrival in Troy (which preceded the Aulis episode). Each of these songs has a strong dramatic element, and it is easy to imagine the men in the *choros* not only singing the words, but also miming the action. Indeed, given the Greek view that the dramatist's medium was a blend of music, words and *rhythmos* (i.e. bodily movement), it is surely safe to assume that the dancing of the *choros* was representational (or mimetic, to use Aristotle's special term), miming the events of the story, and expressing the emotions of the singers in what is now called body-language. There would be little place for the purely ornamental and formal style of dancing familiar to us from nineteenth-century ballet.

The conventional view of the early form of tragedy, which was held by most scholars in the first half of the twentieth century, was suggested to them by the very prominent part assigned to the *choros* in the *Suppliant Women* of Aeschylus. For many years this was believed to be the oldest surviving tragedy, dating from around 500 BC; but evidence came to light in 1952 which shows that it was in fact written during the last twelve years of Aeschylus' life.[24] But then again, the *Agamemnon* belongs to the very end of his life, and he still uses some very old-fashioned narrative techniques in that play, where it suits his purpose to do so.

There is also quite clear evidence in the surviving plays that the actors in the earliest tragedies had a smaller part to play, and that for most of the performance there was only one 'on stage' at any one time. This means that, although four or five characters might appear at various times, they could all be played by the same actor. We do not know precisely when a second actor was added to the cast; but where there are two speaking actors in conversation, the less important of the two is very commonly a narrator or bringer of news rather than a character involved in the action. A number of Aeschylus' plays consist almost entirely of choral songs, or dialogue between the *choros* and one actor, or narrative speeches by a messenger. The introduction of a third actor, an innovation which Aristotle attributed to Sophocles,[25] made it possible for the playwright to present a clash of personalities on the stage, such as the famous arguments between Creon and Antigone in Sophocles' play (*Antigone* 441–525) or between Jason and Medea in Euripides' (*Medea* 446–626). The effect of these developments was to curtail the musical element, by reducing the amount of the performance time occupied by the *choros* songs, and by taking away some of the functions earlier entrusted to the *choros*. In Sophocles they no longer act as narrators, that function usually being transferred to the prologue spoken by an actor. The result of this is not merely to change the personnel, but also to transform the mode of narration. In their songs, the *choros* did not tell the story in the leisurely, diffuse manner of the epic poets, with plenty of detail and an ordered sequence. Instead, they tended to use a very selective technique, picking out the moments of climax in the story and presenting them graphically, dwelling on the emotions of the people concerned, and leaving out the mundane details. In fact, the poet often assumes that the listener is familiar with the essentials, and can be relied upon to fill in quite large gaps in the narrative. The same technique was employed by Pindar in those stanzas of his victory odes in which he tells an illustrative or admonitory story. There could hardly be a sharper contrast with the rather prosaic, matter-of-fact way in which (to give one example among many) the god Apollo speaks of the events leading up to the opening scene of Euripides' *Alcestis*, spelling out the details and explaining the situation in a way which might have tried the patience of the quicker minds in the audience.

However, the loss of the narrative function from the *choros* songs was partly compensated for by a simplification of their role. In some of the early plays there is an awkward inconsistency between some passages in which the *choros* sing of events with the poet's own understanding and interpretation, and other passages in the same play where they appear to be bewildered and mistaken. In the later dramatists, though they expound a good deal of generalized morality, they do not stand apart from, nor always fully understand, the action which they see on the stage. Sophocles is particularly fond of exploiting the irony of a situation in which the *choros* believe that events are moving to a happy conclusion – when the true parentage of Oedipus is about to be revealed, or when Creon decides to rescue Antigone from the cave in which she is imprisoned. Their elation and joy would be closely reflected in the musical setting of their song and in their dance movements, and both would contrast sharply with the dirge-like tones and movements of the next song – in the *Oedipus Tyrannos* when they reflect on the awful truth that has been told, and in the *Antigone* when Creon returns with the body of his son.

So far we have mentioned only two 'modes' in Greek tragedy – the dance-songs of the *choros* and the spoken words of the actors. There was another, which might be described as intermediate between the two. It is indicated by words written in a metre called 'anapaest', which consists of short lines, usually twelve syllables, in the rhythm

$$\cup\cup- \mid \cup\cup- \mid \cup\cup- \mid \cup\cup- \mid$$

(for more details see Chapter 4, pp. 117). Groups of these lines may be organized in two different ways, one of which was apparently 'recited' and the other sung. We have evidence that some passages in comedies written in this metre were accompanied by an *aulos*, and on this basis it is generally assumed that similar passages in tragedy were so performed. We cannot be sure whether the words were sung, chanted or spoken, but there is one argument from probability which may be useful. The power of the speaking voice is very much less than that of the singing voice, and (as we shall see in Chapter 2) the notes of the *aulos* were loud and penetrating. It is likely that even a *choros* of twelve or fifteen men speaking would have been drowned by the accompaniment, and not clearly audible.[26] I am therefore inclined to believe that the words were chanted, perhaps on one note, or on a short, simple repeating pattern of notes.

When are these anapaests used? In early tragedies, exemplified in Aeschylus' *Persians* and *Suppliant Women,* the opening words sung or chanted by the *choros* as they make their entrance at the start of the play are written in this metre, and presumably this was the old tradition. However, Aeschylus makes the *choros* of women in his *Seven against Thebes* enter in a panic, and use a variety of strange metres, so there was apparently no fixed rule. The later tragedians tended to write a prologue scene, spoken by an actor or actors, before the entrance of the *choros*. When they do enter, they embark straight away on the first song, without any preliminary anapaests. Later in the play, certain passages which cover stage movements – entrances, exits and dramatic crises – may be written in anapaests. A characteristic example is the moment when Agamemnon enters in his chariot in triumph, in Aeschylus' *Agamemnon*, lines 782–809. Throughout the fifth century, the words sung or chanted by the *choros* as they left the theatre at the end of the play were normally written in anapaests. As the ancient theatre was open-air, and had no curtain, this was the way of signalling to the audience that the play was over.

From early times the playwrights used at least one 'combined mode' – an exchange between an actor on the stage and the *choros*, in which either or both sang their words. In a number of plays this occurs after the main tragic event, and consequently takes the form of a lament. Aristotle used the term *kommos* (which means 'lament', being derived from the word for beating the breast) for such songs; but the word is sometimes used in a more general sense for any exchange between actor and *choros* which is partly or wholly sung. The distinction between spoken and sung words is very clearly indicated by the Greek text; spoken words are almost invariably in six-foot iambic lines – the normal rhythm for all the dialogue – but the sung words are written in a variety of complicated rhythms. Sung words are also, in many such scenes, written in matching pairs of stanzas – that is, they are 'strophic', a term discussed in Chapter 4 (p. 124).

This seems a convenient point at which to raise an interesting musical question. All the actors in the ancient theatre were men, at least down to the third century BC, and all the female roles created by the great tragedians were intended to be played by male actors. The supposed sex of the *choros* in roughly half of the surviving tragedies is female, although the *choros* singers were all men. How, then, did they and the actors manage the sung passages? It may be that we are inventing a problem here which did not exist for the Greeks. We do not know how serious an attempt was made to give the actors in female roles a feminine appearance. No doubt the masks and wigs (which were worn by all actors in all roles) would help, and to some extent the clothes. Comic actors playing female roles certainly wore false breasts, though we cannot be sure about the tragic actors. But it was the universal convention, familiar to the audience since time immemorial, that actors were in fact men, and if Antigone or Clytemnestra were to sing in a tenor, or even a baritone voice, I doubt very much if anyone noticed, much less worried about it. Those of us who have watched performances of Greek tragedy with a male actor playing a female role know that it seems a little strange for a few lines at the start, but the oddity is soon forgotten. If we had encountered tenor or baritone heroines in every play we had ever seen, surely there would be no problem at all. Conversely, the audiences of later centuries did not trouble themselves over Gluck's Orpheus being a contralto, or Handel's Julius Caesar being a *castrato* treble.

In some of the later plays of Euripides a device is used which was, in its day, an even more exciting musical development. There are a number of extended monologues spoken by actors in the earlier tragedies, usually containing some narrative of past experiences (for example, Deianeira's speech in Sophocles' *Trachiniae*, lines 531–587). But Euripides sometimes cast them in the form of a *monōdia*, or solo song – something like an operatic aria. Without the music for any of these pieces, it is impossible to say what they sounded like; but we have the words for a few (e.g. Kreousa's song in Euripides' *Ion*, lines 881–922) and a very amusing and interesting parody of the style in the *Frogs* of Aristophanes (lines 1331–63). It seems that the playwright/composer exploited new musical techniques, and was inclined to sound rather avant-garde, so lending himself to the mockery of a traditionalist comic poet. One device in particular is parodied – the division of a single syllable between several notes, which the Greeks called *melisma*; by the conventions of writing this is indicated by the repetition of the syllable (*eieieieieilissete*) in the text. This is of course very familiar to us and, if we judge by the standards of Handelian opera, seems a very modest adventure; but when it was heard for the first time, it seems to have had a considerable impact. It is also noticeable that these solo songs were not usually written in matching pairs of stanzas, as the *choros* songs were. This reflects two features of the performance; first, that the actor did not dance, or move about much during the song (in one famous example, sung by Andromeda in Euripides' play of that name he could not, as he was supposed to be chained to a rock!) and second, that the rhythmic pattern of the words could be much more freely and loosely constructed.

One final comment on the *monōdiai* which, though it comes from a comic poet, has a nucleus of truth in it: in the *Frogs* of Aristophanes, Euripides claims that when he took over 'The Lady Tragedy' from Aeschylus, she had an obesity problem. He put her on a slimming course, by which he means that he attenuated the high poetic style, and cut down on the long, sonorous compound words of which Aeschylus was very fond. Having thus made her slimmer and healthier, he 'fattened her up' on *monōdiai*.[27]

It is by no means easy to tell from an English prose translation how much of the text of a Greek tragedy was spoken, and how much sung. In order to give a general impression of the proportions, I have analysed the *Ion* of Euripides, a fairly representative play of the later fifth century. The analysis is crude, being based on a line-count, but is not, I believe, misleading. The whole play has 1,622 lines, and would take, at a guess, most of two hours to perform. About two-thirds of this time would be taken up with spoken dialogue, the rest (something like 40 minutes) being wholly or partly sung or chanted. The fully sung part, which consists of (a) all the *choros* songs, (b) Kreousa's *monōdia*, and (c) the opening song, shared between Ion and the *choros*, may have lasted about 24 minutes, and the passages in anapaests, together with the *kommos* bits which were partly sung and partly spoken, would have taken about 10 minutes. For the mathematically-minded reader who may have spotted that there are about six minutes unaccounted for, it should be said that there are about 84 lines written in a metre called the trochaic – longer lines which were probably spoken rapidly. They occur at dramatic moments of action in the play, and since Aristotle describes the metre as 'suitable for dancing', those lines may well have been spoken or chanted with a musical accompaniment.[28]

Ancient Greek comedy, which grew up with tragedy in the same theatre and at the same festivals, had its own important musical element. In fact, because the nature of early comedy allowed the actors to make frequent references to themselves and their theatrical setting, we gain much of our information on theatre music from this source. For instance, in a number of Aristophanes' comedies there is a section known as the *parabasis,* which occurs roughly halfway through the play. In this section the *choros* 'come forward' and address the audience directly, often making some claims on behalf of the poet. The opening lines of this section were written in anapaests – the metre which we have already met – and in one play, the *Birds*, the *choros* actually ask the aulos-player to 'lead us into the anapaests' (lines 682–4). It appears from some expressions in the text of this play that the player may have gone on to the stage, and engaged in some by-play with the actors (lines 665–75), though it might be argued that a non-speaking extra played the part of a 'pretty little bird' (Procne, the wife of Tereus the King of the birds) and mimed the action while the real aulos-player played in his usual place. We have no direct evidence of where this was, and the issue is confused for the English reader by a change in the meaning of the Greek word *orchēstra*. This meant a 'dancing-platform', and referred to the circular area in front of the stage where the *choros* performed. In Roman times, if not earlier, when the *choros* ceased to have any importance, this area was used for seating, and in modern proscenium theatres those seats came to be called the 'orchestra stalls'. The musicians sat at the front of these stalls in the 'orchestra pit', and in the end the word orchestra was transferred to them. It is generally believed (for lack of any evidence by which to check) that in the ancient theatre the aulos-player and the kithara-player (if there was one, which is disputed) stood at the back of the dancing-platform, perhaps one either side of the stage. This is consistent with a very unusual feature in the text of Aristophanes' *Birds*; there are virtually no stage directions preserved in the texts of ancient drama, but at line 223 of the *Birds* there is a marginal note which says 'someone plays the aulos from behind the scene' (in Greek, *endothen*, 'from within'). This suggests that the aulos-player was normally in view of the audience, and that here we have a special effect. In the text of the songs sung by the *choros* of birds there are quite a lot of bird-song noises (e.g. 'tio-tio-tinx' or 'kikkabau, kikkabau'), and we may be fairly sure that the aulos-player contributed his share of bird-like trills and warbles.

In the majority of the surviving comedies the *choros* were dressed as human groups – men from Acharnai, for example, or women at a festival; but in a few plays they appear in animal costume, as birds or frogs, and in another play they are disguised as clouds. It is clear from vase-paintings of a century before Aristophanes that dancing by an 'animal *choros*' was a very ancient ritual, dating from a time long before the emergence of comedy in the form in which we know it. There are pictures of men dressed as cockerels, or riding on dolphins (perhaps real ones, or men dressed as such) and a very striking picture of a *choros* of men riding 'piggy-back' on others who have horses' heads and tails. The inscription nearby, which reads 'EI-OKHI-OKHI' would of course have been intelligible to a Greek horse. On first sight, this would appear to be an illustration of a performance of Aristophanes' *Knights*, but it was painted a century earlier than that play (Figure 1.9).

There is one very significant feature of all these choruses – they are led in their dances by an aulos-player, and this must surely have been true of a *choros* in fifth-century comedy.

The latter part of a typical Aristophanic play has a number of short (sometimes very short) scenes of a knockabout character, interspersed with short songs by the *choros*, most of them closely bound up with the plot of the play, though some contain satirical comment on contemporary affairs.

As a final comment on the importance of music in Aristophanic comedy, it should be said that a number of plays end with a musical celebration, by contrast with the tragedies which end with the *choros* chanting the anapaests as they leave the scene (see p. 16 above). The *Acharnians* ends with the triumphal song celebrating the hero's victory in

Figure 1.9 Animal *choros*

a drinking-contest, and the *Birds* with a marriage ceremony – a very blasphemous fantasy in which the disreputable old Athenian is married to Universal Sovereignty, formerly the partner of Zeus. At the end of the *Wasps*, the plot more or less disintegrates, and a troupe of three dancers are brought on to do a vulgar dance (the *kordax*, roughly the ancient equivalent of the can-can, but danced by men) and so round off the play with a sort of cabaret turn.

Up to now we have been considering only the fifth-century comedy as we know it from the works of Aristophanes. In the fourth century BC a number of developments took place, some of which are already foreshadowed in the last two of his surviving plays, the *Women in Parliament* and *Wealth*. These led to a different form of comedy, known as the 'New Comedy', in which the musical element was much less important. As it was the forerunner of early Roman comedy, it will be examined in detail in Chapter 8.

Beside the tragedies and comedies, there was another type of play which was regularly performed at the Dionysia, the great drama festival. This was known as satyr-drama, and was a most peculiar art-form. First of all, it should be stressed that it had nothing whatsoever to do with satire, in the ancient or modern sense of that word. The drama got its name from the fact that the men of the *choros* were always dressed in the same costume – that of satyrs. These were strange creatures of the Greek imagination, part human and part animal, usually represented with human body but with horses' ears and tails, and a characteristic face marked by a high bulging forehead and snub nose, in complete contrast to the familiar elegant 'Greek profile'. There are abundant Greek vase-paintings of 'real' satyrs, in which they are characterised as drinkers, dancers and uninhibited lechers, a feature which is very explicitly shown by the Greek artists. There are other vase-paintings which show actors dressed as satyrs about to take part in a satyr-play. They wear masks with the appropriate features – snub nose, horses' ears and hair which looks rather like a mane, and a pair of shorts covered with animal hair, with a tail on the rump and a large, obtrusive artificial phallus on the front.

The most remarkable feature of this type of drama was that it was written by the tragic poets. Three such poets were chosen each year to have their works performed, and each had to contribute three tragedies, which were performed consecutively, followed by a satyr drama. Aeschylus tended to favour the trilogy: a sequence of three tragedies which formed a saga, dealing with the fortunes of a single family through two or three generations, followed by a satyr play which had some sort of connection with the story. The later dramatists preferred as a rule to write three separate tragedies and a satyr play with unconnected stories. So the audience listened to a total of four plays by one author on each of the first three days of the festival. It is an interesting comment on the character of the Greeks that they liked to have the light relief at the end of the day, and not earlier.

The form of the satyr-drama was similar to that of tragedy, with prologue, entrance-song of the *choros* and so on, but the mood and tone were totally different from those of tragedy, despite the fact that the text was written and the music composed by tragic poets. The *choros* of satyrs were characterized as drunken cowards, with none of the virtues of the characters in tragedy, and with no capacity for endurance. Unlike the plots of comedy, which were usually invented by the poet, the plots for these plays were taken from mythological stories, as were those of the tragedies. Naturally, the stories chosen were of a light and comical kind, to give the satyrs plenty of opportunity to show their unheroic characters. In one play by Aeschylus, of which only fragments survive, they are required to go into training for the Isthmian Games, a prospect which appals them. In Euripides' *Cyclops* (the only complete satyr play which has survived) they are asked to help Odysseus to deal with the monster, which they are most reluctant to do. In Sophocles' *Trackers* (*Ichneutae*) they are struck with terror on hearing for the first time the notes of a lyre, which has just been invented and constructed by the infant Hermes.

This brings us conveniently back to the musical element in the satyr-drama. In vase-paintings of scenes of Dionysiac worship, in which 'real' satyrs and maenads (ecstatic female devotees) dance around the god, music is often featured. Satyrs play the aulos, occasionally the kithara, and most often the lyre or its 'big brother', the *barbitos*. Maenads usually play the hand-drum (*tympanon*, see p. 81 below). It is not surprising, therefore, to find that in representations of satyr-drama the members of the *choros* are shown with various instruments, most commonly the lyre or a particular variant of it (see p. 67). But the most valuable pictorial evidence comes from a vase of the very late fifth century BC known as the 'Pronomos Vase' (Figure 1.10).

The side of the vase shows on three levels a troupe of actors preparing for a satyr-play; Figure 1.10 shows four figures from the lowest 'level'. The one on the right of the picture is wearing his shorts but carrying his mask in one hand. The one on the left has put on his satyr mask and is practising the typical hopping dance of the satyr *choros*, which was called the *Sikinnis*. In the row above (not shown in Figure 1.10) are several actors dressed for the main roles, but carrying their masks. It is easy to recognize Dionysos, Ariadne and Herakles, and to their right a 'senior satyr' called Papasilenos, who is the leader of the *choros*. But most interesting of all are the two central figures in the lower row. One appears to be a 'main part actor', who is carrying a lyre, and presumably played it during the drama. The other is an aulos-player, dressed in very luxurious costume and seated on an elegant chair, who is named as Pronomos, a famous virtuoso player who came from Thebes. He was responsible for important developments in the design of the aulos (see below, p. 36). This seems to suggest that an outstanding soloist might be engaged to play for a theatre production, even a satyr-play. What is not so clear is whether the actor with the lyre actually played it, or whether he mimed the action while a kithara-player performed 'off-stage'; it is doubtful whether the sounds of a lyre would be loud enough to carry throughout the very large theatres, though their acoustics were excellent.

So, taking all the evidence together, it is clear that the theatrical experience of the Greeks in the Classical period involved a considerable element of music, singing and dancing. It is very difficult for the producer of a modern version, especially in translation, to replace this lost music. All that survives of the music of the three great tragedians is a very small fragment of Euripides' *Orestes* and an even smaller scrap of his *Iphigeneia in Aulis*, and of Aristophanes not a single note. Some attempts have been

Figure 1.10 Four figures from the Pronomos Vase

made to compose music which sounds vaguely like ancient Greek; but the only substantial remains we have are the Delphic Hymns (see Chapter 10), which are liturgical music, and can hardly give us any reliable clues to the nature of theatrical music three centuries earlier. The Theatre of Dionysos in Athens is silent, and we shall never hear more than a few fleeting notes of the music which sounded there.

2(a)

THE AULOS

The instruments used by the Greeks and Romans may be conveniently divided into the same categories that are used for modern instruments; to avoid irritating argument over fine-drawn definitions, I shall use the terms woodwind, stringed, brass and percussion. In this chapter the instruments will be dealt with in the order of their importance or popularity, which means that they are not necessarily treated in the historical order of their first appearance.

The aulos

In the woodwind category there was one instrument which spanned the whole history of Greek and Roman music, and which appears more commonly in illustrations than any other – a double, reed-blown pipe, called *aulos* in Greek and *tibia* in Latin.

For many years it has been the practice of Classical translators, including some very distinguished ones, to use the word 'flute' for this instrument.[1] This is extremely misleading and inaccurate, in two respects. First, the *aulos* did not look like a flute; it was a double pipe, the two pipes being held out in front of the player (Figure 2a.1a). There was an ancient instrument which really was a single pipe of the flute type, and was held transversely, as a modern flute is held. It was called the 'transverse aulos' (*plagios aulos*, or *plagiaulos* in Greek, *obliqua tibia* in Latin, Figure 2a.1b).

The *plagiaulos* was entirely confined to the pastoral environment, and it does not appear in Greek literature or art until the Hellenistic period (third century BC onwards). The translation 'flute' should, therefore, be restricted to that instrument alone, and not used for any other type of *aulos*; nor should it be used with reference to any earlier period. Second, the ordinary *aulos* was, beyond reasonable doubt, a reed-blown instrument, and we can be quite sure that it did not sound anything like a flute. The two pipes spoke together, perhaps in unison, and ancient writers describe its sound variously as 'shrill', 'blaring' or 'booming', none of which would be appropriate to the sound of a flute. It is more difficult

Figure 2a.1a Aulos

Figure 2a.1b Flute

to play two pipes than to play one, and the range of notes on each pipe is limited to six, whereas it could be much greater on a single pipe; but the Greeks and Romans were prepared to accept both these limitations in order to produce the brilliant and exciting effect of the two pipes sounding together.

So it is easy to show that the words aulos and *tibia* should not be translated as 'flute';[2] but to suggest a good alternative is not so easy, because there is no well-known instrument in modern use which corresponds on all three points – a double pipe, with double reeds and a cylindrical bore. In Europe the technique of double-piping survives only in folk music of remote regions, and to translate aulos by the name of (say) some Caucasian double pipe would be to explain the unfamiliar in terms of the unheard-of. For a technically accurate prosaic translation 'reed-blown double pipe' is perhaps the best available; for less exact requirements 'pipes' will do, given an explanatory footnote for Scottish readers that bagpipes are not indicated. In this book from now on, the instrument will be called aulos, which is to be regarded as a loan-word; but I shall retain the Greek plural auloi, as being less troublesome than 'aulosses'.

We cannot now discover the date or circumstances of the first introduction of the aulos into the Greek world. A marble sculpture from Keros in the Cyclades, dating (despite its curious resemblance to a modern sculpture) from between 2800 and 2300 BC clearly shows such an instrument;[3] but the island's culture at that time may have been Carian, not Greek.

The earliest surviving painted illustration, dating from about the fourteenth century BC, is on a sarcophagus found at Hagia Triada in Crete, in the context of a ritual in honour of the dead.[4] It shows an unusual type of aulos, with pipes of about equal length, one of them fitted with an upward-curving bell. This instrument, dating from the late Minoan period, bears no close resemblance either to the double pipes shown in near-contemporary Egyptian illustrations, or to the earliest representations which can reliably be called Greek, which are in vase-paintings of the Geometric period from the early seventh century BC.

The two earliest mentions of the aulos in literature also date from that same period or a little earlier; they are in Homer's *Iliad*.[5] However, both these passages are slightly suspect, and it is very noticeable that there are many more references to stringed instruments in the Homeric poems. This is hardly surprising, since only stringed instruments were used by bards, both in real life in Homer's day and in the stories in which they portrayed their predecessors in the heroic age. The Greek myths relating to the invention or discovery of the aulos are discussed in Chapter 6: if they preserve a genuine folk-memory, which is possible but by no means certain, they suggest that the aulos was imported into Greece from Asia Minor. It may also be significant that, while the principal stringed instrument – the kithara – was associated with Apollo, who in the eyes of the ancient Greeks was the most Greek of all the gods, the aulos was closely connected with Dionysos, believed by the Greeks to have been an Asiatic deity whose cult was imported into Greece and later Hellenized. Indeed, it has been suggested that the reason and occasion for the introduction of the aulos to the Greek mainland (along with the hand-drum, *tympanon*) was the arrival of the Dionysiac cult and its ritual. However this may be, the aulos established itself in Greece as a very popular instrument, the use of which was by no means confined to cult; it appears in almost every department of Greek life, from the most solemn religious occasion to the most dissolute orgy (Figure 2a.2).

The aulos is shown in a developed form in Greek vase-paintings of the sixth century BC, and its outward appearance (or, at any rate, the way

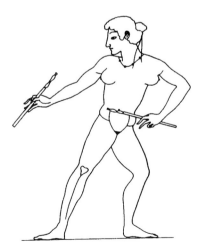

Figure 2a.2 Aulos not-so-solemn

of representing it) seems to have changed little during the following century.

Each pipe of the instrument was usually made in five separate parts – the body (usually in two parts), the two bulbs and the reed mouthpiece (Figure 2a.3). The stem of the reed was inserted into the top bulb and, as it was particularly vulnerable, it was removed when the aulos was not in use. The pipes were carried around in a long, narrow double pouch, usually depicted as made from the skin of a dappled animal (a leopard, or perhaps a deer) and the reeds were stored in a small oblong box fixed to the side of the pouch near the top. Its size was about $5 \times 1^{1}/_{2} \times 1^{1}/_{2}$ ins ($12 \times 4 \times 4$ cm) and it was called a 'reed-carrier' (*glōttokomeion* in Greek). The same word was also used for any 'long box' including (with a touch of dark humour) a coffin (Figure 2a.4).[6]

These parts will be treated in order, starting from the mouthpiece and working downwards.

In the great majority of vase-paintings the aulos is shown actually being played, with the most interesting and vital part of the instrument,

Figure 2a.3 'Exploded' diagram of aulos

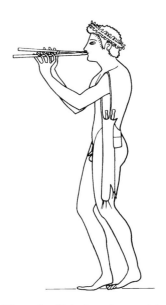

Figure 2a.4a Aulos carrying-case 'de luxe'

Figure 2a.4b Aulos-player with spare pipes in readiness

the reed, hidden in the player's mouth. Usually the lips cover the reed to the top end of the upper bulb. In the few pictures in which the pipe is shown out of the player's mouth, the reed appears to be something like a modern bassoon reed in size and shape (Figures 2a.5 and 2a.6).

These pictures quite certainly represent double reeds, and not single ones (as used in the drones of Scottish bagpipes), which would appear as long, thin tubes with rounded tips. And apart from the pictorial evidence, there are other good reasons for believing that the reeds used on the aulos were double reeds.[7] We also have some literary evidence, albeit vague and difficult to interpret, on how they were made. This is mainly derived from an account in Theophrastos' *Researches into Plants* (Bk 4 Chapter 6) of how the 'aulos-reed' (*aulētikos kalamos*) was grown and prepared for reed-making. This plant has been identified as the species *arundo donax*, or a species closely akin to it, which still grows in large quantities all around the Mediterranean basin, though not in central or northern Europe, and is used to make the reeds for most modern woodwind instruments.[8]

The general gist of Theophrastos' account is as follows. He says that in early times, when the technique of aulos-playing was 'natural' or 'unforced' (in Greek, *aplastos*), the reeds were cut about mid-September in the second year of their growth, provided that the marsh in which they grew had not dried out during that season. (If that occurred, the reeds were presumably discarded as useless.) These reeds were not ready for use until 'quite a number of years later', and needed a long period of

Figure 2a.5 Reed seen from above   *Figure 2a.6* Reed (side view)

manipulation and playing-in before they would speak properly. The openings of the reeds 'tended to close up easily', a feature which was useful for the early technique of playing.[9]

When aulos-players changed over to a 'forced' or 'artificial' technique (*plasis* in Greek) the reeds were cut earlier in the season – late June or early July – and they became usable 'after two or three years'. It is surely significant that in modern times the reed-makers' cane grown in the south of France is cut and stacked for two to three years before use. The change-over to *plasis* was associated with Antigeneidas, a famous virtuoso player from Thebes, who was active in the late fifth and early fourth century BC. The word itself literally means 'moulding' or 'shaping', and would be appropriate for any technique by which the pitch or tone was modified by the player's embouchure, such as a glide from one note to another (glissando) or a tremolo or vibrato effect. It might possibly refer to the production of harmonics; this is discussed later.

One possible explanation of the change from one technique to the other is that the older one involved putting the whole length of the reed-tongues inside the mouth, leaving them free to vibrate without any control from the lips. For this purpose, it is indeed necessary to have reeds which 'close up easily' – if they do not, they cannot be made to vibrate. The later 'forced' technique should then be interpreted as the modern one, used on an oboe or bassoon, in which the reeds, which are much stronger and more open,[10] have to be squeezed in order to make them speak; this is done by inserting only about half the length of the reed-tongues into the mouth, drawing the lips inward over the upper and lower teeth, and then squeezing the reed-tongues between the lips. The great advantage of this 'forcing' is that the volume, pitch and tone of the instrument can be varied, whereas with the reed uncontrolled in the mouth there can be little variation of loudness between *pianissimo* and *fortissimo*, and only very limited control of pitch.

Unfortunately, it is not possible to discover from Theophrastos' text the exact method by which the reeds were made.[11] In this context, he is dealing strictly with the choice and preparation of the material, and he writes on the assumption – perfectly justified – that his readers know exactly what the finished product looks like. It is unlikely, however, that the modern method, which involves splitting the cane longitudinally into three segments, bending one of them in the middle and binding its ends on to a metal tube (called a staple) was used. It is much more likely that the end of a short section of cane was softened by some process (perhaps by steaming), and then flattened and scraped into the characteristic double-reed shape.

A number of other terms which relate to the control of the reed and embouchure are used in the literary sources, and some are apparently illustrated in vase-paintings. Some authors speak of 'separating' the pipes and 'putting them alongside', and players in vase-paintings are shown holding the pipes at various angles of divergence, up to about 45 degrees at the extreme (Figure 2a7).

According to the literary sources,[12] these movements were used for delicate adjustments of pitch, which was sharpened by separating the pipes, and flattened by bringing them together. They might have brought about a very slight adjustment of the embouchure; the aulos-player had no thumb-rests, and it must have been very difficult to control the position of each reed on the lower lip with one hand only. Incidentally, the ability of the player to separate the pipes is a strong argument against the use of single reeds, which are by their construction necessarily much longer than double reeds, and would surely have collided inside the player's mouth. There is a rather incredible story told by an ancient commentator on Pindar *Olympian 12* about an aulos-player whose reeds stuck on the roof of his mouth, and were so badly damaged that he had to play the two pipes as though they were pan-pipes. The first part of the story would be quite credible if they were double reeds, but the reed-tongues of single reeds, which are cut in the sides of the tubes, would have been protected by the closed tips of their tubes from such damage. (One should never be too sceptical about stories of remarkable achievements by woodwind players: on being told this one, an oboist friend removed the reed from her instrument and, to my great surprise, played it as a trumpet.)

In the treatise on acoustics attributed to Aristotle (see p. 138) there are two references to tightening the embouchure, which he calls 'squeezing

Figure 2a.7 Aulos pipes held wide apart

the reeds' (*piezein ta zeugē*).[13] The word *zeugē* means 'pairs' (in the plural), and this must surely mean two double reeds.

Many illustrations show an aulos-player wearing a mouthband made of leather, which the Greeks called *phorbeia;* the word was also used to mean a strap or halter used to tether a horse to its feeding-trough or, more probably, to tie its nosebag on. The version worn by an aulos-player consisted of a broad strap with two round holes, looking rather like a highwayman's mask, but worn over the mouth and around the cheeks. In the great majority of vase-paintings it is shown in profile, but where the player is drawn full-face, the reed mouthpieces can be seen emerging from the holes. The strap tapered towards the back of the player's neck where, presumably, there was some kind of buckle or hook, and a thin cord ran from the cheekpieces up over the top of the head, to prevent it from sliding down on to the chin (Figure 2a.8).

A number of explanations have been offered for this device. Some ancient scholars said that it was to prevent the cheeks from bulging, but this is hardly satisfactory; the cheeks can normally be held in without any such aid, and an explanation so closely tied up with the story of Athena's rejection of the aulos must be suspect (see p. 154). I have suggested another explanation for the *phorbeia* which seems much more satisfactory. In all illustrations (leaving out a few ambiguous ones) the player wearing it is male, and he is taking part in a public competition, or at least playing out of doors. This would require strong, open reeds, and the lip muscles which control the embouchure (and, incidentally, restrict the bulging of the cheeks) would be subject to fatigue after a short time – present-day players of the shawm would testify to this. I do not know of any

Figure 2a.8 Aulos-player wearing *phorbeia*

undisputed illustration of a woman wearing a *phorbeia*, presumably because women normally played indoors, and used softer, weaker reeds. The *phorbeia* could, I believe, have been used to put pressure on the lips, squeezing them together and keeping them in position over the teeth, thus taking some of the strain off the lip muscles. The pressure could be varied and controlled to some extent by movements of the head, and in fact the illustrations usually show the chin thrust out; this would be the natural way to increase the tension in the strap. Moreover, when the *phorbeia* is used, the pipes are usually held well up in front of the player – horizontal or even higher. In a few exceptional cases the pipes slope downwards, but this is clearly artist's licence, intended to improve the composition of the picture.

There is ample evidence to show that the behaviour, or rather misbehaviour, of the reed was as much of a problem as it is today. The Greeks had two words for the odd noises made by beginners on the aulos – *krizein* (to squeak) and *chēniazein* (to blow a goose). We are also told of aulos-players who drew frantic applause in a crowded theatre by 'playing with a slack embouchure and blasting out a lot of repetitive, off-key shrieks' – early practitioners, it would seem, of a punk rock style.[14]

Between the reed and the body of the aulos there were normally two bulbs, sometimes only one. They took one of two forms, as shown in Figure 2a.9.

Two Greek words were used for these parts of the mouthpiece section – *holmos*, meaning 'mortar' (the kitchen utensil), and *hypholmion*, meaning 'mortar-stand'. Aristotle remarks on the similarity of shape between this part of the aulos and the egg-cases of dogfish, popularly known as mermaids' purses (Figure 2a.10).[15]

Some illustrations which show only one bulb give it a cone-shaped extension, making the mouthpiece as a whole thistle-shaped. This is exemplified in illustrations of the post-classical period, and in the Pompeian pipes. The function of this part may have been to act as a 'pirouette', to give support to, and relieve strain on, the lip muscles. If so, it would have been an alternative to the *phorbeia*.[16]

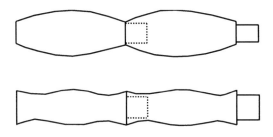

Figure 2a.9 Two types of bulb (*holmos*)

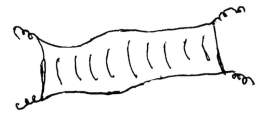

Figure 2a.10 Dog-fish egg-case

What was the function of the bulbs? We cannot be sure. They may have been purely decorative (there are pictures of auloi without any) or they may have contributed somehow to the balancing of the instrument – a difficult problem for the player, with only one hand to control each pipe. Where they appear to be larger in diameter than the body of the pipe, they may have served to protect the reed when the aulos was laid down on a flat surface: on some instruments, particularly the Reading aulos, the bulb is quite large.[17] It is unlikely that they had an acoustical function; the internal bore is the same as that of the rest of the pipe, and they could hardly have influenced the pitch or the tone of the instrument.

The material most commonly used for the body of the aulos in the classical period was the same species of reed (*arundo donax*) that was used to make the reed mouthpiece, except that it was cut at a much later stage of growth, when the stalks had reached an internal diameter of about 9–15 mm (0.3–0.6 in.). The length between two knots on the stem would usually be sufficient to make the body in one piece. Other woods were used, particularly one which they called *lotos*, probably to be identified as the nettle-tree, *celtis australis*. (It was native to north Africa, hence both the wood and the aulos made from it are referred to as 'Libyan'.) Two pipes in the British Museum, the 'Elgin auloi', were made from sycamore wood, which shows that solid stems could be used as well as hollow ones.

Unfortunately, instruments made from these materials do not as a rule survive. Bone was almost as commonly used, though a more difficult material to work in. The tibia bones of small animals such as sheep or deer were most suitable, and the portion of such a bone which can be bored out and shaped is usually not more than about 9 cm (3.5 in.) long, which means that the aulos body has to be put together from two or three sections. These were jointed together, as are the sections of a modern instrument, with tenons and sockets. There is some doubt whether the tenons were padded with some soft material, or lapped with thread, as they sometimes are on modern instruments. I am inclined to think that they were not, because the sections were permanently glued together. The carrying-case is almost always shown as being long enough to hold the complete instrument without its reed.

Bone is a much more durable material than wood, and a number of bone sections of auloi survive, giving us some valuable information on the instrument-maker's art. (Ivory was also used, which is sometimes very difficult to distinguish from bone.)[18] For example, we know that down to the middle of the fifth century BC the inside of each bone section was bored out to an exactly cylindrical bore, but the outside surface was usually left unworked, preserving the grooves left in the bone by the muscle attachments. Then, as lathe technique improved, the outside was shaved down to an exact cylinder, polished, and decorated with incised lines. Eventually, the bone sections were given a thin outer shell of bronze or silver. But this pattern of development is less useful than it may seem for the purpose of dating surviving fragments of auloi, because crude and simple instruments continued to be made to the old-fashioned pattern long after the refinements had been introduced.

The fingerholes were bored in the wood or bone with something like a modern centre-bit, probably rotated by a bow. It could cut a very clean and exact circular hole, as can be seen from some surviving fragments. On instruments made of wood or bone the outer surface was filed or gouged out slightly around the holes which were to be stopped by the player's fingers, so as to make a better 'seating' for the finger, and from the depth and position of the hollows made in this process it is sometimes possible to tell whether the pipe was designed for the left or the right hand. This shaping might have been done by the player himself, or by the maker on a custom-made instrument. The player used the flat of the finger near the last joint to stop the holes, and not the tips of the fingers; this makes the shaping of the holes even more important. Later instruments which had a casing of bronze (for example, the Reading aulos) could not be shaped in this way.[19] There is also evidence for 'under-cutting' – removing a small sliver of bone from the interior edge of the hole, for fine correction of pitch (see note 18).

Throughout the early Classical period, and down to the middle of the fifth century BC, the aulos apparently had five fingerholes, with or without a sixth hole further down the pipe, which could not be covered by the fingers. This is known as a vent-hole, and was used to sound the lowest note on the pipe.

Figure 2a.11 shows the typical arrangement, with hole I on top (stopped by the index finger), the thumbhole T underneath, and II, III and IV for the middle, third and little fingers respectively. The vent-hole V, if there is one, can be distinguished by its sharp outer edge, not shaped for the player's fingers. This arrangement imposes a limit on the distance between I and IV; the maximum stretch, even for a player with large hands, could not have been much more than about 15 cm (6 in.). Each pipe would normally be supported on the player's thumb; but when the thumbhole had to be uncovered, wholly or partially, the little finger was

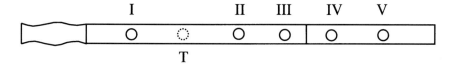

Figure 2a.11 Fingerholes on early aulos (total length about 35 cm, fingerholes about 9 mm diameter)

apparently tucked under the pipe to support it. It must have taken a lot of skill to do this (usually with both pipes at once) during a rapid piece of music.

The arrangement of holes would enable each pipe of the aulos to play a scale of six 'natural' notes, with the option of raising the pitch of five of them by a small amount. This was done by raising the finger slightly from the edge of the next hole above; so the note from the vent-hole could be modified in this way, but the 'natural' from the top one (I) could not. The small interval by which the pitch was raised was called a *diesis* in Greek, and in this context it means a 'leak' or 'escape'. (It is interesting that this seems to be the only term for an interval which is based on the playing technique of a wind instrument; all the note-names in the scales (see p. 54), and the names of the other intervals – for example, *dia pente,* 'across five' for the fifth – were based on the layout of stringed instruments.) The amount by which the pitch was raised (i.e. the size of a *diesis*) could vary between a quarter-tone and a semitone, according to the scale being used. If the finger were raised a little further, the pitch would rise by one more *diesis.* It would therefore be possible to play a scale of six notes, with a cluster of three closely-spaced notes (called a *pyknon* in Greek) based on each of them except the highest one. This, however, was not part of normal musical practice, though it might have figured in exercises set to pupils by aulos teachers. The Greek scales, which will be discussed in detail in the next chapter, allowed only one *pyknon* in any 'tetrachord' – a group of four notes, which normally spanned the interval of a fourth.

Apart from raising the pitch by means of 'leaks', the aulos-player could lower the pitch of some notes by cross-fingering. This involves closing holes below the open one which is sounding the note. Obviously, this technique is available only on holes I, T, II and III, and would in practice be very difficult to achieve on T (one should never say 'impossible' of any technique supposed to have been used on a woodwind instrument!). It has the advantage that the lowering of pitch, though very slight, is quite accurate, unlike the hit-or-miss technique of 'leaks'.

According to good literary evidence, there were three ancient aulos scales, the Dorian, Lydian and Phrygian, and down to the middle of the fifth century BC there were three types, or sizes, of aulos, one bored for each of the scales. In order to change from one to another, the player had to change instruments, just as a clarinettist today may have to change from a B flat to an A clarinet in order to play in a different key. The nature of these scales, and their relationship to later systems, are discussed in Chapter 3. For the present, it will suffice to say that they probably differed in three respects – the pitch of each scale as a whole, the number and range of notes, and the patterns of intervals within that range.

A development took place some time about the middle of the fifth century BC whereby it became possible to play any of these three scales on the same instrument (i.e. pair of pipes). This 'invention' is ascribed to Pronomos of Thebes, a famous virtuoso player, who was active in the middle years of the century, and who in the 430s attempted (poor chap!) to teach the art of aulos-playing to the notorious aristocratic tearaway Alkibiades.[20] Unfortunately, the literary sources do not give any details of his innovation, but we can assume that he modified the design of the instrument, and perhaps transposed one or two of the scales to a different 'key' in order to make them overlap to a greater extent. It might then have become possible to play the three scales on an aulos with (say) eight fingerholes fitted with a form of keywork by means of which the holes which were not required for the scale being used could be closed off. The problem with this hypothesis is that the earliest surviving examples of instruments fitted with keywork date from a much later period. But the surviving instruments are not a representative selection. They have mostly been found in rubbish deposits (e.g. wells in the Athenian Agora), and while we might expect to find cheap or damaged instruments in such a context, we are not likely to find an expensive instrument casually discarded by a professional player. (The Brauron aulos is a different matter; it was thrown into an underground spring, probably as a thank-offering.) The best examples of keywork that we possess come from Pompeii, and of course date from centuries later. They probably represent the private collection of a musician, or perhaps instruments in a maker's workshop at the time of the volcanic eruption. As for the lack of contemporary pictorial evidence, that is easily explained by the nature of the keywork itself.

The mechanism is quite simple. The body of the aulos is covered with a thin layer of bronze or silver, and the holes are bored through it and the bone or ivory beneath. On the outside of this layer are fitted sleeves of metal which are tight enough to seal off the air, but loose enough to be rotated around the body. Each has a hole which can be made to coincide with the hole in the aulos body, or turned away from it so as to close it off. Each of them looks rather like the air regulator on an old-fashioned Bunsen burner, and they work in much the same way. Figure 2a.12 shows two sleeves, with the left one in the 'open' position and the other closed; there would normally be a minimum of eight.

This system of keywork is, of course, much simpler and much less effective than that on a modern oboe or clarinet. To begin with, no more

36

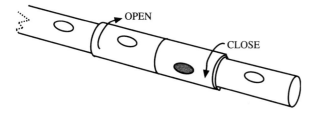

Figure 2a.12 Key mechanism of aulos

than six holes could be used at any one time, and the distance between I and IV was restricted to the span from the player's index finger to little finger, i.e. about 15 cm (6 in.), though the vent-hole could be at any distance below. Some later auloi (from the second century BC onwards) had long bronze rods which moved back and forth along the body, and caused half-sleeves or pads to slide up or down, so as to cover or open holes which were beyond the player's reach.[21] To give the sleeve extra strength and stability, it was bent around the body of the instrument (the one in Figure 2a.13 has quite a large bore) and held in place by staples, which were soldered into the bronze body (Figure 2a.13).

It might have been possible to manipulate one of these rods while playing, but it must have been very difficult indeed to twist the sleeves around and change the scale except during a pause in the music. On the remains and in illustrations of much later instruments there are small knobs on the sleeves, and on others there are sockets, perhaps for the insertion of a short lever, which would have made it easier; but no such details appear in Greek vase-paintings of the Classical period. Without them, of course, the sleeves would have been quite inconspicuous, and this would account for the fact that the artists did not bother to show them.

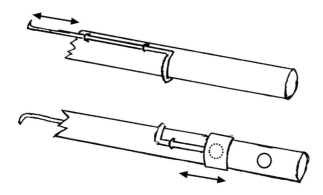

Figure 2a.13 'Remote-control' key on aulos, seen from above and below

We do not have any literary evidence about the exact nature of Pronomos' invention, but we do have two passages which testify to its effectiveness. One is from Simonides (perhaps mid-fifth century BC) and the other from Plato, writing in the 380s but pretending to report conversations in the last decades of the fifth century.[22] Both of them use the word *polychordos* ('many-stringed') in connection with the aulos. Plato is seeking to restrict the musical education of his 'Guardians of State' to the 'mood' or ethos associated with two particular scales (this is discussed in Chapter 3) and he mistrusts the aulos, because it is capable of playing all the notes needed for several other scales, and can therefore skip about from one ethos to another, in a way which he found highly objectionable. The lyre and kithara are the only instruments acceptable to him, because they could not change scale without pausing and retuning. The strange thing is that both of these writers should use the word 'many-stringed' to describe a wind instrument, though we have already seen that virtually all the terms relating to notes, scales or intervals were derived from the structure or playing techniques of stringed instruments, with the single exception of *diesis*, which was derived from the aulos. It seems probable that the ability to modulate (as we would say) had been encountered earlier than the mid-fifth century in instruments of the harp type (to be described later), which were literally 'many-stringed', having perhaps twenty strings as compared with the seven on a lyre or kithara; as a result the word *polychordos* may have been already established as a technical term simply meaning 'versatile' and applicable to any type of instrument.

Mention has already been made of the possibility of playing harmonics on the aulos, and this whole question must now be investigated.

It would be very surprising indeed if the Greeks had failed to discover that by 'overblowing' and tightening the embouchure it is possible to make a reed instrument play the same pattern of intervals as its normal scale, but in a higher register. Because the aulos had a cylindrical bore, this higher register must have been 'at the twelfth' – that is, an octave and a fifth higher, as it is for the same reason on a modern clarinet. (The recorder and the flute both have a cylindrical bore, but can produce the octave harmonic; this is because they are not reed-blown, and are open to the air at both ends of the air-column.) There is some ancient evidence, dating from the mid-fourth century BC, that aulos-players made use of this technique. The most telling evidence comes from Aristoxenos' *Harmonics*, where he is talking about the upper and lower limits of pitch in practical use in music.[23] Having said that the total range of the human voice from low bass to high treble is more than three octaves, he says that an even greater range of notes can be played on an aulos by the use of a device which he calls a *syrinx*. This word is the regular name for the pan-pipe, a rustic instrument of the flute type, which will be discussed in detail later. But in this context it probably signifies a device analogous to the 'speaker' on a modern clarinet, which makes it much easier to obtain the harmonics. The word itself can be used to mean any kind of tube or pipe, which gives some clue to its shape. The same device is also mentioned in the work on acoustics attributed to Aristotle (see Chapter 5), which was probably written at about the same time, mid- to late-fourth century BC, and by one or two other authors.[24] The only real problem is that the authors disagree as to whether the *syrinx* was 'drawn down' to obtain the higher register (Aristoxenos) or 'drawn up' (Aristotle, Plutarch). An ingenious answer to this problem was given more than a century ago by A.A. Howard.[25]

He suggested that the *syrinx* was a small tube which fitted around the upper end of the aulos body, similar to one of the sleeves but without a hole in it. This would normally cover a small 'speaker hole' drilled in the body of the pipe. When the upper register was needed, the *syrinx* might have been moved either up or down on the pipe, so as to uncover the speaker hole – hence the apparent disagreement in the evidence. The Aristotelian work mentions 'stopping' (with the finger) as an alternative to drawing down the *syrinx* to obtain the lower register, saying that it 'increases the volume of sound, just as with thicker strings'. Aristoxenos also uses a verb *syrittein* (derived from the noun *syrinx*) meaning to 'play on the upper register', as against *aulein*, to 'play on the normal register'. There is also some evidence to support this interpretation to be found in the surviving fragments of auloi. One from the Athenian Agora, which is clearly a bulb (*holmos*), has a small hole drilled in it at about the right distance from the mouthpiece end.[26] Another similar fragment from Delos has a similar hole, about 1.5 mm (0.06 in.) in diameter – obviously much too small, and in the wrong position, to have been a fingerhole. The Reading aulos also has a slightly larger hole in the mouthpiece section above the bulb. It is difficult to say with any certainty whether these holes are in the right position to act as speakers, but as a speaker hole does not determine the pitch of the notes, but merely prevents a full pressure-wave from building up in its vicinity, its position is not critical.

Even if there were such a device on the ancient instruments, however, it cannot be compared with the speaker key on a modern clarinet. Almost invariably, it would be necessary for the player to alter the setting of the sleeves when changing register (unless he were playing a musical phrase immediately followed by the same phrase a twelfth higher or lower, which seems unlikely). It is much more credible that such changes would be made during pauses in the music. If, as Aristoxenos suggested, the total range of an aulos over both registers was more than three octaves, there must presumably have been a gap between them, unless the lower register covered a twelfth, which is hardly possible.

There is one other interesting passage which sheds a little light on the *syrinx*. In the treatise on music attributed to Plutarch[27] we are told of an aulos-player called Telephanes from Megara, who disapproved of the *syringes* (plural) to such an extent that he would not allow the instrument-makers to fit them on his instruments (or on any instruments – the Greek is ambiguous) and for that reason he refused to take part in the musical competitions at the Pythian games. There are two possible interpretations of this. One is that he disapproved of the special ear-piercing effects which could be obtained by their use (perhaps during the 'Pythian *nomos*' to imitate the dying hisses of the serpent, see p. 5), regarding them as 'gimmicky'. The other is that he was himself able to play the harmonics without them, and regarded them as a cheap trick by which inferior players could appear more skilful than they really were.

This brings us to the general question of range. The early, simple form of the instrument was bored to play in one of the old aulos scales – Dorian, Lydian or Phrygian. The compass of these scales is not known for certain, but it was probably about an octave or less (see Chapter 3). The scale system and the aulos key system presumably developed together and along the same lines, and by the time the Aristoxenian two-octave 'complete system' had been evolved (see p. 88), the aulos probably had a potential range of at least an octave and a half, not forgetting, of course, that at any one time only six of the possible notes would be available, all of them within the reach of the fingers and thumb. By this time the old scale-names had come to denote little more than key or pitch (again, see Chapter 3) and a new set of names for the aulos types came into use. There were apparently five of these, listed in descending order of pitch:

(1) *parthenikos*, or 'girl' aulos, presumably 'soprano'.
(2) *paidikos*, or 'boy' aulos, presumably 'treble' – perhaps of about the same size and pitch range. At a guess, these were probably about 25–30 cm (10–12 in.) long, and would have a lowest note about a fourth or a fifth above middle c (about 356 Hz).
(3) *kitharistērios*, or 'aulos-to-go-with-the-kithara'. This was almost certainly the instrument occasionally shown being played with the kithara, and which presumably had about the same pitch range. It appears to have been about 35 cm long, and would have had a lowest note just below middle c (about 244 Hz).
(4) *teleios*, or 'complete' aulos – either because it had the range of an adult male voice (*teleios*), or because it could play any selection of six consecutive notes from the 'full' system (*systēma teleion*) of two octaves. The Pompeian instruments were probably of this type; the longest of them is about 54 cm (21 in.) which, allowing 3 cm (1.2 in.) for the reed, would have a lowest note around e flat below middle c (about 150 Hz) – roughly the lowest note of a modern B flat clarinet.
(5) *hyperteleios*, or 'super-complete'. This appears only in a few illustrations, the best being a wall-painting from Herculaneum, thought to be based on an earlier Greek painting of perhaps the third

century BC. (see Figure 8.14 on p. 199). The pipes appear to be about 90 cm (3 ft) long, which would give a lowest note around G, an octave and a fourth below middle c (about 95 Hz). However, to judge from the picture, the player is using a group of notes played from holes about two-thirds of the way down (i.e. from about d upwards); if he used the note from the whole pipe, which the Greeks called the *bombyx*, or 'boomer', it would have been a sort of pedal note a fifth lower.

In addition to the types of aulos named from the scale they were designed to play (Dorian, Phrygian, etc.) and those named from their range of pitch, there is a bewildering list of some 35 other types. Some were apparently named from a particular feature of their construction, such as the *hēmiopos* or 'half-holed' aulos. Ancient scholars explained this as meaning 'half-size', or 'with half the usual number of holes', taking the second element of the word to refer to fingerholes. But this is to strain the sense of the Greek, and it is much more likely to have meant 'with half-size bore' – perhaps a pipe with a 'throat' or diaphragm with a small central hole at the lower end, to make the tone softer and more mellow. If this is so, the type-name *hypotrētos* ('not fully bored') may have meant the same instrument, and a mysterious device called the *pantreton*, which is referred to only once,[28] may have been a key or lever by which the full bore of the aulos could be opened up, and its tone made much louder and clearer. Another interesting type-name is the *magadis* aulos. Until recently it was thought that the *magadis* was a stringed instrument of the harp type, with perhaps as many as 20 strings, and that the technical term *magadizein* (to 'magadize'), which meant to double a melody in octaves, was derived from the name of the instrument. Now most scholars agree that it was the other way round, and that *magadis* was a descriptive term meaning 'playing in octaves' (something like our 'diapason') and not the name of an instrument.[29] Some of the other names for types of aulos may in fact be names of compositions for aulos, and most of the rest are unintelligible.

The most vital and difficult question about the aulos has been left until the last. How were the two pipes of the aulos combined? Did they sound together, and if so, was it in unison, or in some kind of counterpoint, or in octaves, or twelfths? This question has been discussed at length by many scholars, but no firm or generally agreed conclusion has been reached. The question is greatly complicated by the fact that the techniques used by Roman tibia-players may not have been the same as those of the Greeks, and evidence from (say) the first century BC onwards may refer to contemporary Roman practice, or may be derived from a Greek source and refer to the Greek practice of two or three centuries earlier, and it may be very difficult indeed to decide which. A specific example of this problem arises in connection with the 'Phrygian' aulos. To the Greeks, this apparently meant an instrument bored to play the Phrygian scale, but otherwise similar in design and appearance to the rest, while to the Romans it seems to have been a different type, with (perhaps) unequal pipes, one or both of them fitted with a horn bell. This question is discussed later, in Chapter 8.

The evidence on which we have to rely falls into four categories. The first, and by far the most valuable, is the pictorial evidence from vase-paintings. This dates from the mid-sixth century BC onwards, and covers a period of more than two centuries, over which there are a number of features which appear consistently, and must surely be significant. The literary evidence is much less satisfactory; in fact, there is no explicit statement about the piping techniques of the Classical period. The surviving instruments and fragments of instruments are of little help, since no two of them can be said with any certainty to have formed a pair.[30] So the one piece of evidence which could settle the question once and for all is denied to us. Finally, there is the evidence drawn from comparative musicology – from the way in which pairs of pipes have been played in folk-music of more recent times. This type of evidence is favoured by many historians of wind instruments, but seems to me to be very unreliable. It cannot possibly 'prove' anything about the ancient Greek practice. At best, it can only show that a given technique is possible; and, unless it is drawn from a musical culture which resembles that of the Greeks in the most important respects, it is of little value. This effectively rules out any non-European culture; and it would be difficult to find a folk-music tradition in present-day Europe which has not been profoundly changed over the intervening centuries.

In dealing with this very complex question, it seems best to begin with what is, in my opinion, the most credible theory, discussing the evidence which supports it and that which may tell against it, and assessing its implications for Greek music. The other theories which have been put forward will then be reviewed in turn, with discussion of the evidence offered in support of them, and of the serious objections which can be raised against them.

The pictorial evidence suggests that the two pipes of the aulos sounded together, and in unison. In the vast majority of pictures the pipes appear to be of equal length. One may appear to project further than the other, but this is almost invariably the artist's way of trying to indicate that it is nearer to the viewer – a crude attempt at perspective drawing. The player's hands are shown in exactly corresponding positions on the two pipes, and where fingers are shown raised, it is normal for the same ones to be raised on each pipe, indicating that the fingering position is the same. And finally, in the few illustrations which show the fingerholes uncovered, they appear to correspond in position on the two pipes, so as to have sounded the same notes. However, there must have been a very good reason for using two pipes rather than one. The player had to prepare and manipulate two reeds, and most woodwind players would agree that one reed gives more than enough trouble. He also had to blow much harder, and had to control the embouchure on two reeds, using a region of the lips on each side which is less supple and less sensitive than the central region. Why then go to all this trouble, merely in order to play the same note on another pipe? The reason is that the two pipes together produce a totally different tone quality. The two notes are very nearly, but not exactly the same pitch, and this produces a beating or tremulant effect; a similar sound is made by the *vox humana* stop on a modern organ, which has two metal reeds for each note, one very slightly out of tune with the other. The degree of pitch difference, and hence the speed and intensity of the 'beats', could be controlled by a skilful player, and no doubt contributed to the mood or ethos of the music. The technique of 'separation' and 'putting together' of the two pipes (see p. 30 above) may have been used for this purpose. By contrast, the double pipe most commonly used in the Middle East today, the *zummara*, has its pipes fixed together, and has single reeds which are not very effectively controlled by the embouchure. I have only encountered one illustration which is seriously inconsistent with this theory.[31] It shows a scene of Dionysiac revelry, with the unusual combination of aulos and kithara, both played by satyrs. The one playing the aulos is shown in profile, but the right-hand pipe, nearer to the observer, is actually shorter than the more distant one, and the right hand seems a good deal further down the pipe than the left (Figure 2a.14 p. 44).

Although the drawing is meticulous enough to show the little finger of each hand tucked under the pipe to support it while the thumb is taken off the thumbhole, it is still possible to see the hand position as a mistaken attempt at perspective, which may have been partly due to yet another odd feature. In accordance with the convention of black-figure painting, the flesh of female figures is painted white, but so also are the pipes of the aulos. Putting the hands in line would have created a confusing mess of black fingers and white pipes, which the artist may have wished to avoid.

Of the other theories which have been advanced on the use of the two pipes, four deserve mention.

(1) It has been suggested that one pipe was a drone, sounding a single note throughout a piece of music. This is hardly a tenable theory. All the evidence cited above shows that both pipes had more than one fingerhole, and both were fingered at all times. It is scarcely credible that the fingers of one hand would be wasted in an unnecessary operation, limiting the 'chanter' or melody pipe to six notes, when other much better arrangements were possible. The word *bombyx*, which for the purposes of this theory was interpreted to mean 'drone',

Figure 2a.14 Aulos-player's hands not in line

in fact means the lowest note obtainable on the aulos, or any other bumbling or buzzing noise.

There is, however, another technique which involves a drone note, which might be reconciled more easily with the evidence. It is used on several folk-instruments with double pipes (e.g. the Sardinian *launeddas*), and is therefore favoured by those who rely on evidence from comparative musicology. The technical name for it is an 'articulated drone', and it works as follows. The two pipes have a range of (say) six notes each, the two lowest on one pipe overlapping with the two highest on the other (c' and d' in Figure 2a.15).

When the melody (I use the term loosely) rises above these notes, it is played on the higher pipe, the other one sustaining one of the overlapping notes as a drone; when it falls on one of the overlapping notes, it is played on both pipes in unison, and when it goes below those notes it is played on the lower pipe, while the higher one sustains the drone note. Anyone listening who could not see the player's fingering might think that he had a pipe with a range of ten notes and a drone pipe with two. The objection to this theory is that pipes designed to play in this technique are usually unequal in length, the difference being quite unmistakable, and this is not what the vase-paintings show. Even if we hold that the pipes were made equal for the sake of a symmetrical appearance, the player's hands ought not to be level on the two pipes. Apart from the awkward example discussed on p. 43, the evidence is against this.

Figure 2a.15 Two pipes playing with articulated drone

(2) The theory offered in the older textbooks was that one of the pipes played the 'melody line' and the other played an 'accompaniment'. There is, in fact, some evidence to show that when two notes sounded together in harmony, the melody was the lower of the two, so perhaps 'descant' would be a better term. The main evidence in support of this theory comes from Varro, a Roman writer of the first century BC, and should, in my opinion, be disregarded as evidence for the Greek techniques. It is discussed in Chapter 8, in relation to the Roman musical practice. It is entirely reasonable to suggest that on occasion (at a cadence, for example, or at the end of a piece) the two pipes might sound a fifth apart, a fourth apart or an octave apart, these intervals being regarded as harmonious by the Greeks; but there is virtually no evidence for polyphony (in any real sense of the term) in Greek music.[32]

(3) It has also been suggested that the two pipes did not sound together – that the player stopped one from speaking, either by tonguing the reed, or by some key device, and that the two pipes between them were thus able to play an extended scale. This, I believe, should be discounted on the grounds of improbability. A single pipe, fingered by both hands, is capable of a greater range of notes, because it can be held more easily, and there are more opportunities for cross-fingering. Also, as was said earlier, the difficulties of using two reeds would have been avoided if possible.

(4) Finally, there is the theory that the two pipes played the same melody, an octave apart. This is open to the same basic objection as the articulated drone theory – that the pipes should not be of the same length (in fact, one should be twice the length of the other) or at any rate that the hands should not be level. This has been answered by the suggestion that the two pipes were of the same length, but that one of them was played in a higher register. However, as we have already seen, the aulos had a cylindrical bore, and the higher register, produced by the use of the *syrinx*, was not an octave but a twelfth above the lower register. This would have given a strange sound, which does not seem to have any parallel in other double-piping traditions. I am inclined to think that the octave effect was used at times, but that a special type of aulos, the *magadis* aulos, was designed

for the purpose. It is possible that this is the instrument mentioned by
Herodotus, and called 'the female and male aulos', used to accompany
the soldiers of Alyattes the king of Lydia on the march.[33] In Chapter 8
it will be argued that this may have been the ancestor of the 'unequal
pipes' of Roman music, introduced via the Etruscans who, according
to the ancient tradition, had Lydian connections.

2(b)

KITHARA AND LYRE

The most important stringed instrument used by the Greeks was called *kithara* in Greek, and, since there is no obvious equivalent among modern instruments, will henceforward be called kithara in English. This is the normal practice among translators of the Classics, though many use the Latin spelling cithara.

There were two distinct basic forms of the kithara, the earlier one of which had a round base (Figure 2b.1).

This form appears very early in the pictorial evidence. It is shown in a painting on the Hagia Triada sarcophagus dating from the fourteenth century BC or earlier[1] and in geometric vase-paintings from the Greek mainland from the mid-eighth century BC onwards. As these vase-paintings are roughly contemporary with Homer, it is generally held that the stringed instrument played by the bards in his narrative was of this type. He uses two names for it: *kitharis*, an older form of the word kithara (also used by later poets who wish to sound archaic), and *phorminx*; his choice between the two seems to depend only on the rhythm of the

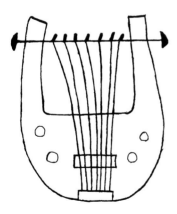

Figure 2b.1 Round-based kithara, seventh century BC

verse. As the instrument has the general appearance of a horseshoe, I propose to call it the 'horseshoe-kithara', though other names have been used.[2]

A great deal has been written about the earliest forms of this instrument, and its probable ancestry in similar, older instruments of the near East. The only important question as far as Greek music is concerned is whether there was a stage in its development when it had only four strings. The trouble is that, though some early pictures clearly show four strings, we cannot be certain whether this represents the reality, or whether the number of strings is limited by the artist's medium or technique. In vase-paintings the four lines representing the strings occupy most of the available space between the arms of the instrument, but are as thin as any in the picture. The same limitation applies to a few surviving miniature models in bronze – at this stage of the art, the strings could not have been made thinner. This problem is complicated still further by the fact that some of the earlier Mycenaean paintings are of a superior artistic quality, and show a more elaborate design of instrument, with more ornamentation than the later ones, and apparently as many as eight strings. The horseshoe kithara is the only one to appear before about 520 BC. After that, however, the flat-based type seems to take over as the standard instrument for the professional musician – indeed, for the great divine musician, Apollo himself.

The horseshoe type more or less disappears for a time, but then re-emerges in a different context – that of indoor, informal music-making in a relaxed atmosphere. Curiously enough, it is commonly shown hanging on the wall at the back of a scene, but not so often being played as part of an ensemble; it should therefore perhaps be viewed as a 'scene-symbol' rather than an actual instrument, comparable to the mirrors which indicate a lady's boudoir, or the gravestone which indicates a funeral context without necessarily being a physical part of it. In the meantime, it has undergone a slight change of shape, whereby the arms seem to be set a short distance from the outer edges of the curved base. Whether this is a change of design, or a more accurate drawing of the older shape, it is difficult to say. By this date it has seven strings, like the flat-based version (Figure 2b.2).

A few vase-paintings show a variant of this design which has a bar across the front of the strings, fixed to the arms each side. Its function is doubtful, but it may be significant that it appears to be about one-third of the vibrating length of the string above the bridge. If so, it might have been possible for the fingers of the left hand to use it as a fret by pressing the strings against it, and to play all the notes of the normal register a twelfth (that is, an octave and a fifth) higher. If, as I shall suggest later, the octave harmonic could also be sounded, this would greatly increase the range of notes (Figure 2b.3).

Figure 2b.2 Round-based kithara, fifth century BC

The flat-based kithara was the 'concert instrument' of the Classical Greek world, through antiquity until the late years of the western Roman empire. It was the instrument of the solo kitharist (*kitharistēs*), the kithara-singer (*kitharōdos*) and the accompanist for a *choros* in all its various functions. It first appears in vase-paintings about 520 BC, and the fact that a number of representations by various different artists show close

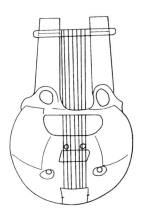

Figure 2b.3 Round-based kithara with 'cross-fret'

similarities suggests that the design was standardized (Figure 2b.4).

The flat-based kithara seems to have been made in five distinct parts. The soundbox (A), rather larger than that of the horseshoe kithara, has a flat bottom and straight sides which diverge up to a point about one-third of the height of the instrument. Instead of the wide, solid-looking arms of the older instrument, this type has two pointed extensions (B), which are sometimes shown as obviously jointed into the top of the body. Rising from the tops of these, which slope at an angle of about 30 degrees, there are two vertical posts (C), of about the same height as the body of the instrument. They extend well beyond the height required by the length of the strings – the cross-bar (D) runs between them about half-way up. There appears to be a curiously weak point where the body extensions join the vertical posts, and a quite elaborate wooden structure (E) is inserted between the top of the body and the bases of the vertical posts, presumably to reinforce the structure as a whole. The central part of this wooden structure is in the form of a horseshoe turned on its side (F); this is braced from the top of the body by a curving strut (G), and a round or mushroom-shaped element (H) is wedged between the top of the 'horseshoe' and the base of the vertical post. It seems hardly credible that this elaborate design was merely decorative. There is no inherent reason why the body of this type of kithara should not have extended upwards into two wide arms, exactly as the early horseshoe type had done, and as the 'Italiote' kithara (see p. 168) did later. We must assume, therefore, that it had some acoustical function; but it is difficult to see what that might have been. It has been suggested that the instrument was deliberately designed to bend at the apparent weak point when extra stress was applied, and then to resume its former shape exactly when the extra

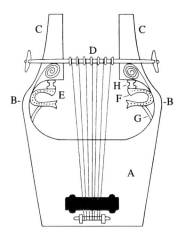

Figure 2b.4 Flat-based kithara

stress was removed. This will be discussed later, in connection with the playing technique (see p. 60 below).

In some of the earliest pictures (of Mycenaean date) the strings are bunched together at the lower end, and diverge towards the crossbar at the top, but in the classical period they are shown exactly parallel. They were anchored at the bottom end to a 'string-stretcher' (*chordotonon*) which apparently consisted of two vertical pieces with a round metal rod stretching across between them. In contrast to the bridge, this part is drawn in outline, and not blocked in in black by the red-figure vase-painters, which suggests that it was metal – not surprising, since it had to take the tension of all seven strings.[3] The exact shape of the bridge cannot be determined with any certainty from the two-dimensional drawings, but it seems to have been remarkably large. Its width from side to side was obviously determined by the spacing of the strings, but from top to bottom it appears to have been at least 5 cm (more than 2 inches) as compared with the bridge of a modern guitar, which is about 1 cm, and usually has a sharp metal ridge across its centre. It is not possible to say whether the top surface of the bridge on which the strings pressed had a clearly-defined ridge, or a gentle curvature. This might affect the tone of the vibrating string to some extent, but would certainly not cause the rattling effect of the Indian *sitar* strings, which are steel wires. It has been suggested that the vertical lines at each end of the bridge in some illustrations represent legs which stand on the soundboard, and support the bridge itself a short distance above it, looking like a miniature coffee-table when seen from the side. In other pictures the bridge seems to rest on its own top and bottom edges, and curve up like an arch between them.

A further problem, created by the preference of the vase-painters for painting a 'full frontal' kithara, is that we cannot be sure whether the front of the instrument was straight and flat, or concave. Certainly, there are some sculptures which show a very marked vertical curvature, but these belong to the Hellenistic period at the very earliest (third to second century BC) and most of them are Roman. Another feature which can be seen in some illustrations is a vertical ridge down the centre of the back, which makes the base, when viewed from below, look triangular. This feature may well go back to the earliest instruments.[4]

The strings ran over the bridge and up to the crossbar, which the Greeks called the 'yoke' (*zygon*). Here we come to one of the most problematic areas – the tuning mechanism, which was apparently the same for the lyre and the kithara. There is no doubt whatsoever that it was situated on the crossbar, since a number of illustrations show a player tuning the instrument, usually plucking the string with the left hand while making some adjustment with the right hand on the crossbar. But here, instead of a consistent and recognizable pattern, the vase-painters show a variety of different arrangements, some with round black tabs, some with round dots above and below the bar, some with the string in line with the tab and others with the string to one side of it. What are we to make of them?

There are two general considerations which must be borne in mind. First, it is surely unwise to assume that there was only one method of tensioning the strings, and to insist that all the illustrations must be reconciled with one and the same device. Since the subtle intonations of Greek music required very accurate tuning, it is likely that the mechanism was developed and improved over a period of three or four centuries, and its appearance may have been changed in the process. Second, when studying the vase-paintings we have to deal with an artist's impression, not a technical draughtsman's diagram. Just as an artist, for his own reasons, might have drawn the aulos to look more elegant than it really was, so the tuning mechanism of the kithara may appear in illustrations to have been much tidier than it was in real life.

As it happens, there is a mention of the tuning device, which was called *kollops* in Greek, as early as the seventh century BC, in the *Odyssey* of Homer.[5] Odysseus is described as having strung his bow 'as easily as a skilled kitharist and singer stretches a string on to (or around) a new *kollops*', which tells us at least that it was something which might wear out and need replacement. It also tells us (in the next line) that the string was made from twisted sheep-gut, which seems to have been the material most commonly used on Greek instruments. Cord made from flax fibres (*linon*) was a possible alternative, and so also was animal sinew (see p. 141). Commentators from much later times[6] give us the information that a *kollops* was a strip of hide cut from the neck of an ox. It has been suggested that some vase-paintings show this. The tabs which appear above and below the crossbar represent the ends of a tongue-like strip, bound to the crossbar by a criss-cross set of thongs, so that it could be pulled up to sharpen the pitch, or downwards to flatten it. But I find it difficult to believe that the hide would not stretch after adjustment, unless it was hardened by some process. There is also the problem that leather (whether cured or raw) extends and contracts with changes in humidity, and this would put the tuning out very badly.

Another explanation of the tuning mechanism depends on an expanded version of a commentator on Homer, according to which the strips of leather from the neck of an ox 'still had the fat adhering to them'. This suggests that the string was somehow interleaved with the greasy strip of hide, and both were rolled around the crossbar. Comparative musicologists assure us that this method is used on the *kissar* (a lyre-type instrument from Ethiopia). It is difficult to see how an accurate tuning could be achieved, but apparently it is possible. A similar method, using strips of cloth instead of leather, has been successfully used on a reconstruction of the Greek lyre by Dr Psaroudakis. With the leather strips there is the added problem that the fat would eventually dry out, and (presumably) allow the *kollops* to slip; perhaps that is why the Homeric bards, if they really used this method of tuning, might have had to fit a new one from time to time.

Another suggested explanation of the word *kollops* is based on a passage in Aristotle's *Mechanics*.[7] Here a detailed analogy is drawn between the *kollops* (which apparently rotates around the crossbar of a kithara) and a form of capstan, called a 'donkey' (*onos*). The point of the comparison is that in each device the force required to turn it depends on the length of the lever or handle – the longer the handle, the easier it is to turn. In fact, the text might possibly be taken to mean that kitharists used an extension arm of some kind to help in turning the *kollopes*, which might have been wooden collars of some kind. They must have fitted tightly enough around the crossbar to prevent slipping, and may perhaps have been rubbed with resin. A slight problem is that the handles of the *kollopes* would normally be at various different heights when the strings were tuned, whereas they appear on one level in the vase-paintings; but this may be artistic licence. A relief sculpture on the 'Ludovisi Throne' shows a lyre-player (who would have used the same tuning mechanism) with what look like wooden collars on the crossbar, and they are not neatly in line. Finally, the explanation derives some support from rude popular slang. The comic poets of the late fifth and early fourth century BC use the word *kollops* and the derived verb *kollopeuein* to refer to the homosexual activities of young aspiring politicians, 'running around and making friends', as the ancient dictionaries politely put it.[8]

Another interpretation of the tuning mechanism has been put forward by Dr Helen Roberts.[9] The word *kollops* is sometimes confused by ancient writers with the word *kollabos*, which apparently meant a kind of bread roll.[10] This may be a simple confusion of similar-sounding words, but it may have more significance. The *kollopes* may have been short wooden rods, shaped roughly like a baguette, about 8–10 cm (3–4 inches) long. They could have been placed against the crossbar, with the top end of each string anchored to the middle of its rod, and wound around above and below the crossbar in a particular way, so that turning the *kollops* would adjust the tension.

This explanation is commended by the fact that it has been used by Dr Roberts on reconstructed models of the kithara and lyre, and was found to work effectively. Once again, there is the problem that the rods should be in various different positions, and not in a neat line as they usually appear, but once again, artistic licence can be invoked.

The crossbar runs across between the arms, some distance below their tops, and the vase-painters seem quite concerned to show that it was a separate element, jointed or slotted in some way on to the arms as though it was made to be removable. I have previously thought that it fitted into slots on the front faces of the arms, but after a meticulous examination of a section of the Parthenon frieze in the Acropolis Museum Dr Psaroudakis concluded that the arms actually pass through rectangular slots in the crossbar. I have since examined more carefully the kithara shown in a black-figure vase painting[11] which gives (most unusually) a rear view. The crossbar cuts across the backs of the arms of the instrument exactly as it does across the front in the usual view. This would give a firm fixing, and would enable the tuning mechanism to be rotated around the crossbar without any danger of the bar itself twisting. It would also, since the arms are straight and parallel, allow the crossbar to be moved a short distance up or down the arms, which might be useful (assuming that the strings had enough spare length) for re-tuning the whole instrument to play in a higher or lower key. It is certain, however, that the spirals which are often shown on the arms below the crossbar were purely decorative, and could not have represented any sort of device for moving the crossbar up and down.[12]

The two vertical lines near the ends of the crossbar represent two round discs, which may have had the effect of transmitting to the air vibrations of very high pitch, which the main mass of the instrument would tend to absorb owing to its inertia. The fact that they are discs can only be inferred from much later illustrations in sculpture, since the vase-painters almost invariably show the front face of the instrument. They were probably made of metal for high speed of sound transmission; they correspond to the very small cones in modern hi-fi loudspeakers, which transmit the very high audio frequencies.

In the vast majority of vase-paintings of the Classical period the kithara has seven strings, and the old names given to the strings were regularly used by the musical theorists for the notes of the basic scale; they are in fact feminine adjectives, with the word for string (*chordē*) understood. Some useful information can be gleaned from them.

1	2	3	4	5	6	7
Hypatē	Parhypatē	Lichanos	Mesē	Tritē	Paranētē	Nētē

The string nearest to the player (i.e. on the left in frontal pictures, which never show a left-handed player) was called *hypatē* in Greek. This means 'highest', or 'first', but the string of this name sounded the lowest note, which is slightly confusing. The reason is that the Greek words for 'high' and 'low' never had any reference to pitch. The Greek word for high-pitched is *oxy*, meaning 'acid' or 'sharp' (hence our use of that word for a note a semitone higher) and the word for 'low-pitched' is *bary*, meaning 'heavy'. (By the way, why is it 'flat' in English?) So the word *hypatē* means the 'first' string, played with the left thumb which, incidentally, is also called the 'highest' of the fingers. The meaning 'highest' is more obviously appropriate for the corresponding string of the lyre or *barbitos* (see below) which was often held sloping away from the player. A modern guitar preserves the same arrangement – the uppermost string is the lowest in pitch. Conversely, the string at the far end from the player was called *nētē*, meaning 'last' or 'lowest', and sounded the highest note. Two more strings were named in relation to these – *parhypatē* meaning 'next to *hypatē*' and *paranētē*, 'next to *nētē*'.[13] The central string of the seven, logically enough, was called *mesē*, the 'middle'. The names of the remaining two are interesting. The third one from the player, between *parhypatē* and *mesē*, was called *lichanos* which, despite its appearance, is also a feminine adjective – the 'index-finger string'. It could, of course, be played with the index finger of either hand. The string between *mesē* and *paranētē* was called the 'third' string (*tritē*), one of a number of indications that the Greeks normally counted the notes in descending order of pitch.

Although the techniques of holding and playing the kithara are copiously illustrated in the Classical period, it is not easy to give a detailed account of them. The reason is that a playing technique is essentially a set of movements, whereas the vase-paintings show static poses. What is more, the artist chooses a particular point in the player's movements for his own reasons – to give an impression of dramatic flourish, perhaps, or languid elegance, or soulful inspiration. There may, in fact, be very few pictures which make an honest attempt to show what a kitharist in action really looked like. However, there are some certainties. Both hands were used, although the movements of the left hand were limited by a sling, which passed around the left wrist and around the far arm of the instrument, and was used to hold the kithara against the player's left shoulder and chest. This sling was made from cloth, and sometimes had ornamental tassels (Figure 2b.5).

The player is almost invariably shown standing upright, unlike the players of the lyre and *barbitos*, who may be shown stooping or seated. Despite the load on the left hand, its fingers and thumb were apparently able to reach, pluck or damp the strings as required. The nomenclature of the strings suggests that the thumb was used for the nearest string (*hypatē*), the index finger for the third string (*lichanos*), the middle finger for *mesē* and the third finger for the fifth string. The little finger would obviously be used for the seventh string (*nētē*), and probably for *paranētē* also. The thumb is sometimes shown bent into the palm of the hand, suggesting that it could reach any of the first four strings. The right hand is normally shown holding a plectrum, which looks rather like a teaspoon, and is attached to the kithara (usually at the base) by a cord about 2–3 ft (60–90 cm) long. The obvious explanation of this is that the plectrum

Figure 2b.5 Support sling on kithara

might have to be dropped while the fingers of the right hand were used to pluck the strings, but when it was needed again it could be rapidly retrieved. These two methods of playing were distinguished by two different words in Greek – *krouein*, to 'strike' (with the plectrum), and *psallein*, to 'pluck' (with the finger). We know from the literary sources that the plectrum was normally made of animal horn. There is a hint in the treatise on acoustics ascribed to Aristotle (see Chapter 5, pp. 140–1) that kithara-players sometimes used the plectrum very close to the bridge, in order to obtain a harsh, penetrating sound with strong harmonics. Modern string players achieve the same effect by bowing *sul ponticello*. The two playing techniques would obviously produce two different tone qualities – the plectrum a clear, loud, brilliant sound and the fingers (of either hand) a softer tone, with fewer of the high-pitched overtones. Since the majority of kithara-players were singers who accompanied themselves on their instruments, it would be natural to assume that the fingers were used for the accompaniment, which would for most of the time be in unison with the voice, or doubling at the octave. The notes played with the plectrum would probably be loud enough to interfere with the voice, and would be used mainly for introductory passages (called 'preludes', *anabolai* in Greek) or link-passages between sections of a work.

One difficult problem posed by the vase-paintings is that the favourite position for a player using the plectrum is 'at the follow-through', with the plectrum high in the air to the right of the instrument, and the playing arm almost straight. Should this be taken to mean that the plectrum was dragged across all the strings at each stroke? If so, it must be assumed that the left hand damped out all the strings except the one which was required to sound; and though there are a few vase-paintings which apparently show this, there are some which show several strings free and undamped.

Though the technique is well illustrated in other musical cultures, and therefore attributed to the Greeks by comparative musicologists, it seems rather clumsy, and it is difficult to see what quality it would add to the sound, apart from a rather tuneless jangling.[14] The vase-painters' favourite position may have been chosen simply for dramatic effect, or to reveal fully the instrument itself and the player's left hand.

Another piece of evidence has been adduced to suggest strumming. In a parody of Aeschylus' musical style in Aristophanes' *Frogs*, Euripides offers two specimens of *choros* song. The first is introduced by a short prelude on the aulos (played by the theatre piper)[15] and has a repeating refrain. This is quite in accordance with Aeschylus' practice in his tragic choruses. In the second specimen Euripides intersperses the lines with the words *tophlattothrat, tophlattothratt*. There is a problem here: the lines are in fact garbled reminiscences of Aeschylus' *Agamemnon* and other plays (which would have been sung by a *choros* with aulos accompaniment) but Euripides says they are 'worked up from kithara-singers' compositions'. This is usually taken to mean that Euripides is parodying a kithara-singer and, having no kithara on which to accompany himself, imitating its sounds vocally ('plink-plank-plonk', so to speak). But we must beware of the English dimension here. If the words are pronounced 'tofflatto-thr-r-ratt' they do indeed suggest strumming, but it is now accepted that the Greeks pronounced the aspirates as two separate sounds, 'top-hlattot-hrat', and there is no good evidence for a Scottish-style trilling of the 'r'. Incidentally, Dionysos, the patron god of the drama, who has a prominent (though not very dignified) role in the play, compares this song to a 'work-song he picked up from Marathon or somewhere', not to a kithara-singer's work.[16] Does this suggest an element of folk-music in Aeschylus' compositions?

We also know of a technical term, *katalēpsis*, used in relation to kithara-players. The word means 'grip' or 'hold', and its effect is described as 'preventing the prolongation of the note'. The exact meaning of the passage is obscure, but it appears that the string could be struck with the plectrum and then almost immediately damped out, making a sound rather like a violin played *pizzicato*.[17]

This brings us to the question of the tuning of the strings and the range of the instrument, both of which have been the subject of much controversy. The basic problem is that the kithara is shown throughout the fifth century BC with seven strings (in a few exceptional cases, eight), but the literary sources, in particular Plato, suggest that kitharists played florid and elaborate passages,[18] which hardly seems possible if only the seven open notes were used. Also, since it is almost certain that the seven strings were tuned to a continuous scale, its range is likely to have been about an octave, or a ninth at the most. The material from which the strings were normally made – sheep-gut – also imposes some limitations on the pitch range. The strings were all of the same length – about 30–40 cm (12–16 in.) – and it would have been difficult to create enough tension in a thin string of that length, even assuming that the tuning mechanism would stand it, to raise its pitch higher than about an octave above middle c (say about 500 Hz). At the lower end, a thicker string cannot be made to give a loud or sustained note unless its tension is above a certain minimum, which would probably have given a note in the region of f below middle c (about 170 Hz). The terminology used for the *harmoniai* (see Chapter 3), which described the high-pitched scales as 'tight' or 'tense' (*syntonōterai*) and those of lower pitch as 'relaxed' or 'slack' (*aneimenai*), if it is to be taken literally, suggests that the general location of the notes was within the range of about a twelfth (f to a′).

A number of scholars have offered theories which claim to explain how the kitharist might have obtained more than the seven open notes from the seven strings of his instrument. One of them has been effectively refuted, but it has found its way into some of the textbooks and encyclopaedias, and must therefore be discussed. It was put forward in the 1920s by Curt Sachs,[19] and was largely based on a phenomenon to be seen in the instrumental notation, as preserved by Alypius (for more details, and the true explanation, see Chapter 9). There are a number of groups of three notes, separated by two small intervals, which are represented in this notation by the same symbol in three different positions, 'normal' for the lowest note, 'lying on its back' for the middle one, and 'reversed' for the highest. Sachs observed that the notes corresponding to the 'normal position' symbols formed a pentatonic scale, such as can be obtained by playing the black notes on a modern keyboard instrument, with two other notes of variable pitch among them. He therefore argued that the Greek lyre and kithara were tuned to a scale of this type. The fact that the symbols were used in three positions indicated, he thought, a system of fingering whereby two additional notes could be obtained from each string, the 'second position' (denoted by the symbol on its back) being used to indicate the open-string pitch raised by a small interval, and the 'third position' (symbol reversed) to indicate a further rise of about the same interval. In other words, this notation is in the form of a tablature, which gives direct instructions to the player on the fingering positions. According to this theory, the seven strings of the kithara would have a range of more than an octave (despite its name, the pentatonic octave scale has six notes) and offer the player a possible choice of 21 notes.

The theory was meticulously examined by Winnington-Ingram.[20] He pointed out a number of illogicalities which cast grave doubt on Sachs' argument. But the argument really founders on the question of how the strings were manipulated to produce the higher notes. There is not one single illustration which could be claimed reliably to show the operation. Sachs supposed that the left hand was used to stop the string (perhaps increasing its tension at the same time); but that could hardly be done except by reaching up and over the crossbar, to press on the string a short distance down its length. It is pretty clear that almost all the illustrations which show the left hand in that area are in fact concerned with the manipulation of the *kollopes* in order to tune the instrument, and not with the actual playing. Also, since there was no fingerboard for the string to be pressed against, the notes obtained by this method must have had a less satisfactory tone, and less reliable pitch, than those from the open strings. They too must have sounded rather like a violin played *pizzicato*.

An alternative solution was offered by O. Gombosi.[21] He suggested that the pitch of any string could be raised by using the plectrum to press on the non-sounding portion between the bridge and the tailpiece, and thus increase the tension, a technique which can be paralleled from the Japanese *koto*. But this also is unsatisfactory. It means that only the left hand could play the sharpened notes, the right hand (and the plectrum) being limited to the open strings. And, once again, reliable pictorial evidence is completely lacking.

Yet another attempt was made by Ingemar Düring to suggest how the number of notes obtainable on a seven-stringed kithara might have been increased.[22] The comic poet Pherecrates, who was roughly contemporary with Aristophanes in the late fifth century BC, wrote a highly amusing (if rather rude) comedy called *Chiron*, of which a short fragment survives. It clearly dealt with musical trends in the second half of the century, 'Music' being personified as a woman who has suffered a series of indecent assaults, and the various composers' innovations being described in terms which could have a musical or a sexual significance. The one in question here is Phrynis, who is accused of 'inserting his own special *strobilos*-thingy, and bending and twisting me until I was completely undone; and he had twelve *harmoniai* on five strings'. The word *strobilos* has the basic meaning 'twister', and can signify a whirlwind or eddy; hence it was taken by earlier scholars to be a musical term meaning 'turn' or 'excursion'. Düring took it to refer to a mechanical device on the kithara, which functioned in the same sort of way as the double action on a modern harp, raising the pitch of some of the strings by a small amount, and thus enabling the player to obtain 'twelve scales from five strings'. Incidentally, the passage makes much better sense if, as Düring suggested, the number five is amended to seven. But *strobilos* could also mean a spinning-top or a pine-cone which, in conjunction with the word 'insert' would sound suggestive to the more schoolboyish minds in the audience. Also, the expression 'twelve scales' is in itself suspect; two other composers are accused of employing twelve strings on their instruments, and (bearing in mind the style and spirit of the passage) the number twelve might well have been pornographically suggestive.[23] Perhaps it would be safer to treat this item of evidence as a comic poet's extravagance. In any case, Düring's hypothesis depends on assigning a technical meaning to a single word in one context, and there is no reliable pictorial evidence to support this hypothesis.

A totally different theory has more recently been advanced by Bo Lawergren.[24] He suggests that the rather peculiar design of the kithara, which we have already examined, was intended to make the whole structure elastic. One or more of the strings could be pressed by the thumb of the left hand, so as to increase the tension in those strings and compress the whole frame of the instrument. This would reduce the tension in the remaining strings and lower their pitch. This is an attractive hypothesis, and can be supported from some pictorial evidence, but there are a number of difficulties involved.

First, there would be a serious danger that the string or strings used to compress the frame might be stretched, and not return to their original pitch.

Second, they must have been pressed against some resistance, either the sling (i.e. away from the player) or the shoulder (towards the player). It would be difficult to apply the right pressure to more than one string.

Third, the most natural way for the arms to bend, given the structures supporting them, would be inwards; but the crossbar would prevent them from doing this. Moreover, the apparent thinness of the crossbar suggests that it would bend more readily than the more substantial parts of the body.

Fourth, this theory cannot easily be reconciled with the evidence of the instrumental notation, which Sachs regarded as very important. The 'normal' position of the symbol denotes the lowest of the three notes, and the 'modified' positions indicate notes which are sharpened to a higher pitch. According to Lawergren's theory, the modified notes would have a lower pitch. My own explanation of the notation, which I believe to be correct, is that it refers to the aulos, and not to a stringed instrument at all (see pp. 207–9).

Fifth, since this technique depends specifically on the design of the kithara, it could not have been used on the lyre or the *barbitos* (see p. 61). It is true that professionals usually played the kithara, and that its playing techniques required more skill, but it is difficult to imagine that ambitious amateurs would be satisfied with a very restricted range of notes on the other instruments.

In view of these difficulties, it seems wise to regard the theory as 'not proven', though we should keep an open mind about it.

Finally, one technique should be examined which could have extended the range of the kithara and of the lyre and *barbitos*, which has been proved to be workable by experiments, and which may be shown in some vase-paintings. It was called 'division' (*dialēpsis* in Greek), and involved the production of harmonics in much the same way as they are produced by a modern harpist. A finger of the left hand (the kitharist could use any finger) was allowed to rest lightly on the central point of the string, and was removed immediately after the string had been struck by the plectrum. This causes the two halves of the string to vibrate, each at twice the frequency of the open note, thus sounding an octave higher. My own experiments on a monochord, and those of Dr Helen Roberts on reconstructions of the ancient instruments (see note 3) have shown that the tone quality of these harmonics is almost as good as that of the open string, unlike that produced by stopping. Here, then, is a technique which could have doubled the range of the kithara, enabling it to play a scale of fourteen notes over a range of two octaves or more. It may also be significant that above a certain pitch both notation systems use octave marks (see p. 212), a feature which may have been added to the basic system when the technique of *dialēpsis* became popular.

Among the woodwind instruments, the aulos was clearly the king, and no other instrument had anything like its popularity or range of use. But there were two other stringed instruments which almost rivalled the kithara in popularity – the lyre and barbitos, two instruments which were, in effect, the alto and tenor versions of the same instrument. Here we meet an interesting phenomenon. They differed from the kithara in size and loudness of tone, but apparently had much the same range of pitch, and were played with similar techniques. The social attitudes towards them, however, were in sharp contrast. A kithara-player (*kitharistēs*) was almost invariably a professional musician who dressed in a florid costume when performing at public ceremonies; many kithara-players were also teachers of music, and though they naturally played a lyre when teaching their pupils to do so, they were none the less called 'kitharists'.[25] The proper instrument for the amateur – that is, for the free-born man who did not earn his living by playing – was the lyre or barbitos.

In many respects the lyre-type and the kithara-type instruments were very similar. The essential difference was that the soundbox and frame of the kithara formed a single structure, all made of the same material, whereas the lyre had a soundbox made from tortoiseshell and animal hide, with wooden arms jointed into it. So important was the choice of this material for the soundbox that the words for 'tortoise' (*chelys* in Greek and *testudo* in Latin) were regularly used as poetic alternatives for 'lyre' (*lyra* in both Greek and Latin).

Our evidence for the lyre is copious, and extends over a long period. The earliest representation in a vase-painting dates from about 700 BC, and there is a very useful piece of literary evidence in the Homeric Hymn to Hermes, in which the poet gives an account of the invention of the instrument by the infant god. That poem is usually dated to the early sixth century BC at the very latest. The type of tortoise used in the making of lyres was not the familiar type kept nowadays as pets, but a larger

*Figure 2b.*6 Lyre (front view)

*Figure 2b.*7 Tortoiseshell body of lyre

variety called *testudo marginata*, which when fully grown may be as long as 10–12 ins (26–30 cm). It is native to Greece, but rarely found in other places. This has been used as evidence that the instrument originated in Greece, and was not imported. It also fits the evidence (such as it is) of the myth, which placed the birth of Hermes and his invention of the lyre in Arcadia, in the central Peloponnese (see p. 161).

Though couched in poetic language, the account of Hermes' achievement can be interpreted with some confidence. He first killed the tortoise and scooped the flesh out of its shell. Then he 'cut reeds to the correct length and fitted them inside' – an obscure operation to which we must return later. He then 'stretched ox-hide around it by his ingenuity, and inserted arms and jointed a yoke on to both of them, and then stretched seven guts of female sheep on it'. From this it is quite clear that the ox-hide formed the sounding-board on which the bridge stood, while the tortoiseshell acted as a hollow resonator behind it. The use of animal hide for this purpose is common in primitive stringed instruments, and survives in many primitive cultures today. But there is a serious problem involved here. The shape of the underside of a tortoise is a plain oval, and if the ox-hide was 'stretched over' it, the sound-box should appear oval when viewed from the front. But although some early and crudely-drawn illustrations show this shape, the characteristic picture in fifth-century vase-paintings, which are very carefully drawn, is rather different (Figure 2b8).

The most natural way to interpret the poet's phrase 'inserted the arms' would be to suppose that the two curved lengths of wood passed through the recesses in the rim of the shell where the animal's hind legs had been (the shell was probably used upside-down, with the 'head' end at the bottom), and extended to the rim at the base, where they were probably jointed together. This would ensure that they, and not the tortoiseshell, bore the stress caused by the tension in the strings.[26]

However, the lyre body in the classical vase-paintings has 'wings' or 'ears' towards the top, and the arms appear to be fixed to them, and to extend no further down the front of the instrument.

This leads me to suggest that these pictures represent a change in the construction, involving the use of a wooden frame, shaped on the outside as it appears in the vase-paintings, with the hide stretched over the front, but with an oval hole inside, into which the tortoiseshell was fixed at the back. The arms could have been fixed on the front surface by means of

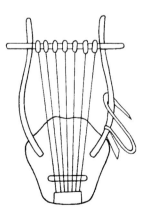

Figure 2b.8 Shape of lyre sounding-board

dowels. This arrangement would take all the stress off the tortoiseshell itself, and transfer it to the frame. It may be objected that such a frame would greatly increase the weight of the instrument, and it must be admitted that some pictures show players waving a lyre about with one hand in a way that implies a very light instrument, but I am not sure that the objection is decisive.

In the illustrations of the lyre we are faced with the same problem as with the kithara. They are, almost without exception, frontal views, and it is impossible to tell whether the arms were bowed in one dimension only, as shown in the flat plane of the illustrations, or whether they also curved forwards towards the viewer. If they did, the vase-painter would have had no possible way of showing it except in a side-view or three-quarter view. As it happens, there is one such illustration on a 'white-ground lekythos' dating from the middle of the fifth century BC.[27] There is some controversy over the interpretation of this picture. At one time I was convinced that it was not a lyre, but after having taught Greek vase-painting for some years, and having come to respect the perspective skills of the painters in the 'white-ground' technique, I now think that it is. The fact that the arms (the far one is faintly visible) appear to be bowed has been taken by some (especially West) to indicate a bowed or arched harp; but the strings of that instrument are at various distances from the sounding-board, and would all be clearly visible, whereas here the artist has shown just enough to indicate that there are more than one. The cross-bar is seen end-on – something which a red-figure vase painter would find difficult to show – and the arms extend beyond and above it, while at the bottom there is quite unmistakably a bridge and tailpiece, both of which are inappropriate for a harp.

There is another important piece of evidence which suggests that the arms of the lyre were bent both inwards and forwards. The philosopher Herakleitos, renowned for his obscurity, spoke of the unity of all things in the world as 'a *harmonia* of contrary tensions, like that of a bow or a lyre'.[28] He has just said that 'by pulling itself apart, it pulls itself together'. This analogy with the lyre (interesting that he should use the word *harmonia*) would be much more effective if the arms of the lyre appeared to be 'bowed' and in tension themselves.

The Homeric hymn tells of Hermes 'cutting reeds to the correct length and fitting them inside (or across) the shell'. There are also a few allusions in fifth-century literature to something called a 'reed under the lyre', and a phrase used by Sophocles suggests that 'taking away the reed from under someone's lyre' was an expression roughly equivalent to 'taking the ground from under his feet'.[29] The first explanation which immediately suggests itself is that these lengths of reed were sound-posts, propped against the tortoiseshell body at the back, and under the ends of the bridge to prevent it from depressing the surface of the hide sounding-board. But this is not acceptable, because they are said to have been put in place before the arms were inserted or the hide fixed on the front. It is better to assume that they were some kind of reinforcement for the tortoiseshell, placed horizontally and vertically across to prevent it from distorting when under stress.

The arms of the lyre (the Greek word was *pēchys*, which strictly means 'forearm') have a fairly standard and simple shape, being curved symmetrically. There is one significant variation; some early pictures show S-shaped arms which taper to a point. This probably represents an archaic design in which large animal horns were used for the arms.

In most other respects the lyre seems to have been closely similar to the kithara. The fixing of the crossbar may have been the same (it is drawn in the same way) but there is the problem in the lyre that the arms are not parallel at their top ends, and the crossbar could not have been slid over them. The tuning mechanism appears to be the same, and the lyre regularly has seven strings. The techniques of playing also appear similar, both hands being used. However, because the lyre was much smaller and lighter, it could be played standing or seated, and though a sling around the left wrist was used to support it, it was not necessary to hold the instrument upright. In many pictures it is shown sloping away from the player at an angle of 45 degrees or even more (Figure 2b.9). It was altogether a less exacting and more comfortable instrument.

It is difficult to assess the pitch range of the lyre with much confidence. Its structure was not strong, so the maximum tension allowable in the

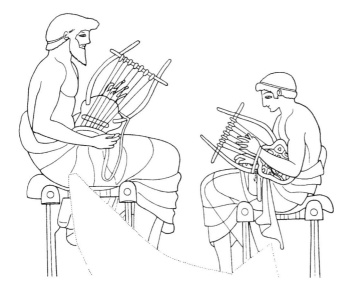

Figure 2b.9 Seated lyre-players (teacher and pupil)

strings could not have been high. A reasonable guess would be an octave somewhere around a–a´, about 216–432 Hz.

The version of the lyre which had longer strings and a lower range of pitch was called the *barbitos* (sometimes *barbiton*). It is found in a lot of the contexts in which the lyre is seen, and a few others which are specific to it. The regular instrument for musical instruction in school scenes is the lyre, and the *barbitos* is not to be found there; however, it is more common than the lyre in scenes of revelry, such as the *kōmos*, or band of revellers going home from a party, or going from one party to the next – a favourite subject with the vase-painters. It is also, rather surprisingly, often played by 'real' satyrs in Dionysiac revels (as opposed to actors dressed for satyr-plays, see p. 22). The 'solo lyric' poets Sappho and Alkaios are shown playing the *barbitos* in Figure 1.8 on p. 11. On this basis Winnington-Ingram humorously suggested that Sappho sang contralto.

The name '*barbitos*' was almost certainly a foreign word, and ancient attempts to give it a Greek etymology should be ignored. According to tradition, it was 'invented' by Terpander, who lived in Lesbos in the mid-seventh century BC, but this may simply mean that it was imported from a musical culture in Asia Minor at about that time. It was very similar indeed to the lyre, except that the arms were shaped differently, and its strings were about half as long again as those of the lyre. The body was made from a tortoiseshell of the same size as that used for the lyre, but because the arms are proportionately longer, it appears smaller. Instead of a uniform curve, the arms have a special shape (Figure 2b.10).

For the first two-thirds of their length the arms are almost straight, diverging to about two and a half times the width of the body. Then they curve inwards quite sharply through a quarter-circle to the horizontal, their ends being about the width of the body apart. Two vertical bars about 4–6 ins (10–15 cm) long are jointed at right-angles, with forks to

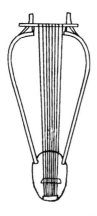

Figure 2b.10 Barbitos

support the crossbar, making the strings apparently longer than those of a kithara. As the structure of the instrument is lighter and less robust than that of the kithara, it is likely that the tension in the strings was less, so that the lowest note may have been about an octave below middle c (about 128 Hz). This would make it ideal for accompanying a baritone voice in the comfortable part of its range. It is also significant that of all the combinations of woodwind and stringed instrument shown in vase-paintings, that of aulos and *barbitos* is by far the most popular.

Finally, there was a variant of the lyre which could be called the 'Thamyris-lyre' or 'Thamyris-kithara' according to taste. It is so called because it appears in a vase-painting depicting the famous musician who was punished for his presumption (see p. 152). It is also referred to as the 'Thracian' kithara or lyre. Two players are shown in Figure 2b.11.

It is difficult to be certain whether these are 'real' satyrs or actors dressed for a satyr-play; there is an aulos-player standing in front of them (not shown in Figure 2b.11) which would suggest a theatrical context. The differences between this type of instrument and the standard lyre are:

- The sound-box is not made from a tortoise-shell, but probably of wood (hence, perhaps, it should be called a kithara). It has a flat base (we cannot tell what the back was like) and a semi-circular top edge, with quite a lot of decoration.
- The strings run from a 'stretcher' (*chordotonon*) over a bridge to the

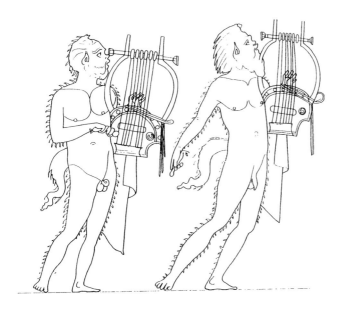

Figure 2b.11 'Thamyris' or 'Thracian' kitharas

67

crossbar, as on a lyre, except that the bridge is higher up on the soundboard. They are not very carefully painted, but the instrument on the left has got eight, the one on the right the usual seven.

- The arms are of different shape, much nearer to arcs of a circle, and they appear to enter the body behind the soundboard instead of being 'pegged' on the front. The extensions which go beyond the crossbar are parallel, so that the crossbar might have been adjustable to different heights, but there is nothing obvious to suggest how.

2(c)

OTHER INSTRUMENTS

The remaining instruments in general use may be dealt with much more briefly. They do not appear in vase-paintings with anything like the same frequency as the aulos, kithara or lyre, and the literary references to them are comparatively few, some of them confined to specific literary genres. For the sake of variety, let us return to the woodwind instruments.

The *Syrinx*

The aulos was a reed-blown instrument; but the Greeks used two wind instruments which worked on the flute principle – that is, the oscillations in a tuned pipe were set up by so-called 'edge tones', generated by the player blowing a stream of air on to a fixed edge at or near one end of the pipe. The most important instrument of this kind was the pan-pipe, called *syrinx* in Greek and *fistula* in Latin. This instrument was perhaps among the very first to be used by primitive peoples, being the most simple of them all. Indeed, it was probably not invented by people, but copied from nature, as told in the charming Greek myth of its origin (see Chapter 6). It is occasionally mentioned in literature down to the end of the Classical period, almost invariably in connection with herdsmen or their patron god, Pan. It is even used by the divine herdsman Argos in the Io story in Aeschylus' (?) *Prometheus Bound* (574–5). This presumably reflects the restricted use of the instrument in real life in a pastoral setting, which even Plato is prepared to allow in his Ideal Republic.[1] The earliest illustration of it is on the François Vase, dated about 575 BC, where it is shown being played by one of the Muses at the wedding of Peleus and Thetis, and almost the only literary evidence for its use in such a setting is in a choral song written nearly two centuries later by Euripides,[2] which happens to refer to the same event. It did not really come into its own as a serious instrument until the third century BC, when Theokritos developed the genre of pastoral poetry. From then on, it became a powerful symbol of the pastoral poet's art. This is discussed in Chapter 7.

The Greek version (Figure 2c.1) was made with all its pipes of the same

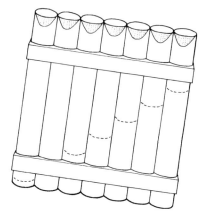

Figure 2c.1 Syrinx (Greek form)

length, the tuning being effected by filling them up to various depths inside with beeswax. The same material was also used to fix the pipes together, though illustrations appear to show some signs of binding with criss-cross twine or straw. This use of wax gives rise to a curious error among the writers of late antiquity. Theokritos, describing the construction of the instrument, regularly uses the verb *pēgnymi*, meaning 'fix' or 'solidify', and the adjective *pēktos*, meaning 'fixed together (with wax)'. There was an instrument called *pēktis*, which was almost certainly one of the harp family (discussed on p. 75), but owing to the similarity of sound the term came to be used mistakenly for the *syrinx*.[3] The pipes themselves were made from the ubiquitous reed (*kalamos*), or from fennel-stalks, or any other plant with hollow stems. Most of the illustrations suggest that the pipes were fixed together in a straight line. The Rumanian *naiu*, which is a direct descendant of the Roman form, is made with a curve of about a foot radius, and it is certainly easier to move rapidly from one note to another as a result. There is only one slight suggestion, in a rather vague phrase of Theokritos,[4] that the Greek version was curved. There are frequent allusions to 'rubbing the lip' on the instrument, which may be a problem for the player, because the near side of the pipe has to be filed away at its top to make a sharp edge, over which the player's upper lip forms the embouchure, and the lower lip then has to be pressed against the area from which the smooth outer skin of the reed has been removed. The range of pitch was apparently quite small: larger instruments with a greater number of pipes were not developed until Roman times. The characteristic number of pipes in Greek illustrations is seven, some earlier pictures showing five or even fewer. Because the pipes of the Greek version were necessarily 'stopped' pipes (closed at the bottom end), the pitch of each pipe would have been the same as that of a flute of twice the length, and only the odd-numbered harmonics (3rd, 5th, 7th, etc.) would be produced. This gives a pungent, penetrating tone which, though it lacks the fullness and roundness of the flute, has a certain plaintive and mysterious quality, especially if the player uses a *vibrato* breathing technique. The range of contrast between the loudest and softest notes (the 'dynamic range') is fairly limited. The instrument can be 'overblown' so as to produce harmonics, but the upper register is a twelfth higher, and on an instrument with seven pipes there would be a gap of about a fifth between the registers. In any case, the upper register is something of an ear-splitting whistle, and for occasional special effect the ancient players are more likely to have used a technique of partial overblowing, which combines the fundamental pitch with the third harmonic – a husky, wheezy sound, much loved in the 1980s by makers of natural history films.

The *plagiaulos*

The other instrument of the flute type used by the Greeks was the 'transverse aulos', called *plagios aulos* (or in shortened form *plagiaulos*) in Greek and *obliqua tibia* in Latin. Like the *syrinx*, this instrument had strong pastoral connections; the simplest explanation for this is that it was originally a modified form of the *syrinx*, developed in the same environment and used by the same players.

In a number of textbooks and articles[5] it is suggested that the *plagiaulos* was a reed-blown instrument, the reed being inserted into a socket near one end, either at right-angles or at an obtuse angle to the pipe. This suggestion is based on a misinterpretation of a passage in the work on acoustics attributed to Aristotle (see pp. 141–2) where the text is almost certainly corrupt, and also on a misinterpretation of sculptural evidence from later periods. In fact, a reed cannot be made to function in this way – it must be 'end on' to the resonant tube, and its stem must be of the same diameter. As a result of this mistake, a few surviving instruments (for example, the so-called 'Maenad Pipes' in the British Museum) have been wrongly described as *plagiauloi*.[6] There are a number of illustrations in Egyptian art from an earlier period of an end-blown flute, which is no more than a single pipe of a *syrinx* with fingerholes bored along its side. It can be held vertically in front of the player, or sideways like a flute, the latter position being preferred. But virtually all the illustrations in Greek, Etruscan and Roman art show a flute of the modern type, with an embouchure hole near one end, over which the player blows. Its sharp edge (on the far side from the player's mouth) is used to create the 'edge tones'. Figure 2c.2 is based on a Roman mosaic, but that is thought to be based in turn on a Greek wall-painting of two or three centuries earlier.

There are three important implications of this design. First, it is

Figure 2c.2 'Nude Youth Fluting'

impossible to play a pair of such instruments, and the technique therefore cannot have been the same as that of the aulos. Second, it is possible to employ as many as nine fingerholes, with or without a vent-hole, since both hands are used on the same pipe, and only one thumb need be used all the time to support the instrument. This makes possible an extended scale of ten notes, covering a range of more than an octave. To judge from later illustrations, some of these instruments were almost the same size as a modern orchestral flute, and must have had a lowest note in the region of middle c (256 Hz). The third implication of the design is this: the *plagiaulos*, though it was blocked above the embouchure hole, acted as an 'open' pipe, and sounded an octave higher than a 'stopped' *syrinx* pipe of the same length. It also produced the even-numbered harmonics as well as the odd, and would have had a tone not unlike that of a modern flute. For the same reason, it would have overblown the octave instead of the twelfth, and since it had an extended range anyway, there would have been no gap between the upper and lower registers, which between them might have covered at least two octaves, with all the notes available all the time. But the *plagiaulos* never ousted the aulos as the virtuoso woodwind instrument, and we must ask why. Presumably by the late fourth century BC the potential range of the 'complete' aulos had been extended to something like two octaves though, as we have seen (p. 36–7) only a limited part of the range of any aulos was accessible at any given time, owing to the design of the keywork. But despite this disadvantage, the characteristic sound quality of the aulos, which depended on both pipes sounding at once, seems to have been preferred.

Bagpipes

Did the Greeks use bagpipes, or any similar instrument? This is a vexed and difficult question. There was a Greek word *askaules*, which literally means 'bag-piper', but it does not occur in a Greek context until long after the Classical period. It is almost entirely confined to Latin writers of the first century AD, when the instrument seems to have enjoyed some popularity in Rome. There is only one piece of Greek evidence which has been interpreted as referring to bagpipes, but there are grave doubts about its meaning. In the *Akharnians* of Aristophanes a salesman arrives from Boeotia (line 860) to barter with the hero. He says (to render the vulgarity in full) '. . . and you pipers, who have come with me all the way from Thebes, with your bone pipes blow up the dog's arse'. A few lines later the hero Dikaiopolis begs them to stop, calling them by a specially coined word *bombaulioi* – 'bumble-pipers'. This has led one scholar[7] to suppose that they were playing bagpipes which had bags made from dogs' hides, the blowpipe being inserted into the rear orifice. But this is most unlikely, unless the instruments were stage props specially made for the sake of this crude and very feeble joke. Of course, it is tempting for a translator to choose a Scots dialect to represent the Boeotian dialect in the original Greek; and given that he is a visitor from the North, accompanied by pipers, the rest springs readily to the English mind. But in fact, 'The Dog's Arse' was probably a song-title, or a parody of a song-title, and the pipers were probably playing quite ordinary auloi.

Harps

The minor stringed instruments fall into two categories – the harp types and the lute types. Two types of harp appear regularly in vase-paintings from the fifth century BC onwards. One has a flat base which acts as a sounding-board resting on the player's thigh, and a curved vertical arm from which the strings run either vertically or at a slant to the base (Figure 2c.3).[8]

The number of strings varies between sixteen and twenty-two, so it is easy to see why it was referred to as a 'many-stringed' instrument (*polychordon*). It may well have been able to double a melody in octaves. The representations in the fifth and fourth centuries are fairly consistent, and show a plain curving arm; but in vase-paintings of the late fourth century from South Italy there appears a very ornate version, with moulding or carving on the outside edge, which is usually painted white on the vase, making it look a bit like an iced cake. Also, in a few cases, there is a 'prop' inserted between the end of the curving member and the soundboard (making, in effect, a third side to the frame) which may be quite plain, or may be elaborately carved in the shape of a large bird, probably meant to be a heron or a crane.[9]

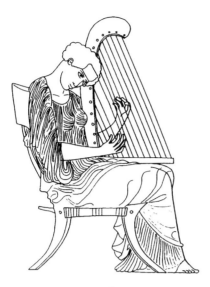

Figure 2c.3 Type of harp (exact name uncertain)

The other type of harp always has three sides, roughly in the shape of a right-angled triangle, with the longest side sloping away from the player and the strings running from that side vertically down to the base, which likewise rests on the player's thigh and acts as a sounding-board. The number of strings is about the same. The most obvious difference apart from the shape is that on this instrument the shortest strings are furthest from the player, while on the curved type they are nearest (Figure 2c.4).

There were a number of Greek words for instruments which were almost certainly of the harp type. Unfortunately it is difficult to assign these names to the various shapes, except that we may be fairly sure that *trigōnon* (meaning 'triangle') indicated the type shown in Figure 2c.4. There is also a generic term *psalterion* which seems to mean any stringed instrument played without a plectrum. Until recently it was thought that *magadis* was the name of the instrument shown in Figure 2c.3, but it has now been established that the word is a descriptive adjective, meaning 'able to double in octaves' and not the name of a specific instrument (compare the name *magadis aulos*, discussed on p. 000).[10]

About the *sambykē* (*sambuca* in Latin) we have a few hints. There was a form of siege-engine, carried on two ships fixed together to form a sort of catamaran, with a ladder which could be lowered forward over the bows on to fortifications on land, thus enabling an assault-party to scale them and get over. The description is in Polybius,[11] who tells us that the ship and ladder when seen as a whole resembled the musical instrument. As a result, it was called a *sambuca* in services' slang. It is difficult to find a

Figure 2c.4 Type of harp – *trigōnon*

design of harp which would fit the various requirements, though various types have been suggested.[12]

As we saw earlier (p. 000) the name *pēktis* was mistakenly applied to the *syrinx* or pan-pipe. It seems originally to have been the name of a kind of harp, but there is no instrument of that type with which it can be reliably identified. If its name has any etymological significance, it should mean a wooden construction which is 'pegged together'. This might suggest the 'horizontal angular harp' found in Near Eastern illustrations which resembles a long boat with a mast, from which the strings run down at an angle to the 'deck', which is the sounding-board (Figure 2c.5).

The problem is that there is, so far as I know, no illustration of this type of instrument in Greek art.

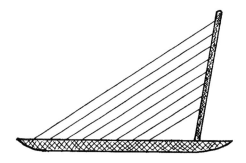

Figure 2c.5 Horizontal angular harp

Illustrations of the harp types from the fifth century BC have certain significant features in common. The players are, with very few exceptions, women. In many illustrations they appear to be perfectly respectable women – even the Muses on occasion play such instruments – and the most characteristic setting for the *trigōnon* is shown on a type of vase called a 'wedding cauldron' (*lebēs gamikos*), where the bride is shown playing a *trigōnon* rather nonchalantly while the preparations for the ceremony go on around her. Figure 2c.4 is taken from a scene of this kind. However, in literature of the fourth century BC and later the terms *psaltria* and *sambykistria* (female players of the psalterion and sambyke) come to mean 'courtesan', just as *auletris* (female aulos-player) had earlier.

One frustrating feature of the illustrations is that none of them clearly shows the nature of the tuning apparatus. The harp shown in Figure 2c.3 (mid-fifth century BC) shows a row of very small circles on the curving vertical arm, which correspond roughly, but not exactly, with the top ends of the strings. They may perhaps be tuning-pegs, but it is difficult to see how they could have been twisted around. Some pictures of the *trigōnon* have a number of knobs or studs on the slanting side, but there are far too many to allow us to suppose that they are tuning pegs.

There is one solitary illustration which shows another kind of harp, sometimes termed the 'bow' or 'arched' harp (Figure 2c.6).

This instrument is much smaller, and must have had a much higher range of pitch. The details are difficult to discern, but it appears that the body is made of wood, with a hollow resonator under the sounding-board which makes it look rather like a lute. But it is not a lute, since the strings can be seen running directly from the 'neck' to the sounding-board, and they are graded in length, the one running from the end of the neck to the far end of the sounding-board being at least twice as long as the one nearest to the sounding-board. Incidentally, the lady player seems to be tuning its strings to those of an 'Italiote' kithara (see p. 168) which she is playing with her left hand. The dating of this picture also presents problems. It was found at Stabiae near Pompeii, where it was buried by the eruption of Vesuvius in AD 79, so the actual painting probably belongs

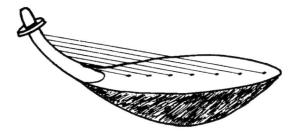

Figure 2c.6 'Arched' or 'bow' harp

to the first century BC at the earliest; but many Pompeian wall-paintings are known to have been based on Greek originals of two or three centuries earlier.[13] So we cannot say with any certainty when the instrument first made its appearance in Greek music. It certainly does not seem to have been at all popular, and should not, in my opinion, be identified with the *sambykē*.

The lute

This leads conveniently to the last category of stringed instruments – those of the lute type. These instruments differ in a number of important respects from the kithara types and the harp types. Like the kithara types, they have strings which are stretched over a bridge, and transmit their vibrations to a sounding-board by this means, whereas the strings of a harp are attached directly to the sounding-board. Also, the strings of a lute are all at the same distance from the sounding-board, in a plane parallel to it, whereas those of a harp are at various distances from it. But unlike the kithara, the simple lute has only three or four strings at the most, and it has a fingerboard which enables the player to shorten the string lengths by stopping with the fingers of the left hand, thus obtaining at least five notes from each string. Almost all the representations of this type of instrument in Greek art are in statuary or terracotta figures. This may be a coincidence, or it may be due to the fact that there is very little vase-painting evidence for the period to which they belong – the late fourth century BC. The evidence has been carefully assembled and analysed by R.A. Higgins and R.P. Winnington-Ingram.[14]

Figure 2c.7 'Square' lute

Figure 2c.8 'Pear-shaped' lute

Two distinct types of lute can be distinguished. One has an oblong soundbox and straight-sided fingerboard (Figure 2c.7).

As this is a relief carving, it is possible to see that there was a longitudinal ridge down the back of the sounding-box, looking rather like a ship's keel; the same effect is shown on the back of a kithara nearby. The other type is more or less pear-shaped, with no clear demarcation between sounding-board and neck (Figure 2c.8).

It is not possible to discern the strings in any of the illustrations, or to say with confidence how many there were, but literary evidence suggests that there were three or four. Nor is there any clear indication of the tuning mechanism. Two names are listed by the ancient authorities which may be assigned to this type of instrument – *pandoura* and *skindapsos*, both probably non-Greek words.

Brass instruments

In relation to Greek music, the term 'brass instrument' is loosely applied, and requires explanation. No instruments were actually made of brass (an alloy of copper and zinc, not extensively used until the first century BC) but some were made of bronze, and played in the same way as a modern trumpet or bugle. On the modern instruments the player's lips are squeezed into a cup-shaped mouthpiece, and act in much the same way as a double reed, setting up oscillations in a resonant tube. Though the Romans used a number of these instruments, made in various shapes and materials (see Chapter 8) there is only one commonly found in Greek illustrations and literature – the *salpinx*. It appears in vase-paintings from the sixth century BC onwards, and is referred to frequently in all types of literature, usually in a military context, but sometimes as a 'public address' instrument, used to call for silence at a large gathering, or to give the signal for the start of a race. There are also one or two curious references to its use at drinking-parties, played *pianissimo* to suit the circumstances.[15] But, though there are a few allusions to more than one *salpinx* being played at a time, these are rare, and there are virtually none at all to the *salpinx* being played in combination with any other instrument. Incidentally, it is worth pointing out that the drum had no part whatever in martial music, being confined to religious cult.

The *salpinx* was unlike a modern trumpet or post-horn in several respects (Figure 2c.9).

First, it had a cylindrical bore of constant diameter throughout, unlike the bugle, which widens consistently from mouthpiece to bell, or the post-horn, which expands slightly along its length and flares suddenly at the bell. Second, there is no sign in the vase-paintings of a cup-shaped mouthpiece. The player seems to be using the end of the tube instead, which suggests that its inside diameter must have been about half an inch (1.3 cm) at the least. It must have been more difficult to get a satisfactory tone or a full range of notes by this method. An even more confusing feature in some illustrations is that the player wears a mouthband (*phorbeia*) similar to that worn by aulos-players (see p. 31). It cannot have been used by a trumpeter in the same way, or for the same purpose as it was by an aulos-player. Finally, instead of a flared bell the *salpinx* had a

Figure 2c.9 Salpinx

bulbous lower end, similar to that of a modern cor anglais. This must have affected its tone, but it is difficult to say in what way.[16]

There is, however, one unchanging feature of all instruments of this type – they play a particular pattern of notes, known as the harmonic series. As the length of the *salpinx* shown in vase-paintings is normally about 3 feet (about 1 m) its fundamental note would have been somewhere around B flat, an octave and a tone below middle c. But the fundamental is not normally obtainable on this type of instrument, so the lowest note sounded would have been an octave higher, in the region of b flat (228 Hz). Above this the next two or three harmonics would have been playable, as shown in Figure 2c.10.

As a result, we can assume that the sounds made by a *salpinx*-player on an ancient Greek battlefield must have been very similar to our own bugle-calls. There is an interesting piece of evidence which possibly bears this out: one of the most unusual musical scores ever to come to light. It is also the oldest by a long way, dating from the sixth century BC. It is on a piece of pottery (an *epinētron*) which looks rather like half a thermos flask, and may have been placed on the knee to avoid injury while sewing. It has battle scenes painted on it, including an Amazon playing a *salpinx* with the letters TOTE TOTOTE on the background around her.[17] For many years (it was found at Eleusis in 1883) this was regarded as nonsense, but Annie Bélis spotted that it looked like a kind of sol-fa notation which is mentioned in Aristides Quintilianus and elsewhere.[18] The problem is that this system of notation was devised for singers, and the various vowels (TA, TE (short) TE (long), TO, and possibly some others) were assigned to notes in the tetrachords of the scale. It is not too difficult to see how they might have been allocated to the notes of the harmonic series, since only three or four would have been needed, but we have no evidence to show how they were assigned. There is, however, some evidence that there were traditionally accepted calls on the *salpinx* to indicate 'attack', 'retreat', etc.

We have some information on the date of the *salpinx*'s introduction to Greece. Ancient commentators on Homer observed that he does not

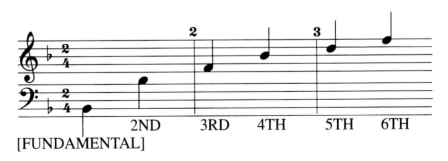

Figure 2c.10 Harmonic series of notes playable on a *salpinx*

describe the use of the instrument in the warfare at Troy, though he refers to it in a simile as being used to give warning of a pirate raid.[19] It was noticed that his similes, being drawn from the familiar sights and sounds of his own day, sometimes contained anachronisms, but that he had been careful (surprisingly so, for an epic poet) to avoid making his warriors use this instrument, which was generally thought to have been 'invented' some centuries later than the Trojan War – perhaps about the eighth century BC.

Percussion instruments

The percussion instruments may be dealt with briefly, and last, which exactly reflects the unimportance of their role in Greek music. There could hardly have been a more wounding insult to the dead Euripides than the suggestion made by his rival in the *Frogs* of Aristophanes that a girl 'rattling bits of pottery together like castanets' could provide an adequate accompaniment for his songs.[20] The only function of a percussion instrument was to emphasize the rhythm which was already inherent in a melody, usually being played on an aulos or *barbitos*, or being sung or chanted; the percussion sounds did not form part of the music in their own right.

One of the most commonly illustrated percussion instruments is the hand-drum, called *tympanon* in Greek, which appears in many vase-paintings of scenes in which women worshippers ('maenads') are dancing in honour of the god Dionysos. Because such dancing was essentially a group activity, the sound most familiar to Greek ears was that of a large number of drums beating together, in a way which could on occasions excite frenzy and mass hysteria – a phenomenon not unknown in our own times. Its use was not confined to the Dionysiac cult. In the opening lines of Aristophanes' *Lysistrata* the heroine complains that none of the women have turned up to hear her plan; 'but if it had been a festival of Pan or Aphrodite, you wouldn't be able to push through between the *tympana*'.

The apparent size of the *tympanon* in illustrations varies between about 12 in. (30 cm) and 16 in. (40 cm) in diameter. It is usually held in the left hand and played with the fingers or palm of the right hand – no kind of drumstick is shown (Figure 2c.11).

In some other illustrations the player is shown striking the decorated back of the instrument instead of the head.[21] This may seem strange, but the action might well produce a low, muffled sound caused by the air pressure evenly applied all over the head (Figure 2c.12).

The literary sources tell us that the head was made of leather[22] but we do not know whether this was rawhide or cured. It was stretched over a bowl-shaped shell, about 6 in. (15 cm) deep at its centre; hence in some older translations it is called a 'kettledrum'. Many illustrations show

Figure 2c.11 Tympanon (played normally)

decorative ribbons attached to the outer rim, but there is no sign of the metal discs which characterize a tambourine, and the sound was a deep, booming drum-beat (the effect of the bowl resonator). It was not shaken like a tambourine, which does not appear until some time in the third century BC. It is repeatedly stressed in the literary sources (particularly in Euripides' tragedy, the *Bacchae*, which is much concerned with the cult of Dionysos), that the *tympanon* provided a rhythmic reinforcement for the ritual songs and cries and the aulos-music of the cult, rather than a sound which was interesting in itself.

Another commonly illustrated instrument was called *krotala* in Greek (a plural word, meaning 'clackers'). They were almost always played in pairs, particularly by female dancers. They consisted of pairs of wooden

Figure 2c.12 Tympanon (reversed)

bars with round recesses on their inner sides, joined by a hinge (presumably leather) which was under tension, and caused them to spring apart when released (Figure 2c.13).

The standard picture which appears in almost every book on Greek music shows a topless girl dancer dancing to the music of an aulos-player. This more unusual one shows a male musician on his way to an engagement, carrying his aulos and bringing a pair of *krotala* in case they might be needed.

The *krotala* were held between the thumb and middle fingers of each hand, and illustrations show that, like modern Spanish castanets, they were played with a lot of movement and flourish. But here again, the function of the percussion instrument was merely to reinforce the rhythm of the melody (another instrument is almost invariably being played in the picture) and, to a lesser extent, to give visual emphasis to the dancer's movements.

Cymbals (*kymbala* in Greek) were less commonly used by dancers. There are a few illustrations of them, and a few pairs of cymbals have survived.[23]

Modern cymbals are made by a sophisticated technical process which was not possible in the ancient world. The ancient ones were much smaller in diameter and much thicker, and their sound must have been more like that of a small bell. The translation 'tinkling cymbal' in the Authorized Version is entirely apt.[24]

Finally, there is a mysterious object shown in a number of vase-paintings which has been interpreted as a musical instrument. It appears regularly on Greek vases from Apulia in southern Italy, in the

Figure 2c.13 Krotala

context of a group of women in the women's quarters of a house, sometimes against the background of an *aedicula* or small pillared porch. It looks like a small ladder, about 18 in. (45 cm) long, with 10 or more rungs (Figure 2c.14).

In the early part of this century this instrument was usually called an 'Apulian sistrum', on the assumption that it was some kind of rattle; but nobody succeeded in explaining what made the rattle rattle. The better-known design of rattle is the one used in the cult of Isis in Egypt, which had a horse-shoe shaped bar with two or three wires stretched across it, and small metal discs with holes in their centres which slid up and down along the wires when the rattle was shaken from side to side. The problem with the 'Apulian' version was that there did not seem to be any moving part which could make a noise. Max Wegner suggested[25] that it might have been some form of xylophone, but was unable to find any picture which showed the 'rungs' of the ladder being struck with a stick or hammer. There were, in any case, two objections to his interpretation. One is that we should expect the 'rungs' to be of various lengths. This is not a fatal objection, as a single note repeated very rapidly might give some sort of pleasure, but the other is more serious. The 'notes' of a xylophone (rectangular strips of wood in the modern instrument) produce their sound by vibrating longitudinally as shown in Figure 2c.15; this means that their ends must be free to vibrate, and cannot be 'anchored' in any way. They are supported on bars which are placed at the quarter- and three-quarter points, the 'nodes' where the vibration is almost zero.

So the mystery remained until the publication of West's book; he shows (Plate 33) a woman holding the instrument up with her left hand, and running the fingers of her right hand up and down the 'rungs'. He correctly interprets the entry in Pollux's dictionary (under the word

Figure 2c.14 Psithyra or 'Apulian sistrum'

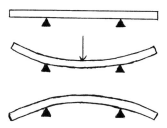

Figure 2c.15 Mode of vibration of xylophone element (movement greatly exaggerated)

psithyra, meaning 'rustle' or 'whisper') as suggesting that this instrument had 'a frame with bobbins drawn through it' – that is, that the 'rungs' had holes through their centres, and could rotate around wires which ran across the frame. This movement created a characteristic sound, aptly described (and imitated) by the word *psithyra*. West does not go on to add that the 'blobby excrescences' (p. 127), if they were weighted and mounted off-centre, may also have served to make the 'rungs' rotate; the instrument could have been shaken with a rotary motion. So now we know the truth about this mysterious instrument.

3

SCALES, INTERVALS AND TUNING

Scales and intervals

The number of scales in general use in European music has varied considerably over the centuries. In the heyday of modal music in the Middle Ages there were the modal scales of the Gregorian system, each containing the same seven intervals but in a distinctive order, which gave each mode its own characteristic sound. In time all but two of them, which evolved into our major and minor scales, were virtually forgotten. That was the situation until the late nineteenth century, which brought experiments with strange scales such as the whole-tone, strange intervals such as the quarter-tone and sixth-tone, and the ultimate resort of atonality, which is, in effect, the abandonment of the concept of a scale.

We have clear evidence from ancient sources that the Greeks employed scales other than the familiar major and minor, and intervals smaller than the semitone. Unfortunately, the history of those scales is obscure. We know that a set of ethnic names, such as 'Dorian', 'Lydian' and 'Phrygian', were used at various times to define patterns of notes or melodic structures, and these structures may have served as the ancient equivalent of scales as we know them. But we have good reasons for believing that the principles on which they were constructed, and the way in which the later Greek theorists analysed them and assigned names to them, changed considerably over the classical period.

It might seem logical to begin by considering the evidence for the earliest scales, but this evidence is very scanty and difficult to interpret. I therefore propose to begin with the fourth century BC, a period for which we have ample reliable evidence, and then consider the earlier scales as possible precursors of the developed system.

The outstanding authority for this period is Aristoxenos, whose life spanned the middle of the fourth century BC, and who was for some years a pupil of Aristotle. He wrote a number of works on music and related subjects, of which the most important surviving treatise is the *Elements of Harmonics* (*Harmonika Stoicheia* in Greek), in three books.[1] In this work,

Aristoxenos sets out a theory of scale structure and a method of analysis which became standard in the ancient world and remained very influential in later antiquity. In fact, via the later Latin encyclopaedists (particularly Martianus Capella, fifth century AD and Boethius, sixth century AD) it became the accepted basic theory throughout the Middle Ages in Europe. It is impossible to say how much of Aristoxenos' work was original, and how much was merely a systematic account of the musical practices of his day. He certainly claims originality in a number of contexts, but it must be said that he is an argumentative writer, highly critical of his predecessors, and it would be unwise to accept him at his own valuation.

Like all good pupils of Aristotle, Aristoxenos begins by defining the various terms that he is going to use, particularly those which have a more general sense in everyday language, but which carry a specific technical sense in music. One such term is *phthongos*, which can be used of any sound produced by the human voice (it is the second element of our word diphthong); in musical terminology it means a note. By way of preliminary to this definition, he explains at some length the different ways in which the voice may rise or fall in pitch.[2] When speaking, it slides up or down over a range of pitch 'without ever seeming to settle at any one specific pitch'. By contrast, when singing, it moves by intervals from one clearly defined pitch to another, so that the intervening pitches are not sounded. (This, of course, is the ideal at which singers should aim; no doubt some ancient Greek singers were guilty of the occasional *glissando*.)

After some tedious and pedantic explanations of related terms, he goes on to discuss range of pitch, and while doing this he gives some information about the capabilities of ancient instruments and singers. For instance, he says[3] that the smallest interval which the voice is capable of intoning accurately is about the same as the smallest interval that the ear can recognize; in ancient Greek music it was in practice an interval which he calls a quarter-tone, which is at, or very near, these limits of the voice and ear. At the opposite extreme, he believed that the ear could assess the difference of pitch between sounds which were further apart than the highest and lowest that an individual voice could produce, 'but not much further'. In a later passage[4] he seems to say that the range of any individual voice or instrument is two octaves and a fifth. If applied to a voice, this seems a remarkable span, and may refer to a virtuoso professional; the notes of the first Delphic hymn, probably written for a male voice *choros*, extend over only one octave and a fourth (see p. 227). He stresses that he is speaking of the range of one particular voice, and not of the maximum possible interval between a young child's voice and a man's, or between the lowest note of a bass aulos and the highest note of a soprano one, or even between the highest and lowest notes of two different registers on the same instrument (see p. 38), any of which could be 'greater than three octaves'.

Next comes the term interval (*diastēma* in Greek), which he defines as that which is bounded, or marked off, by two notes of different pitch. This definition, by its very form, gives an important clue to Aristoxenos' thinking – he seems to have conceived the interval as a magnitude or quantity, and not (as did the Pythagoreans) a ratio or proportion. This matter is fully discussed in Chapter 5.

The final definition in this section is 'system' (the same word in Greek, *systēma*) by which Aristoxenos says he means a 'construction' of intervals. It is tempting to translate this as 'scale', but that could be misleading, because a *systēma* could have a range greater or less than an octave, and was probably regarded by Greek musicians as a spectrum of notes from which a segment was chosen to form the scale for any particular composition.

In constructing a 'system', Aristoxenos did not in practice start from the interval as the unit or building-block. He started from a basic group of intervals, called a tetrachord, which (by definition as well as by name) consisted of four notes with three intervals between them. Moreover, it was by no means allowable to put together any intervals at random to form a tetrachord. The total sum of the three intervals must be a fourth (for example, d–g or e–a) and the lowest of the three was usually a small interval. There were a number of patterns for the tetrachord; the one which sounds most familiar to us was known as the diatonic, and consisted of a semitone and two tones in ascending order. For a simple mnemonic, the first four notes of the Londonderry Air (or, to be politically correct, Danny Boy) form this pattern

| | ¹/₂ tone | | | tone | | | tone | | |
| e | | f | | | g | | | | a |

(These notes are merely an example – they could be in any key.)

But it should be stressed that this was the fourth-century practice as described by Aristoxenos. We have reason to believe that pairs of intervals totalling a fourth were used in earlier music, and were referred to by later theorists as trichords.[5] By then the concept of the tetrachord had become so firmly established that the older scales were regarded, mistakenly, as defective or incomplete.

The tetrachord was, by Aristoxenos' definition, the smallest system. His method of constructing larger systems was quite simple. Tetrachords could be linked together in two ways, which he called 'conjunction' (*synaphē* in Greek) or 'disjunction' (*diazeuxis*). In conjunction, the top note of the lower tetrachord was the bottom note of the higher one, giving a scale of seven notes with a compass of a seventh. With disjunction, there was an interval of a major tone between the tetrachords, giving an octave scale of eight notes. Names were given to the notes in these pairs of tetrachords, based on the names given to strings of the lyre or kithara (see p. 54), with an extra one (*paramesos*) for the lowest note of the disjunct.

Conjunct: ⌐¹/₂ ⌐ 1 ⌐ 1 ⌐¹/₂ ⌐ 1 ⌐ 1 ⌐

Disjunct ⌐¹/₂ ⌐ 1 ⌐ 1 ⌐ 1 ⌐¹/₂ ⌐ 1 ⌐ 1 ⌐

There were apparently three 'systems' in use, known as the 'Lesser Complete System', the 'Greater Complete System' and the 'Greater Complete Non-Modulating System' (this will be explained later) containing three, four and five tetrachords respectively, joined by conjunction except for the two central ones. In order to make the lower part of each system up to an octave below *mesē* one more note, called the 'taken-on-in-addition note' (*proslambanomenos*) was added at the bottom, a tone below the rest. There was no set pitch or key for these systems; choosing d' (arbitrarily) as the pitch for *mesē*, the notes would be as in (a), (b) and (c) below. The same names for the notes above and below *mesē* were kept, but with the addition of a second term which denoted the tetrachord in which the note stood. This second term is in the form of a genitive plural in Greek, meaning 'of the – 's', and the tetrachords were named:

1) *Hypatōn*, meaning 'of the highest', but actually the lowest in pitch (see p. 000)
2) *Mesōn*, 'of the middle notes'
3) *Synhemmenōn*, 'of the conjunct notes'
4) *Diezeugmenōn*, 'of the disjunct notes'
5) *Hyperbolaiōn*, 'of the excess, or over-the-top notes'

As these words are a bit of a mouthful for the non-Greek reader, I shall call them by shorter names, (1) 'Low', (2) 'Mid', (3) 'Con', (4) 'Dis' and (5) 'Top'.

(a) The Lesser Complete System

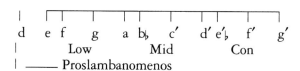

| d e f g a b♭ c' d' e'♭ f' g'
| Low   Mid   Con
| —— Proslambanomenos

(b) The Greater Complete System

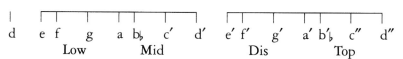

d e f g a b♭ c' d' e' f' g' a' b'♭ c" d"
  Low   Mid   Dis   Top

(c) The Greater Complete Non-modulating System

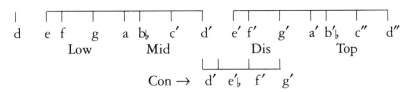

All the tetrachords shown above are of the diatonic pattern, but any or all of them could be modified in accordance with certain principles. It would be natural to assume that all the tetrachords in the system in use at any given time were the same, but the first Delphic Hymn and other surviving pieces clearly show that this was not always so.

Aristoxenos describes in some detail a scheme of three basic tetrachords, which he calls the *genera* (*genē* in Greek). Two of them had permissible variants, known as 'colours' (*chroai* in Greek). Since the rule that the outer notes should form the interval of a fourth was strictly applied, any variation was confined to the inner two notes; as a result, the outer notes were known as the 'fixed' notes, and the inner two as the 'moving' notes (*phthongoi kinoumenoi*). The three basic tetrachords were called the diatonic, the chromatic and the enharmonic. These terms may sound familiar, but it must be strongly emphasized that the term 'chromatic' did not have the same meaning that it bears in modern musical terminology – i.e. having a complete succession of twelve semitones – nor did the term enharmonic, which means something totally different nowadays.

Diatonic	$^1/_2$	1	1

Chromatic	$^1/_2$	$^1/_2$	$1^1/_2$

Enharmonic	$^1/_4$	$^1/_4$	2

These versions of the tetrachord involved the use of intervals smaller than the semitone, and expanded, diminished and composite intervals of a kind not normally encountered in orthodox Western music. It is difficult to discuss these intervals, since they cannot be indicated in normal notation (most writers on the subject invent their own), nor can they be played on a keyboard instrument. (I have written a computer program in BASIC which reproduces them, but I cannot claim that the result was a musical treat.) Nor can they be accurately described in any terms other than the rather repulsive technical jargon which I have deliberately confined to Appendix 1. The Greeks used the term *hemitonion* exactly as we use the term 'semitone' to describe any interval which is about half a tone; and just as we have major semitones and tempered semitones, so they had

90

several intervals of roughly, but not exactly the same size, all of which they called *hemitonion*. The term *diesis* was used for any interval smaller than a semitone, sometimes with a descriptive term such as 'smallest' or 'smallest chromatic' to distinguish between the various sizes. Aristoxenos uses these terms, but he also refers to the smaller intervals as arithmetical fractions of a tone, and he gives the patterns for the three basic tetrachords in that form. He writes as a musical expert, and bases his description of the various intervals on the evidence of his ear; a semitone to him was simply an interval which sounded like half a tone, and a tone (his unit of measurement) was the interval you got if you tuned up a fifth from any note, and then down a fourth. His use of fractions, arithmetical sums and differences is really an attempt to give an appearance of numeracy to what is really a non-mathematical account based on an assessment of sound quality. There were Greek acoustical scientists who fully understood the mathematics of the subject, and who realized that an interval must be thought of as a ratio between the notes which enclose it, and not as itself a quantity which can be added to or subtracted from another interval, or divided into fractions. Their findings are fully discussed in Chapter 5.

However, despite Aristoxenos' shortcomings, I have decided to use his terms to describe the various intonations. A 'quarter-tone' does at least mean something to the non-expert; one can play c followed by c sharp on a piano, and imagine (perhaps even sing) a note half-way between them. Even a third-tone is not inconceivable – one can play c and d and imagine two more notes equally spaced between them. But the terms 'an interval in the ratio 81:64' or 'an interval of 408 cents' are musically meaningless to anyone but a trained expert.

The diatonic had two forms, the one shown above, called the 'tense' diatonic (*syntonon*), and a variant called the 'soft' diatonic (*malakon*) in which the note next to the top was flattened by a quarter-tone, giving the sequence:

$^1/_2$	$^3/_4$	$1^1/_4$

The chromatic lent itself most readily to adjustment or 'colouring'. The form shown previously:

$^1/_2$	$^1/_2$	$1^1/_2$

was called the 'one-tone' chromatic (*toniaion* in Greek) because the lower two intervals added up to one major tone. Aristoxenos gives two variants of this – the *hemiolion* chromatic (i.e. the 'one-and-a-half', so called because its *diesis* of $^3/_8$ tone was $1^1/_2$ times the $^1/_4$-tone *diesis* of the enharmonic), and the 'soft' chromatic (*malakon*), with a *diesis* of $^1/_3$ tone.

91

Chromatic *hemiolion* | $^3/_8$ | $^3/_8$ | | $1^3/_4$ | |

Chromatic *malakon* | $^1/_3$ | $^1/_3$ | | $1^5/_6$ | |

The enharmonic did not apparently admit of any variation, but Aristoxenos' attitude to it is rather puzzling. The very small intervals which it employs must have been difficult to intone and to recognize. He says that it is rarely heard nowadays, since the performers tend to enlarge the small intervals, and assimilate the intonation to that of the 'soft chromatic'. There is an element of nostalgia in this ('ah, they don't sing the way they used to') but there is also the possibility that Aristoxenos is airing his knowledge of older intonations, and that the enharmonic may have been a 'dead letter' for some time previously. The notation system apparently did not distinguish between the chromatic and the enharmonic (see p. 208), and it may well be that musicians followed their own inclinations, or adopted whichever intonation happened to be fashionable at the time.

Tuning instruments

How did a Greek musician tune his instrument? If it was an aulos, the holes were bored so as to sound the 'natural' notes (see p. 35). All of these could be flattened or sharpened by pushing in or drawing out the reed mouthpiece, but they would be detuned by different amounts, which would distort the intervals. All the intervening notes were produced by partially uncovering the next hole above, which sharpened the note by one *diesis* or two *dieses*. Thus the intonation was entirely under the control of the player, which was both a privilege and a challenge. It accounts for two phenomena – the considerable number of different intonations in use, and the fact that the notation does not distinguish between them, leaving the choice to the aulos-player.

But how did a kithara-player tune the strings of his instrument for the various tetrachords? Let us imagine that he had eight strings, and required two disjunct tetrachords. In the 'tense diatonic' (starting with this because it contains familiar intervals) the notes required, taking *mesē* arbitrarily as a′, would be as shown below. The pitch for *mesē* (a′) might be set by 'absolute pitch', or perhaps by the use of a small pitch-pipe, resembling one pipe of a *syrinx* (see p. 69), which was the ancient equivalent of a tuning-fork. (Of course, if he were playing together with a wood-wind player, he would take his pitch from the aulos.) All the remaining notes could be found by the process called 'acquiring by concord' (*lēpsis dia symphonias*), that is, by tuning in fifths and fourths. The process is shown in the following diagram:

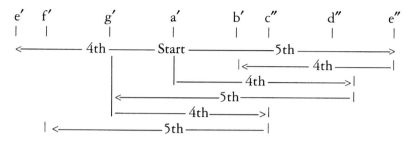

By this method of tuning, all the fifths and fourths are 'perfect', all the tones are major tones, and the semitones are the 'remainder' (*leimma* in Greek) left after taking two tones away from the fourth. Though a musician would be quite happy to call this 'half a tone', the ancient scientists were aware that it is in fact less than half a tone.[6] There are two composite intervals to be found in the scale, the ditone (f'–a', g'–b' and c"–e") and the 'tone and a half' (e'–g', a'–c" and b'–d"); in this context these two intervals should not be thought of, or named, as major third and minor third, which to us are non-composite and harmonious intervals. The Greeks regarded them as 'discordant' (*diaphona*). To them, the only concords (*symphona*) were the octave, the fifth and the fourth.

One of the variants of the diatonic mentioned by Aristoxenos had intervals which he calls $^1/_3$ tone, 1 + $^1/_6$ tone and 1 tone, a mixture of *genera*, with the note next to the bottom taken from the 'soft' chromatic and the one next to the top from the 'tense' diatonic. This pattern is also listed by the mathematician Archytas, and we can be pretty sure therefore that it was in actual use. The tuning would be the same as for the normal diatonic, except that the note next to the bottom would be flattened by a small amount, reducing the lowest interval in the tetrachord and enlarging the middle one to what Aristoxenos called 1 + $^1/_6$ tones, and we call a septimal tone. This can be occasionally heard in our music, being the interval between the seventh and eighth harmonics in the sequence of open notes played on a brass instrument – hence the lower note of the two is sometimes called the trumpet seventh. How the strings were tuned at this interval is a mystery. Perhaps the Greek ear could judge the septimal tone and recognize when it had been found, or perhaps the 'lower moving note' was first tuned two tones below *mesē* by the process described earlier, and then adjusted to a more harmonious, slightly lower pitch. The lower two intervals in the tetrachord taken together would form the same discordant interval of 1 + $^1/_2$ tones as found in the 'tense' diatonic, but the interval between the top note of the tetrachord and the note next to the bottom would sound more pleasant, being a third from the harmonic series instead of the harsher ditone. A similar effect is found in other intonations listed by Archytas, and may perhaps tie up with the Pythagorean theory of concordance, which is discussed in Chapter 5 (pp. 144).

The variants of the chromatic and enharmonic raise a lot of problems, but a few reasonably certain suggestions can be made. First, Aristoxenos tries to show that the two small intervals at the bottom of the tetrachord, which taken together were known as the *pyknon*, or 'clutch', were normally equal. In practice this probably meant that the player tuning his instrument had some means of tuning the top note of the *pyknon*, and then tuned the middle note to a pitch which he judged by ear to be at the mid-point of the *pyknon*. Some of the ratios for the small intervals given by the acoustical scientists look as though they were worked out mathematically, and not found experimentally by listening to players and assessing the intervals they were using by measurement on the monochord (see Chapter 5, pp. 132–5). The 'one-tone' chromatic was characterized by two intervals in the *pyknon* which added up to a tone. It would be quite easy to tune the 'upper moving note' a tone above the bottom note (up a fifth and down a fourth), and then tune the intervening note so as to sound half-way between the two. However, Archytas gives numerical ratios which suggest that the note next to the bottom was below the 'centre' of the tone.

According to Aristoxenos, as we have seen, the Greeks employed 'colours' of the chromatic in which the *pyknon* spanned less than a major tone. There is one piece of evidence which tends to bear this out. The so-called vocal notation system (described in Chapter 9) used three successive letters of the alphabet to denote a chromatic *pyknon*, for example the Greek equivalents for K, L and M, M being the lowest. But another note in the same system, known for certain to be a tone above M, is denoted not by K but by another letter, I. (The other system of notation, the instrumental, makes the same distinction.) Of course, this does not prove that the two notes were at different pitches, but it does show that the notations were devised to cope with that possibility.

Finally, there is the enharmonic type of tetrachord, which according to Aristoxenos had intervals of $^1/_4$ tone, $^1/_4$ tone, 2 tones, and did not admit of variations. This could have been 'tuned through the concords', with the top note of the *pyknon* two tones below the top note of the tetrachord, and the middle note at what sounded like the mid-point of the semitone. But Aristoxenos complains[7] that in his day there was a tendency to depart from the 'wonderful old music', of which many were ignorant, and to use a higher pitch for the top note of the *pyknon*, in an attempt to 'sweeten' it (*glykainein* in Greek) and assimilate it to the pitch and characteristic sound of the chromatic. Once again, Archytas the mathematician gives a set of ratios which almost certainly correspond to this 'sweetened' version, which substitutes a major third for the harsher ditone at the top of the tetrachord, and a major semitone for the 'remainder' semitone of the *pyknon* (for the details, see Appendix 1). Once more, this fits with the Pythagorean theory of concord. This agreement between the musician and the mathematician, first evaluated by Winnington-Ingram in a classic article many years ago[8] is most striking, and must surely be taken as reliable evidence.

To sum up, Aristoxenos gives us two intonations for the diatonic, three for the chromatic and one for the enharmonic, with the possibility of three other intonations. One of these was a 'sweetened' version of the enharmonic, and the other two were forms of the tetrachord which were mixtures of the diatonic and chromatic. The mathematician Archytas gives ratios which correspond very closely to three of the nine, and the others should probably be regarded as alternatives used according to the whim of musicians or the changing fashions of the time.

The Greater Complete System, being a two-octave construction, could be used as a spectrum of notes from which a number of octave segments could be selected, each containing the same intervals but in a different order. In Greek theory each of these scales was called a 'species of the octave' (*eidos tou dia pasōn*), and each had its own name. Here a problem arises, because four of the names were the same as those which had been applied to much older and more irregular scales, and this has led to a lot of confusion and argument. On the one hand, it seems unlikely that the use of a name such as Lydian, Phrygian or Dorian for a species of the octave should have been completely arbitrary and without any justification. Surely there must have been some recognizable connection between the early Dorian melodic patterns and the later Dorian species of the octave. In fact, Aristoxenos speaks (disparagingly, as usual) of one of his predecessors having attempted to 'bridge the gap'. The problem is that the earlier melodic structures date from centuries before and were (so far as our evidence goes) odd and irregular, whereas the species of the octave are derived, in a very orderly way, from a developed two-octave scale, and can hardly have been formalized much before the end of the fifth century BC.

Aristoxenos himself does not give the complete scheme of species of the octave, but they are set out in the 'Introduction to Harmonics' by one of his followers, Kleoneides.[9] In the diagram below, the pitch for *mesē* is arbitrarily taken as d′, and all the tetrachords are diatonic; the intervals are marked as tones (1) and semitones (½).

	Low					Mid			Dis			Top	
d	e	f	g	a	b♭	c′	d′	e′	f′	g′	a′	b′♭	c″	d″

| |½| 1 | | 1 | |½| 1 | | 1 | | 1 | | Mixolydian species
| 1 | | 1 | |½| 1 | | 1 | | 1 | |½| Lydian species
| 1 | |½| 1 | | 1 | | 1 | | 1 | |½| 1 | Phrygian species

Dorian species |½| 1 | | 1 | | 1 | |½| 1 | | 1 |

Hypolydian species | 1 | | 1 | | 1 | |½| 1 | | 1 | |½|

Hypophrygian species | 1 | | 1 | |½| 1 | | 1 | |½| 1 |

Hypodorian species | 1 | |½| 1 | | 1 | |½| 1 | | 1 |

At first glance, these octave species look very like the Gregorian modes of mediaeval Church music; but this is misleading. Those modes were devised in the eighth century AD, and the names given to them do not correspond to the ancient Greek species names, nor do the patterns of intervals. What is more, it is very doubtful whether the phenomenon of mode, as it appears in the Gregorian context, was part of the ancient Greek musical experience. The whole question was very meticulously examined by Winnington-Ingram,[10] and after reviewing all the evidence bearing on the matter, he was unable to come to any very firm conclusions. One problem is obvious; the 'tonic', or tonal centre to which the other notes of the scale are related, is at the top and bottom of a modern octave scale, but in ancient Greek scales it was in the middle; in a seven-note scale it was literally the middle note, and in the octave scale (i.e. two disjunct tetrachords) it was the fourth note up, there being no note that was truly central. This is exactly reflected in the Dorian species in the diagram above. There is quite good evidence, in the Greek theorists and in some surviving scores, to suggest that this note had the function of a tonic or principal note; for example, it is said[11] that if any other note in the scale is mis-tuned, that note alone sounds wrong, but if *mese* is flat or sharp, the whole scale seems to be 'out'. But was it also the tonal centre in the Lydian or Phrygian species? It is surely significant that some theorists drew a distinction between what they called '*mese* by function' (*mese kata dynamin*) and '*mese* by position' (*mese kata thesin*). There is much controversy about this, but the simplest explanation seems to be that the '*mese* by function' was the *mese* of the two-octave system from which the octave species had been extracted, while the '*mese* by position' was the fourth note up from the lowest note of the species. In the case of the Dorian species these happen to coincide (on the note d′), but in the Hypophrygian species the tonal centre is still d′, but the 'central note' is f′. It should be remembered, of course, that the feminine form *mesē* was originally the name of a string (*chordē*), and only later came to be the name of a note. This explains why the note above *mesē* varies between the masculine *paramesos* when it is regarded as a note by the theorists, and the feminine *paramesē* when it is a string on an eight-stringed instrument, though this distinction is not always consistently observed. *Proslambanomenos*, however, is never feminine, because it was a note name (*phthongos*, masc.), never a string name.

Why was the 'Greater Complete Non-modulating System' so called? The difference between it and the 'plain' version is simply that it includes the tetrachord *synhemmenōn* (conjunct) which the other does not. The explanation generally offered is this: the conjunct tetrachord seemed to the Greek ear to be in a different key from the rest, or at least to provide a path by which to modulate (as we would say) into another key. The Greek word for 'modulation' was *metabolē*, meaning 'change', and that normally implied retuning the strings of a lyre or kithara; but if the conjunct tetrachord was available, it was possible to enjoy some of the effects of modulation without the bother of having to retune. In other words, it was not so much the 'Non-modulating System' as the 'Kid-yourself-you're-not-modulating' system.[12]

The Greater Complete System did not have a set pitch; as I pointed out earlier, the pitch d' for *mesē* in the diagram was arbitrarily chosen. The time has now come to discuss another important term in Greek theory, *tonos*. (It should be said at this point that what follows is a very simplified – some would say over-simplified – account. Those who wish to delve more deeply should consult Barker II pp. 17–27 and his comments on Ptolemy *passim*, or West, pp. 228–33.)

The basic literal meaning of the word *tonos* is 'tension', as found in a string on a stringed instrument; hence, by a simple shift, it can mean pitch – either pitch in the abstract, or a specific pitch. It was also used, as we use it, to mean the interval of a tone – hence Greek has such expressions as 'a tone higher', or 'two notes a tone apart'. Finally, there was a particular use of the word in connection with scales, which corresponded roughly to our word 'key'.

What this meant in practice was that the note *mesē* in any one of the systems (Lesser, Greater Complete, etc.) could be tuned to a specific pitch, and that the system was then said to be 'in' or 'on' a particular *tonos*. As I have already suggested, the most likely source of a standard pitch would be a wood-wind instrument, and it is probably significant that Aristoxenos, when discussing the relative pitches of the *tonoi*, says that the structure of an aulos may influence some people's assessment of the pitch differences between them.[13] There is an interesting aside here on aulos-players. He mentions some theorists who assess the differences in pitch between keys 'by looking at the fingerholes of auloi', and who conclude from that research that the pitch difference between one key and the next is three *dieses* (with one exception, where it is a tone). There is, I believe, a simple explanation. Most of the fingerholes on an aulos were one tone apart in pitch; the player would on occasion raise the pitch of the note from the lower one by one *diesis* or two *dieses*, but he would not play any note between 'two *dieses* up' and the next hole fully open. Therefore, in his way of talking, there were three *dieses* (quite possibly a third of a tone each) between each hole and the next. This is reflected exactly in the notation system.

But here in relation to the *tonoi* we encounter yet again the familiar ethnic names. They were not only used for the old melodic structures of early music, and later for the species of the octave (whatever the relationship between those structures may have been); they were also used for the *tonoi*, or keys.

The evidence on the *tonoi* and their nomenclature comes from various dates, and is not entirely self-consistent. This suggests that there was a long-term development in the course of which the number and range of the *tonoi* was gradually extended. Aristoxenos tells of disagreements between his predecessors as to the number of *tonoi* and their relative pitches; he seems to suggest that five or six was the accepted number. In the latest of the ancient sources we find a complete run of fifteen tonoi covering a range of a ninth (one octave and a tone) in semitone steps. There are, however, three *tonoi* which are present in all the lists, and in the same order of pitch – the Lydian, Phrygian and Dorian, usually described as being a tone apart, and corresponding roughly to the keys of d′, middle c and b flat respectively. The table on p. 99 gives a general picture of the development.

It will be seen from this table that a process of simplification and standardization took place over a period of time. The earlier names employ the prefixes *hypo-*, *hyper-* and *mixo-* in an inconsistent way, whereas the final scheme uses *hyper-* consistently to mean one fourth above and *hypo-* to mean one fourth below. The *mixo-* prefix, which was used in the very old scales, and must surely have meant some kind of combination of scales, is abandoned in the later key-names, and the whole scheme is tidied up. At the same time, two names, Aeolian and Ionian, which were used for the earlier melodic patterns but not for the species of the octave, were reintroduced as key-names to avoid the awkward 'high' and 'low' alternatives.

Another significant feature of these *tonos*-names is the way in which they are related to the names of octave species. If the system is tuned to the Lydian *tonos*, as in the diagram on p. 96 (i.e. the note *mesē* is d′, a tone above middle c) the Lydian species of the octave runs from f to f′, the Phrygian from g to g′ and the Dorian from a to a′. This means that, in order to be able to sing the full octave in any of these three species, a singer

Key	Early name	Later name	Final name	Key
g'			Hyperlydian	g'
f' #			Hyperaeolian	f' #
f'		Hypermixolydian	Hyperphrygian	f'
e'		High Mixolydian	Hyperionian	e'
d' #		Low Mixolydian	Hyperdorian	d' #
d'	Lydian	High Lydian	Lydian	d'
c' #		Low Lydian	Aeolian	c' #
c'	Phrygian	High Phrygian	Phrygian	c'
b		Low Phrygian	Ionian	b
a#	Dorian	Dorian	Dorian	a#
a	Mixolydian	High Hypolydian	Hypolydian	a
g#	Hypodorian	Low Hypolydian	Hypoaeolian	g#
g		High Hypophrygian	Hypophrygian	g
f#		Low Hypophrygian	Hypoionian	f#
f		Hypodorian	Hypodorian	f

requires a range of an octave and two tones. But if the whole system is retuned to the Phrygian *tonos* (i.e. transposed a tone lower), then the Phrygian species will cover the same octave as the Lydian had in the former key, namely f to f'. Again, if it is retuned another tone lower (*mesē* becomes b flat), the Dorian species in the Dorian *tonos* also runs from f to f'. Thus by changing the *tonos*, each of the octave species can be made to cover the same octave in pitch as shown in the diagram below. This is the reason why the lowest *tonos* corresponds to the highest species, and vice versa.

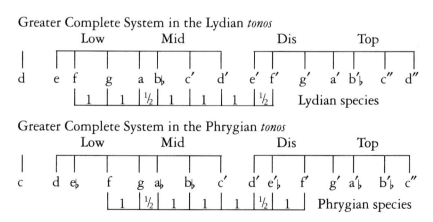

99

Greater Complete System in the Dorian *tonos*

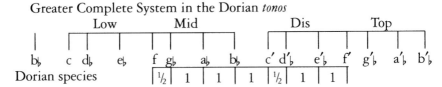

Having looked at the final stages in the development of harmonic theory in the ancient Greek authors, we must now go back in time from a well-documented and fairly self-consistent account to the realms of doubt and conjecture – the old scales, or *harmoniai*, as they were called.

The evidence for these early scales comes from a variety of non-musical texts, from a number of passing allusions in contemporary authors, and from one very important chapter in a musical writer of much later date. The most useful source of information is Plato, who refers to these older scales in a famous passage of the *Republic*.[14] The subject under discussion is the education of the young who, says Plato, must be brought up on a strictly regulated choice of poetry and music, such as would be likely to make them courageous, self-controlled and rational. This implies that any words or songs which convey extremes of sorrow or hysteria, or which condone self-indulgence or sensuality, must be carefully avoided, and that the musical settings appropriate to such songs are also unacceptable, both musically in themselves and intellectually by reason of their association with the objectionable words and sentiments.

Throughout this passage of the *Republic* and in many other contemporary and earlier writers, the term *harmonia* is used, and its meaning must now be examined closely. The root, literal meaning is a 'jointing together', or 'construction'. It can in fact refer to a carpenter's joint between two pieces of wood. In Aristophanes' *Knights* (lines 532–3) the *choros* say of a senile poet that 'he has lost his muscle-tone (*tonos*), and his joints (*harmoniai*) are gaping open' – two ordinary words used with a musical-punning sense. From this concrete meaning comes the abstract sense of a structure of elements with fixed relationships between them, such as the notes in a musical scale. In the same way the verb *harmozein*, which originally meant to 'fit together' (as, for example, in carpentry to make the mortices fit the tenons), came to mean 'attune' or 'harmonize' in the musical sense. Eventually, *harmonia* came to mean the set of notes to which a stringed instrument would be tuned in order to play music of a certain character. There is no real equivalent term in modern music; *accordatura* is the nearest, but is misleading in that the *accordatura* for a stringed instrument (for example, g–d′–a′–e″ for a violin) is normally the same at all times, and does not depend on the character or mood of the music being played.

For Plato, who was very much concerned to draw distinctions between the 'right' and 'wrong' types of music, the *harmoniai* offered a clear and useful criterion. He attached to these musical structures epithets which belonged to the mood or character of the music associated with them, speaking (rather quaintly) of 'mournful *harmoniai*', or 'drunken *harmoniai*', as contrasted with 'masculine *harmoniai*'. He was, for the same reason, deeply suspicious of music which employed a mixture of *harmoniai*, or which (as we would say) modulated from one to another. Reading his account in this passage of the *Republic*, one gets the impression that the lyre and kithara, each with seven strings, could only be tuned to one *harmonia* at any one time, and that any change of *harmonia*, which involved retuning the strings, could be instantly detected by an onlooker. By contrast, the 'many-stringed' instruments (see p. 73 above) could move freely over the whole range of *harmoniai*, producing music of the 'mixed' character which alarmed Plato so much. He therefore ruled out any instrument of this type, specifically naming the *trigonon* and the *pēktis* (see p. 75), and adding that the aulos was as bad as any of them. (This was the result of the developments in its design introduced by Pronomos, see p. 36.) But there is good evidence to show that the kithara-players of the later fifth century, particularly Timotheus, employed a lot of modulations and 'mood-mixtures', and may even have evolved a kithara with as many as eleven strings to facilitate this. Plato, therefore, who is actually writing in the 380s, seems to be harking back to a state of affairs which may have existed fifty or sixty years earlier, but had long since passed into history.

His first requirement is that songs of mourning (*thrēnoi*) must be eliminated; with these songs must go the *harmoniai* traditionally used for them, which are named as the Mixolydian and the Syntonolydian (the 'mixed Lydian' and the 'high-pitched Lydian'). It is clear from what follows that the Lydian *harmonia* had a number of different forms, of which only these two were regarded as 'lamentatory' (*thrēnoides*). One suspects that Plato is being a bit puritanical here, as the Mixolydian is described elsewhere[15] as combining (hence the prefix *Mixo-*) the emotional quality of the Lydian with the nobility of the Dorian, and therefore being suitable for tragedy.

Equally objectionable, in Plato's view, are songs of a convivial character, redolent of drunkenness, relaxation and irresponsibility. The associated *harmoniai*, the Ionian and 'some of the Lydian' (that is, some variants other than the two named above), must therefore be banned also. He applies to them the Greek word *malakos*, which conveys the sense of 'soft' or 'effeminate', with strong overtones of homosexuality. It is curious, and surely not a coincidence, that the same term was used for certain varieties of the diatonic and chromatic tetrachords (see p. 91 above).

Just as we are beginning to wonder whether any of the *harmoniai* are to be allowed, it is pointed out that there are only two left – the Dorian and the Phrygian, and Plato promptly accepts these as being suitable for the best type of character in all circumstances. The Dorian is the 'courageous' mode, suitable for warriors in conflict or in adversity of any kind. The Phrygian is for the same type of character when not under constraint, but acting as he pleases, teaching or advising or exhorting his fellow men, or praying to the gods. The Dorian presents no problems, being frequently mentioned as the musical counterpart of choral lyric poetry of a manly and respectable kind; but the Phrygian is regularly associated with the wild music of orgiastic cults such as that of Dionysos. The only apparent solution to the problem is to suppose that, as with the Lydian, there were a number of different forms of Phrygian, not all of which were of such a type. A few other *harmoniai* are mentioned elsewhere, but very little is known about them.[16]

Is it possible, from this tantalizing glimpse of the various *harmoniai*, to reach any conclusions about the differences between the scales themselves? There is one useful argument which can be applied. The term 'intense' (*syntonon*) is applied to the 'lamentatory' *harmoniai*, and the term 'relaxed', or 'slackened' (*chalaros*) to the convivial ones. It is virtually certain that these terms have both a moral and a musical significance. When 'Music', in the fragment of Pherecrates' comedy discussed on p. 59, complains that Melanippides has 'made her a looser woman' (*chalarōteran*), she is almost certainly implying that he had lowered the pitch of some of the notes in the scales which he was using, or that he had used scales with a low *tonos*. The implications for the human voice must have been the same in the ancient world as they are today; when singing at or near the upper limit of its range, the voice has a strained and agitated quality, whereas in the lower sector it sounds relaxed and calm. In modern terms, the 'mourning' scales had a high *tessitura*, and the convivial ones a low *tessitura*. This corresponds closely with the musical practice of most Eastern Mediterranean cultures to this day.

Are the names of the *harmoniai* in any way significant? In particular, are those which bear the names of Greek tribes (Dorian, Ionian) to be distinguished from those with 'foreign' (that is, non-Greek) names – the Lydian and Phrygian? It is impossible to answer this question with any certainty. Music composed in the Lydian or Phrygian *harmonia* may well have sounded in some way 'eastern' or foreign to the Greek ear. In the *Bacchae* of Euripides frequent mention is made of the fact that the *choros* of female worshippers, who have accompanied Dionysos from Asia Minor, are dressed in 'Eastern' clothing, and come from 'Lydia and Phrygia' and are singing in the foreign-sounding styles of those countries.[17] We must, however, be cautious about taking this at its face value; in fact, the very reason for their repeated assertions might have been that they were not singing in a 'foreign' mode, but were asking the audience to suppose that they were. (The *choros* in Aeschylus' *Suppliants* keep on saying 'there are fifty of us', probably because in fact there were only fifteen.) The Greeks freely acknowledged the importance of musical influences from the Near

East, particularly Asia Minor; but it could be argued with some probability that Greek music in the Lydian *harmonia* was no closer to genuine Lydian music than Tchaikovsky's Arab Dance (in the Nutcracker Suite) is to genuine Arabic music, or Chabrier's 'España' to real Spanish. It was simply Greek music 'with a Lydian flavour'.

However, we do have some more very important evidence about the early scales from a much later writer called Aristides Quintilianus, whose date is unknown. Winnington-Ingram[18] believed him to have lived not earlier than the second century AD, perhaps later. His treatise *On Music* in three books covers a wide range of musical topics, and includes some rather exotic and peculiar metaphysical ideas about the nature of music, and the universe in general. However, on the technical aspects of music he seems to be quite reliable, and his account of the early *harmoniai* is virtually our only direct source of information about them.

In Chapter 9 of the first book[19] Aristides provides a series of ways in which the tetrachord can be divided, which follow the precepts of Aristoxenos almost exactly. He then goes on to say: 'There are also some other divisions of the tetrachord, which the very early musicians used for the *harmoniai*; sometimes they had a compass of an octave, sometimes more, and often less; for they did not always make use of all the notes, for reasons which we will explain later.' He then gives the intervals used in each of six scales, explaining at the end that whenever the term *diesis* is used, it should be taken to mean an enharmonic *diesis*, or quarter-tone. He then gives ('for the sake of clarity') these six scales in the Greek notation.

There are a number of odd features shown by these scales. It is clear that, though a later theorist might regard them as being constructed by tetrachords, with certain notes missing or added, they were not so constructed in the first place. They break a number of the rules propounded by Aristoxenos (for example, that any three consecutive intervals should add up to a fourth) and only three of them are octave scales. Nor are they given in the order in which they appear in Plato, nor again in the reverse of that order,[20] although at the end of the passage Aristides explicitly says that these are the scales mentioned by 'the divine Plato' in his *Republic*, and quotes a few words from Plato's text. (Because references are made in the dialogue to a musical expert called Damon, the scales are often referred to – in West, for example – as the 'Damonian' scales.) But despite all these reservations, there is some useful information to be derived from them. Let us consider them in turn using, as before, Aristoxenos' descriptive terms for the intervals.

Lydian | ¼ | 2 | 1 | ¼ | ¼ | 2 | ¼ |

The Lydian should be regarded with some suspicion, for a number of reasons. First and foremost, it does not, as Aristides has promised, exhibit any divisions of the tetrachord other than the regular enharmonic which has just been described – ¹/₄ tone, ¹/₄ tone, ditone. Its only odd feature is that one quarter-tone interval has been shifted from the bottom to the top of the scale, which is just another way of saying that it is the Hypolydian species of the octave from the two-octave 'system' of later theory, with the tetrachords tuned to the enharmonic instead of the diatonic. A further suspicious feature is that the scale is given in the Hypolydian *tonos* as defined by the later writers. It all seems to tie up a little too neatly with the theory of a much later date, suggesting that it has been rationalized and tidied up. We must return to this later.

| *Dorian* | 1 | ¹/₄ | ¹/₄ | 2 | 1 | ¹/₄ | ¹/₄ | 2 |
| *Phrygian* | 1 | ¹/₄ | ¹/₄ | 2 | 1 | ¹/₄ | ¹/₄ | 1 |

The Dorian and Phrygian scales are given by Aristides in a different *tonos* (the Lydian), and are identical except for the top note, which is a tone higher in the Dorian. This is a serious problem, as it is hardly conceivable that a listener would be able to detect any real difference of character between them. On the other hand, if Plato bracketed them together and fully accepted them both, then perhaps we should assume that they were very alike. But there still remains the problem that they do not show any divisions of a genuine tetrachord other than the regular enharmonic; the Dorian has two disjunct tetrachords (corresponding to the later Dorian species of the octave) with an added note a tone below, making the scale up to a ninth. The Phrygian has this added note too, and it may be significant that the theorists mention a term *hyperhypatē*, meaning 'beyond the lowest note', which, being a string name rather than a note name, is probably more appropriate to this note than *proslambanomenos* would be. The only difference between it and the Dorian is that its top note is a tone lower, making an octave scale.

The remaining three scales are more irregular, and therefore more promising.

| *Ionian* | ¹/₄ | ¹/₄ | 2 | 1¹/₂ | 1 |

The Ionian scale divides in the middle and contains two fourths, one above and one below *mesē* – the framework of two conjunct tetrachords. The lower half is an enharmonic tetrachord, but the upper half would probably have been regarded by later theorists as a 'trichord' – that is, a diatonic tetrachord with one note missing. The scale, consequently, has six notes in all, and a compass of a seventh.

| *Mixolydian* | ¹/₄ | ¹/₄ | 1 | 1 | ¹/₄ | ¹/₄ | 3 |

104

The Mixolydian scale is the oddest of all. It might have been regarded by later theorists as having a lower tetrachord of the enharmonic pattern, with an extra note inserted, dividing the ditone in half, and making a pentachord. Immediately above this (that is, conjunct) is an enharmonic *pyknon*, followed by a single note three tones higher, making eight notes in all, and an octave compass. It was suggested by some Greek theorists that this unique interval should be regarded as the combination of a ditone (which would have made up the enharmonic tetrachord) with a disjunctive tone above it, but this seems little more than a vain attempt to make the older scales fit the later analysis.

Syntonolydian | $^1/_4$ | $^1/_4$ | 2 | $1^1/_2$ |

Finally there is the Syntonolydian scale which, as given by Aristides, is the same as the Ionian without its top note. Here again we have the problem of two scales which can hardly have been distinguishable to the hearer, but which are supposed to have had strongly contrasting qualities.

Some of these difficulties can, I believe, be lessened or removed by taking account of the *tonos* in which Aristides gives the scales. The Dorian and Phrygian are given in the Lydian *tonos* (the 'keynote' is d', a tone above middle c) while the Lydian, Ionian, Mixolydian and Syntonolydian are pitched in the Hypolydian *tonos*, a fourth lower, with *mesē* on a. Though the Dorian and Phrygian may have been in approximately the same area of pitch in performance, it is scarcely credible that the 'slack' Ionian and the 'taut' Syntonolydian should have shared a common keynote. But Aristides' introductory remarks, in which he speaks of 'divisions of the tetrachord', make it clear that he is primarily concerned with the structures of these scales, and not with their pitch, either relative or absolute. It could reasonably be argued that, in order to bring out the similarities in their structures he has transposed the Mixolydian and the Syntonolydian into the same (low) key as the Ionian. I suspect – though this is sheer guesswork – that the Syntonolydian should be at least a sixth, or perhaps an octave higher.

There was one other very early scale, which is not mentioned in Plato's account or in Aristides Quintilianus, but is described in the treatise on music ascribed to Plutarch.[21] It was called the *Spondeion* scale, a name which associates it with the pouring of libations at the end of a meal (see pp. 7–8 above). As with other early scales, it appeared to the later theorists as part of a normal tetrachordal scale with some notes omitted. The basis was a diatonic tetrachord, the tetrachord *mesōn*, with the addition of *paramesē* but with the *lichanos* (one tone below *mesē*) missing.

Spondeion | $^1/_2$ | 2 | 1 |
                    hypatē parhypatē [*lichanos* missing]   mesē   paramesē

105

It is significant that this scale was supposed to have been invented by Olympos, a very early aulos-player – so early that his life story shades off from history into myth (for more details, see Chapter 6, p. 153). The account of his discovery assumes that he had an aulos bored to play the notes of a diatonic tetrachord, and says that he 'passed over' the *lichanos*, finding that the interval between *mesē* and *parhypatē* (an undivided ditone) sounded pleasant, and also that between *paramesē* and *parhypatē*, which is a 'tritone' (3 tones, or an augmented fourth – the same interval as the one found at the top of the Mixolydian of Aristides). By a series of later developments, a note was added at the top of the scale, at an interval of $^3/_4$ tone above *paramesē*, and eventually the semitone at the bottom was divided into two quarter-tones, and so the enharmonic was born. This account should not be regarded as altogether reliable, and there has been much speculation and argument on the subject.[22]

We can only speculate on the original pitches of this scale and those of the other *harmoniai*. We can be reasonably sure that the Dorian scale, and the version of the Phrygian approved by Plato, occupied the middle region of a singer's voice since they were associated with moderation and restraint. The pitch given by Aristides would fit this requirement; it may be significant that the first Delphic Hymn (see p. 227) covers a little more than the range of his Dorian (e flat–a$'$ flat, as against g–a$'$), and is pitched in the Phrygian *tonos*. The Mixolydian and Syntonolydian were presumably in a higher *tonos*, near the upper limits of the voice, and the Ionian might well have been in the key which Aristides gives, in the region of the voice which had a mellow and relaxed sound. There is, however, one factor which makes it difficult for us to be sure. The Greeks do not seem to have distinguished, as we regularly do, between a tenor and a baritone or bass voice. Are we then to assume that there was only one 'male' voice, which was not trained to give the tenor or bass quality which we recognize, but able to cover a wider range with more uniformity of tone? Could any Greek composer reasonably expect his *choros* to get up to a$'$ flat, or down to (say) an octave below middle c$'$, with reasonable ease? (The notation signs go down to F, a fifth lower, but the lowest note in the surviving vocal scores is around c.) We have one or two hints on how it may have been managed. The comic poet Menander (late fourth century BC) in a play of which a fragment survives[23] notes that in a *choros* 'not every man sings'. There may be two or three 'at the end of the line' (or perhaps at the rear) who are there 'just to make up the number', and who dance but only pretend to sing. It may well be that in a normal *choros* those singers who were able to reach the low notes sang a little louder, while the others mouthed the words, and exchanged roles with them when the pitch got too high. There is also another possible explanation: apparently the Greeks regarded notes an octave apart as virtually the same, calling them *homotona*, or 'on the same pitch'. Men and boys singing together

106

presumably sang an octave apart, but were considered to be singing the same notes. That being so, it might have been generally permissible for an adult male singer to go up or down an octave to make things easier; but there is an obvious exception to this in passages where the score has jumps of an octave up or down (e.g. the third section of the first Delphic Hymn), a special effect which would have to be achieved by all the singers.

This, then, is the nearest we can hope to get to the old *harmoniai* which were of such concern to Plato. But Aristoxenos mentions a musical expert who began the process of regularizing and simplifying the old scales, and creating a body of harmonic theory; he and his associates are referred to as the *harmonikoi*. Aristoxenos' criticisms of their work can perhaps give us some clue as to how the evidence which was known to Aristides Quintilianus may have been tampered with. The name of the expert was Eratocles; his date is unknown, but he was at least a generation before Aristoxenos, and probably active in the late fifth century BC.

Aristoxenos has a characteristic whinge about the inadequate treatment previously given to the formation of systems and how it was effected by the juxtaposition of intervals.[24] He intends to define the conditions under which two tetrachords can be joined together, but the earlier writers simply acknowledged that there were two ways (conjunction and disjunction) without defining the patterns of tetrachord which could be joined and those which could not. In another passage soon afterwards[25] he grudgingly admits that Eratocles made one small contribution, although he only examined one *systema* (which turns out to be an octave with two disjunct tetrachords) and he only dealt with the enharmonic form of tetrachord. In view of the statement of Aristides Quintilianus that all the small intervals in the old scales were quarter-tones, we might argue that Eratocles was right to ignore the chromatic and diatonic forms, as these were later developments. He apparently tried to show that there were seven species of the octave.[26] He 'illustrated' them by 'circulation' (*periphora*) of the intervals, which is a rather difficult point to interpret. I suggest that he drew a circular diagram, as in Figure 3.1 on p. 108 (an early precursor of the piechart), and by starting from seven different points on the circle he 'illustrated' the seven species of the octave. If put in this form, it shows the sequences of intervals without any reference to pitch.

Aristoxenos criticizes him for failing to show why the intervals around the circle have to be in a fixed, specific sequence to start with; why can we not jumble them together in any order? Of course, if we did so, there would be many more than seven species – in fact, seven for every possible arrangement of the seven intervals used here, or for any arrangement of seven intervals which add up to an octave, a horrific possibility which is best left to the statistical experts.

In a second attack on his predecessors[27] Aristoxenos complains, without mentioning Eratocles by name, that the *harmonikoi* did not try to discover the reason why certain sequences of notes are melodic and others are not, but concerned themselves only with 'the seven octachord (8-note) scales which they called harmoniai'. This almost certainly refers to the species of the octave illustrated above, and suggests that Eratocles and his school were trying to codify and systematize the old *harmoniai*, and create – for the first time – a body of harmonic theory. From much later sources we learn the names that were given to the seven species, and these names are in themselves significant. They are as shown in Figure 3.1. The first four were names which had been given to the old *harmoniai,* so presumably the *harmonikoi* considered that the species were sufficiently like those scales to be given the same names. However, there were at least three forms of the Lydian (the Mixolydian, the 'intense' Lydian for mourning songs and the 'slack' Lydian for convivial songs), and we do not know which was represented by the second of these species. It is also quite obvious that the scale given by Aristides as the old Lydian *harmonia* is exactly the same as the species here called Hypolydian; in fact, there seems to me to be little doubt that Aristides failed to discover the older form, and used this as the best available substitute.

Three other names are common to the old *harmoniai* and the species of the octave; of these, the Dorian and the Phrygian have undergone very little change in Eratocles' cycle. The extra note a tone below *hypatē* in the Dorian has been lost, while in the Phrygian a tone has been transferred from the top to the bottom, making the lowest interval into a ditone. The Mixolydian has been changed a little more obviously. In the older scale (if

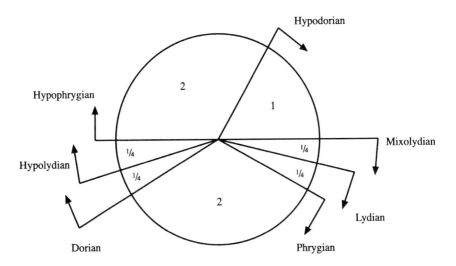

Figure 3.1 Eratocles' 'circle'

Aristides is right) the ditone in the lower tetrachord was divided into two tones, but Eratocles' cycle does not allow for two consecutive tones, so the dividing note is removed, and placed instead so as to divide the peculiar tritone at the top of the scale. This 'normalizes' the upper tetrachord, and enables the whole scale to fit the cycle. It is probable that the suggestion that this was the disjunctive tone in the scale arose from Eratocles' adjustment. In the older scale the undivided tritone was quite probably an important feature, in view of the preference given to it by Olympos in the *spondeion* scale.

It will be seen that at least two of the older scales – the Syntonolydian and the Ionian – have apparently been lost in the course of Eratocles' standardizations. They both involve two conjunct tetrachords, which are only available in two of the seven species (the Mixolydian and the Hypodorian), and the interval of $1^1/_2$ tones, which has no place in the cycle. They were apparently dropped by the theoreticians for this reason, though it is hard to believe that there were not many well-known melodies in these 'modes' which had survived orally from earlier times. Instead, the remaining three species were given the names Hypolydian, Hypophrygian and Hypodorian. Each has a different sequence of intervals from that of the un-prefixed species (compare the Lydian and Hypolydian) but they consistently start from a fourth further round the circle (i.e. a ditone and two quarter-tones, in whatever order). At this stage, their relative pitch is not taken into account; each octave scale returns to its starting-point. It is only later, when the two-octave systems were fully developed, that the circle was 'unrolled' into a linear form, and they were then regarded as starting from a higher or lower note (see p. 96). From then on the prefixes *hypo-* and (later) *hyper-* come to signify a definite pitch relationship, which is eventually fully implemented in the fifteen keys of Alypios' tables (see p. 99). By this time, two of the old names for *harmoniai* (Aeolian and Ionian) had fallen so completely out of use that they could be reintroduced as names for *tonoi*, or keys.

4

MUSIC, WORDS AND RHYTHM

As we saw in the first chapter, a very high proportion of all the music performed in ancient Greece was either singing with instrumental accompaniment, or instrumental music to accompany dancing. Singing means words, and words mean rhythm; and so does dancing of any kind, ancient or modern, in the form of a regularly repeating pattern of beats.

Our knowledge of ancient Greek dance is very limited.[1] Preserved in the literary sources there is a bewildering array of names for various kinds of dance, but these names tell us very little. A few vase-paintings show dances which can be identified by name, such as the *sikinnis* associated with satyr drama (see p. 22) and the *emmeleia* which was associated with tragedy. But vase-paintings are stylized, still pictures in two dimensions, and tell us very little about the movements of the dance, and nothing at all about the rhythm or tempo. T.B.L. Webster, in *The Greek Chorus* (Methuen, London 1970) attempted to link certain dance movements shown in illustrations with certain metres in the lyrics of drama; but his conclusions were highly speculative, and cannot help very much with the re-creation of ancient performance.

When we are dealing with words which were set to music, the situation is different. In the few surviving scores, almost all of which contain vocal music, the signs of the musical notation are written above the words of the text, usually without any rhythm notation. From this it is clear that the words themselves embodied a rhythm which could be 'read' by the singer, and which regulated the length of the notes in the melody line. Only in the later composers (from the late fifth century BC onwards) did the music begin to assert itself over the words, and acquire an independent rhythm of its own, much to the disgust of the old-fashioned orthodoxy. A rudimentary system of rhythm notation then became necessary, and we know some of the signs which were used, both from theoretical treatises on music and from papyrus fragments of music in which they appear. Nor are we totally dependent on our own investigations of the word-rhythms; the works of some ancient writers on the subject of 'metric' – that is, the science of rhythms – have been preserved, and a large body of modern

110

theory has been built up, starting from these works as a nucleus.

Unfortunately from the point of view of anyone who wishes to imagine or re-create the sounds of ancient song, the evidence to be drawn from the words themselves and from the ancient writers on metrical theory is seriously incomplete, because it relates almost entirely to what is called quantity or prosody – that is, to the rules for distinguishing between 'long' and 'short' syllables. The metrical patterns, or line-rhythms, which are set out, analysed and labelled by the ancient metricians are all patterns of 'long' and 'short' syllables. There are some modern scholars, who might be described as purists, who hold that these patterns embody the whole essence of the rhythm, and that no other factors should be taken into account in the study of ancient Greek verse. But there is some evidence which suggests that there were two other factors which influenced the rhythmic pattern – pitch and stress.

In English, and most other European languages, poetry contains patterns of emphasis; the emphasis is effected mainly by loudness, or stress:

> The *cur*few *tolls* the *knell* of *par*ting *day*

The metrical pattern of this line requires ten syllables, with a stress on the second of each pair. But the words themselves as pronounced in normal speech have their own stresses, which in general tend to coincide with the verse pattern, or at least avoid open conflict with it. Gray could not have written the line in such a way that the stress fell on par*ting* or cur*few*. So the rhythm is essentially determined by the stress, or extra loudness, of certain syllables. There is, in English, an in-built connection between this stress and the length or quantity of the syllables, since the stress does not as a rule fall on a short syllable; for example, in the word 'defeat', which has the pattern short + long ($\cup$ —) the stress cannot be put on the first syllable, and in 'conscientiously' (— $\cup$ — $\cup$ $\cup$) it could not be on the second, fourth or fifth. But the position of the stressed syllable is the primary factor in the choice and placing of the words, and any pattern in the quantity or length of the syllables is an accidental by-product of the pattern of stresses.

The principles were quite different in ancient Greek poetry. Instead of a pattern of regular stresses, a line of Greek poetry had a pattern of long and short syllables into which the words, each with its own pattern of long and short syllables, had to be fitted. In normal speech the words had emphasized syllables; but they were emphasized not so much by stress or loudness as by a rise in the musical pitch of the voice. In Classical Greece it was assumed that everybody knew which syllable should receive this treatment, and no indication was given in written texts. But in the third century BC, when pronunciation began to change from a pitch accent to a stress accent (partly due to the fact that Greek was being spoken by foreigners whose native language was stress-accented) scholars wished to preserve some record of older pronunciations or dialect pronunciations, and a system of written accents was introduced.[2] The Greek names of the accents make it quite clear that they were pitch-accents; the one which denoted a rise in pitch (/) was called the *'oxytone'* ('sharp' or 'high-pitch') accent. In a number of Greek words this accent falls on the last syllable, but the Greeks apparently did not like this effect except before a pause, so in any position other than the end of a sentence or clause it is replaced by the *'barytone'* or low-pitch (grave) accent (\), more or less equivalent to a cancellation sign. A third accent (~), called the *perispōmenon* in Greek, or 'circumflex' in English, seems to have been a combination of the two, denoting a rise and fall within the same syllable (Figure 4.1).

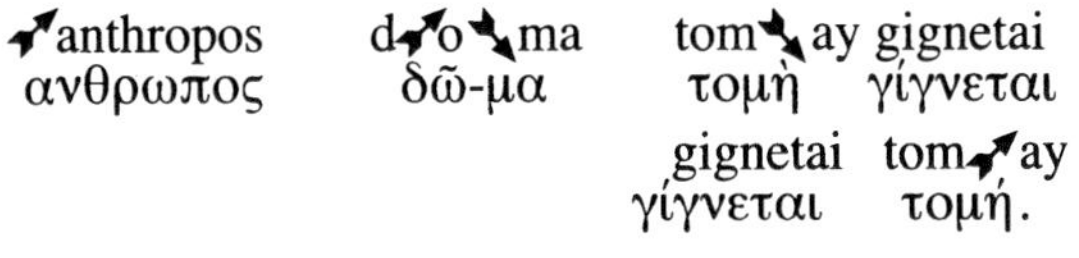

Figure 4.1 Pitch-accentuation of Greek words

Yet further evidence that these accents denoted emphasis by pitch comes from some of the surviving musical scores. In the Delphic Hymns the composers have respected the pitch patterns of the words to such an extent that they might well be said to conform to a rule, according to which a syllable bearing the acute accent is set on the highest note which occurs during the word; there may be other syllables on the same pitch, but none higher. Syllables which bear the circumflex accent are sometimes divided between two notes, in which case the second note is regularly lower than the first. The grave does not necessarily bring about a fall in pitch, but the first syllable of the word which follows it is normally at a higher pitch. Whether this applied to all poetry set to music, we cannot say; in some surviving scores the 'rule' is apparently disregarded, and the explanation of this phenomenon is one of the most difficult problems in the whole subject, to which we shall return later. But in general, there is a perceptible relationship between the pitch-accentuation of the syllables and the musical setting (Figure 4.2).

Just as we have seen a relationship between the position of a stress-accent and the length, or quantity, of syllables in English words, so we can find a relationship between the pitch-accents of ancient Greek and the quantities of syllables. Rather more than half the words in ancient Greek had one acute accent, and its position depended on the length of the last syllable in the word; if it was long, the accent fell on the preceding

Δε-ελ-φί-σι- ιν   Κασ- ταλ-ί-δος   ἐ- ου- ὑδρου   νά- ματ'ἐπ-ι-

Figure 4.2 Correspondence between pitch-accents and musical setting

syllable, and if it was short, on the one before that. If a two-syllable word
had a long followed by a short syllable, the circumflex was generally used
on the first. That accent was also used on many words in which two
syllables have been merged, or 'contracted' into one. The Greek language
also had a number of monosyllables, some of which were not pitch-
accented. There is, however, one very important difference between the
Greek accents and the English. In Greek the pitch-accent may fall on a
long or short syllable, whereas the stress accent in English normally falls
on a long one. As a result, there is in Greek a much less obvious
relationship between the pattern of long and short syllables in the line,
and the musical pattern of the words as determined by the pitch-accents.
This will be seen in the example on p. 114.

So, as we have seen, Greek verse lines had their patterns of long and
short syllables, and the individual words had their patterns of musical
pitch; but did stress, or loudness, play any part in determining the
rhythm? It certainly did not play the main part, as it does in English, but
that is not to say that it had no significance at all. In particular, any kind of
dance music requires a regular pattern of beats and stresses, and it should
be remembered that a Greek *choros*, whether in celebration, worship or
drama, was essentially a group of dancers.

Paradoxically, the best evidence for the importance of stress comes from
a line-pattern which was not connected with dance – the line known as a
hexameter ('six-measure'), used in epic poetry from the earliest times until
the end of the Classical world. Its basic pattern of long and short syllables
was:

$$\left| -\cup\cup \right| -\cup\cup \left| -\cup\cup \right| -\cup\cup \left| -\cup\cup \right| \; -- \left|\right.$$
or $\left| -- \right| -- \left| -- \right| -- \left|\right.$

and it was described by the ancient metricians as consisting of six 'feet'.
Each of the first four 'feet' could be either a 'dactyl', with the pattern — ∪
∪, or a 'spondee', with the pattern — —; the fifth was normally a dactyl
and the sixth a spondee. The words had to be fitted into this pattern of
long and short syllables, and the vocabulary used by Homer and all the
epic poets after him, known as the epic dialect, was custom-made to do so.
It contained a number of specially chosen words, not used in other forms
of poetry which had different rhythms, and a number of words which were

113

used in other poetry, but had been specially modified in order to make them fit the epic rhythm.

(May I please remind the reader at this point that the English version below the Greek is designed solely to reproduce the rhythm as nearly as possible in stress-accented English, and makes no claim whatever to accuracy or poetic merit.)

— ✔︎∪∪	— ∪ ✔︎∪	— ∪∪	— ✔︎∪∪	— ∪✔︎∪	— ∪
hoi d'ho-te	day lim-en	-os po-ly-	benth-e-os	en- tos hi-	kon-to
So, when they	came on a	breeze to the	wa- tery	depth of the	harbour,

— ✔︎∪∪	— ✔︎—	— ∪✔︎∪	——	— ∪∪	✔︎——
his- ti-a	men steil-	an- - to, the	-san d'en	– nay -i me-	lai- nay
furling the	sails they	stowed them a-	way safe	down in the	black ship.

Homer, *Iliad* I, 432–3

In these examples, the pattern of long and short syllables is given above the line, and the pattern of pitch-accents is indicated by arrows (✔︎) preceding the syllables on a higher pitch. It will be seen that there is no clear relationship between them – a syllable emphasized by a rise in pitch could occur at almost any point in the line. Incidentally, the first line shows a feature which is common to all Greek metrical units: the last syllable is normally long in theory, but a short one may be substituted *ad lib*.

There is also some evidence that the hexameter line, in addition to a pattern of long and short syllables, had a pattern of stressed syllables. Quite simply, the first syllable of each foot, which is invariably long, was pronounced a little louder, and in some cases artificially prolonged; in most textbooks this emphasis is called *ictus* (the Latin word for a blow or impact). We need not go into the details of this, but there are many instances of syllables which would normally be shortened because of a vowel at the start of the next word, but which remain long because they are in the emphasized part of the foot. Occasionally a naturally short syllable is artificially lengthened for the same reason.

There is further evidence for the placing of extra stress on certain syllables in the two terms used by the ancient metricians for the parts of a metrical foot – *arsis* and *thesis*. *Arsis* means 'raising' or 'lifting', and *thesis* means 'lowering' or 'putting down'. This must surely have some reference to dance movements; even the word 'foot' (*pous* in Greek) was presumably meant to be a unit of movement as well as a unit of rhythmic measurement,[3] and it is difficult to imagine a dancer (literally) putting his foot down without at the same time giving extra emphasis to the syllable he was singing, though it should be said that a number of modern authorities[4] regard this as an open question. Moreover, we must be very careful not to think of feet as analogous with the bars of modern musical notation; in particular, the *thesis* was not always on the first syllable, whereas the stress is invariably on the first beat of the bar. We shall have to return to this question later.

There is another feature of Greek word-rhythm which must now be investigated more closely. The ancient Greek metricians recognized two lengths of syllable, the long and the short, and they assumed a precise equivalence between them, namely that two shorts equal one long. Thus the two kinds of foot used in Homeric verse (the dactyl — ∪ ∪ and the spondee — —) are exactly equal in length, and interchangeable. For purposes of study, for the analysis of metrical patterns and for the labelling of various kinds of line or metrical unit, this is perfectly adequate. It is also perfectly adequate for the purpose to which a lot of modern metrical expertise is directed – textual criticism. The practitioners of this art tend to favour the argument that if the metrical pattern of the line requires a long syllable in a certain place, and the Greek word in a manuscript has a short syllable in that place, then there must be a fault in the text which requires correction. But if we are trying to imagine what the ancient rhythms sounded like in performance, a scheme which has only two time-values would seem to be a simplified version of the rhythms, which may not provide the full facts. A quite ordinary melody in our own music may require as many as six time-values – semiquaver, quaver, dotted quaver, crotchet, dotted crotchet and minim. Taking the semiquaver as the unit, these represent 1, 2, 3, 4, 6 and 8 units respectively, with a great range of possible interrelations between them. Added to this variety of time-values, we have rests of various durations, for which there are occasional indications in ancient Greek texts, though it is almost certain that they occurred in other contexts where there is no indication. The ancient symbols for rhythm notation (see Chapter 10) allow for four time-values (1, 2, 3 and 4 'units'), and though they may not have become necessary in practice before the fourth century BC, it is very unlikely that the rhythmic variety which they represent had come into being suddenly, or out of nowhere.

One clear example of a rest in Greek rhythm is found in the so-called elegiac couplet, used for various types of poetry (see p. 12). This consisted of a full hexameter line alternating with a shortened version.

$$— ∪ ∪ | — ∪ ∪ \ | — ∪ ∪ \ | — ∪ ∪ \ | — ∪ ∪ | \ — — |$$
(or) $$— \ — | — \ — \ | — \ — \ | — \ — \ |$$

$$— ∪ ∪ | — ∪ ∪ \ | — ▼ | \ — ∪ ∪ | \ — ∪ ∪ | \ — ▼ |$$
(or) $$— \ — | — \ — \ |$$

The second line could simply be described as a hexameter with the second half of the third foot, and the second half of the sixth foot missing.

The ancient metricians had a word for that particular effect – *catalexis*, which means 'fade-out', or 'tail-away'. It normally occurs only at the end of a line, but in the shorter line of the elegiac couplet it occurs twice. As we should expect, it affects the weak, or unstressed part of the foot. There is always a word-division in the middle of the line (or, to put it another way, there is never a word running over the 'missing' syllable). This suggests that there was in fact a pause, or rest, at that point, though there is no indication of it in ancient texts; presumably it was one of many features which were so familiar to everybody that none was needed. It also suggests that in performance the regular six-beat rhythm was maintained in both the longer and the shorter line.

But it could be argued with some cogency that the very act of representing the lines as divided into feet, or in musical notation with bar-lines and with the pattern of stress on the first beat of each bar which this implies, is misleading. The ancient metricians tried to analyse most metres into 'feet', including those which do not lend themselves to such analysis as readily as the hexameter or elegiac couplet. There is a natural tendency for the European ear to expect a regular beat and, where such regularity is interrupted, to restore it by prolonging syllables or adding rests. For example, there is a type of line commonly found in lyric poetry which has the pattern[5]

$$— \cup \cup — \cup \cup — \cup — —$$

This could be analysed as four dactyls, the third 'syncopated' (lacking one of its short syllables) thus:

$$— \cup \cup | — \cup \cup | — \cup | — — |$$

But in order to retain the regular beat, the long syllable in the third foot has to be extended by the length of a short syllable, which would be shown in musical notation as in Figure 4.3.

In order to make do with only two time-values, the time-signature would have to change in the third bar to $^3/_8$, and back again to $^2/_4$ in the fourth bar, which is not easy to accept; but the need for such a change arises entirely from the division into bars. If we can free ourselves from the presumption (it is no more than that) that there ought to be bar-lines, and see the line as a four-beat line with the last beat syncopated,

Figure 4.3 Dactylo-epitrite in musical notation

there is no need for any time-values other than the 'long' and the 'short'.

We have now encountered most of the basic concepts which are needed in order to make some reasonable guesses (and we can do no more than that) about the rhythms of Greek song as they sounded in performance. A detailed description of all the great variety of rhythmic patterns would require a volume to itself, and is beyond the scope of this chapter. Those who wish to pursue the subject in more detail may find the reading list on p. 282 helpful. What follows is a very brief summary of the most common rhythmic patterns, with illustrative examples.

We began with the hexameter, which was perhaps sung or chanted in early times (see p. 9) but may well have been spoken in the Classical period. Another rhythmic pattern, the iambic, was used for the spoken parts of a tragedy or comedy: it regularly had six 'feet', with a few permissible variations:

$$\cup - | \cup - | \cup \mathbin{/\!/} - | \cup \mathbin{/\!/} - | \cup - | \cup - |$$

There was regularly a word-division ('caesura') at one or both of the points marked // above. However, as we are concerned with sung rhythms, the variations of this pattern which come in the musical passages will be dealt with later.

Another common rhythm which may have been spoken, chanted or sung to an aulos accompaniment was also made up from 'feet' which were called anapaests, with the form $\cup \cup -$, which may be treated as a dactyl reversed; there was probably a stress on the second half of the foot, though we cannot be quite sure about this. In the comedies of Aristophanes and his contemporaries there was usually a section in the middle of the play called the *parabasis* (see p. 18). The opening passage of this section was written in anapaests, grouped in lines of eight feet, with 'fade-out' (*catalexis*), i.e. half of the last foot missing. As the metrical stress (*ictus*) apparently falls on the second half of this type of foot, it is the first, unstressed half that gets lost:

$$\cup \cup - | \cup \cup - | \cup \cup - | \cup \cup - \ | \cup \cup - | \cup \cup - | \cup \cup - | - |$$

However, there is no reason to suppose that there was a pause, or rest, between the last two syllables – in fact, they are very often in the same word. Nor is there anything to suggest that the penultimate syllable was prolonged to make up for the 'lost' bit. However, the *choros* presumably danced while chanting these lines, and the eighth dance-beat (or footfall?) may have come after the last syllable, thus maintaining an exactly regular beat.

— —	∪ ∪ —	∪ ∪ —	— —	∪ ∪ —	∪ ∪ —	∪ ∪ —	—
Ex hoo	ge khorois-	in ephes-	tayken	trugikois	ho didas-	kalos hay-mon	
Since first	he produced	comic plays	on stage	for you all,	our illus-	trious auth-or	

— —	∪ ∪ —	— ∪ ∪	— —	— —	— —	∪ ∪ —	—
oo- po	parebay	pros to the-	- atr - on	lex- on	hos dex-	i- os est-	in
too shy	to appear	out on the	stage front,	shout loud,	or claim	to be cle-	ver

Aristophanes, *Acharnians* 628–9

It will be seen from this example that an anapaest is often replaced by a spondee (— —). It was also permissible to substitute a dactyl (— ∪ ∪) for the anapaest (as in the third foot of the second line), and this poses a problem. Was the emphasis, or *ictus*, shifted from the second to the first half of the foot when a dactyl occurred? That is one possibility (I have represented it in the English version). Alternatively, it might have been treated as a spondee with its second long syllable split into two shorts. The technical word for this is 'resolution'. The problem is made more difficult because there is very often a single dactyl followed by a spondee, and a spondee gives no indication of where the stress fell. In the crudest phonetic terms, the very common form of half-line

∪ ∪ — | ∪ ∪ — | — ∪ ∪ | — — |
tiddy tum tiddy tum tum tiddy tum tum

could have been read as

tiddy *tum* tiddy *tum tum* tiddy *tum* tum

or as

tiddy *tum* tiddy *tum* tum *tiddy* tum *tum*

The second version preserves a regular beat; but was there any need to do so? Indeed, might not the first version have produced an out-of-step effect with the dance movements, which might have been quite effective? We can only guess.

We have also seen that in early tragedy anapaests were used by the *choros* when making their entry into the *orchestra* and during the play at certain points, particularly when a new character made an entrance (see p. 16). For this purpose the anapaests were organized in pairs or in groups of four to the line with a word-division half-way, and any passage of more than about eight lines was usually divided into paragraphs (known in the textbooks as 'systems'), usually ending with a 'catalectic' line of three and a half feet.

⏤ ⏤	⏤ ⏤	⏤ ⏤	⏤ ⏤
nun d'ay	-day 'go	kau-tos	thes- mon
Now, now	no more	sad hearts	weighed down

⏤ ⏤	⏑⏑ ⏤	⏑ ⏑ ⏤	⏤ ⏤
ex- o	pheromai	tad'hor- on,	iskhein d'
stay true	to the king	at the sight	so grim,

⏤ ⏑⏑	⏤ ⏤	⏑⏑ ⏤	⏑ ⏑ ⏤
ook- et-i	pay-gas	dyna- mai	dakru- on
nor bitter,	sad tears	any long-	er restrain

⏤ ⏤	⏤ ⏤	⏑⏑ ⏤	⏑⏑ ⏤
ton pan-	koitayn	hot'hor-o	thal-a mon
borne down	by grief	at the sight	of the maid

⏤ ⏤	⏑⏑ ⏤	⏑⏑ ⏤	⏤
taynd' An-	tigon- ayn	a-ny-too-	san.
swept off	to a sleep	that is end-	less.

(Sophocles, *Antigone* 800–805)

Anapaests were also used in the fully sung parts of choral songs; when so used they are known as 'melic' (or 'song') anapaests. As we might expect, they are used more freely in lines which do not always have a word-division half-way through, and may contain two, three, four, five or six 'feet'. Spondees and dactyls are freely substituted for anapaests.

Several other rhythms used by the Greek poets probably had a regular beat, and could usefully be analysed into 'feet'. One was called the Ionic, and differed from the anapaest and dactyl in that each 'foot' contained three long syllables or their equivalent. The most common form in which it appeared was the 'dimeter', a line containing two 'feet':

$$\cup\cup\mathbin{—}\mathbin{—}\mid\cup\cup\mathbin{—}\mathbin{—}\mid$$

The stress or *ictus*, if there was any, probably fell on the central part of each 'foot'; at least, we can be fairly sure that it was not on the last syllable, because in the places where 'fade-out' (*catalexis*) occurs it is the last syllable of the foot which is lost;

$$\cup\cup\mathbin{—}\mathbin{—}\mid\cup\cup\mathbin{—}\blacktriangledown\mid$$

This type of line had a very interesting variation. The ancient metricians called it *anaklasis*, or 'bending back', and it meant interchanging the two central syllables;

thus ∪∪ — —|∪∪ — —|

became ∪∪ — ∪ — ∪ — —

This would mean that in musical notation the normal line would be as in Figure 4.4 and the line with *anaklasis* as in Figure 4.5, except that the stress probably fell on the central syllable of the bar, giving a syncopated effect. It was a favourite rhythm of Anacreon, who composed 'solo lyric' songs (see p. 11); here is an example of his style.

∪ ∪ — ∪ — ∪ — —
Ag- e dyeu- te may- ket' hootow
Let us stop this rough car- ousing,

∪∪ — ∪ — ∪ — —
pa- ta- gow te k'al- al- ayt-oy
sil- ly shout-ing out and brawling

∪ ∪ — ∪ — ∪ — —
Skythik- ayn pos- in par' oinow
like a crowd of lout-ish boozers;

∪ ∪ — ∪ — ∪ — —
mel- et- o- men, al- la kal- ois
but with songs and small- er cups, let

∪ ∪ — —|∪∪ — —
hypopin- on- tes en hymnois.
moderation be the watchword.

Anacreon, fr. 45(a)

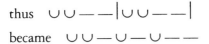

Figure 4.4 Normal Ionic

Figure 4.5 'Anaclastic' Ionic

Note that he uses the modified form except in the last line, which marks the end of a stanza. The same rhythm was used by Euripides in the opening ode of his *Bacchae* to accompany the dancing of a *choros* of Maenads (female devotees of Dionysos), and we may assume that it was traditionally used in the cult in real life. It must have given the dance a curious, shifting rhythmic effect.

Another rhythm which can be conveniently divided into 'feet' is called the cretic or paeonic. It has a $^5/_8$ time, the basic form being — ⏑ —, admitting three variations:

⏑ ⏑ ⏑ —   — ⏑ ⏑ ⏑ and ⏑ ⏑ ⏑ ⏑ ⏑

with no particular preference for dividing into 2 + 3 or 3 + 2. It is a very versatile metre, being used for solemn religious occasions (the Delphic Hymns are in this metre) or, at the other extreme, for bawdy *choros* songs in Aristophanic comedy. It was also the rhythm of the war-chant sung by the Greek sailors as they rowed out to the Battle of Salamis in 480 BC (see Chapter 1, pp. 8–9). I leave it to the naval experts to decide whether the oar-strokes could be fitted to a 2 + 3 or 3 + 2 rhythm![6] This example of the rhythm is from a 'song between episodes' in comedy.

— ⏑ ⏑⏑	— ⏑ —	— ⏑⏑⏑	— ⏑ —	— ⏑ ⏑ ⏑	— ⏑ —| |
O Kyp-ridi	tay kal- ay	kai Kharisi	tais phil - ais	syn-trophe Di-	all-ag- ay
O you lovely	creature, Peace,	Aphrodite's	darling, sweet	part-ner of the	Graces Three,

— ⏑⏑⏑	— ⏑ ⏑ ⏑	— ⏑ ⏑ ⏑	— ⏑ —
hos kal-on ek-	hou-sa to pros-	op-on ar' e-	lanthan-es.
How could I for-	get the stunning	beauty of your	love-ly face?

— ⏑ ⏑ ⏑	— ⏑⏑ ⏑	— ⏑ ⏑ ⏑	— ⏑ —
Pos an em- e	kai se tis Er-	os syn-ag-ag-	oi lab- on;
How I wish that	Er-os could en-	fold us in each	oth-ers' arms!

Aristophanes, *Acharnians* 989–991

Finally, there was one important rhythmic pattern called the dochmiac, which may be regarded as an unusually long 'foot', or as a pattern which can be combined with others to form longer and more irregular patterns. It had a rapid, slightly stuttering movement, and was generally used in scenes of high excitement in drama. The basic form of the dochmiac (the Greek word means 'slantwise' or 'oblique', which tells us nothing) was ⏑ — — ⏑ — ; Sir Richard Jebb gave as an English equivalent 'Rebel, serfs, rebel! Resent wrongs so dire!' (strangely radical sentiments for a nineteenth-century Professor of Greek, but they give the right sound). In theory, this pattern adds up to eight short syllables, divided 3 + 5, and several of the variants can be fitted into this scheme. The one most commonly used divides the long second syllable into two shorts, giving ∪ ∪∪ — ∪ — ('it never stays the same'); several lines in the Orestes music fragment are in this form.

∪ ∪ ∪   — ∪ —   ∪ ∪ ∪ — ∪ —
ho meg- as   olb- os oo   monim-os   em bro- tois
Fortune and wealth are not   certain for mor- tal men

∪ ∪ ∪ — ∪ —   ∪∪∪   — ∪ —
an- a de lai- phos hos   tis ak-a - too tho-as
swirling a-loft they fly   as on a   sail- ing boat. . . .

Euripides, *Orestes* 340–2

So far, so good. We can even contemplate splitting the next long to make ∪ ∪∪ ∪∪ ∪ — (as in 'a very subtle device'), or going the whole hog to make ∪ ∪∪ ∪∪ ∪ ∪∪ ('a little bit of a fiddle'); Euripides was not averse to using lines like this. But then it emerges that instead of breaking up the long syllables the short fourth syllable may be made long, giving ∪ — — — — and also the first, giving — — — — — , and we are faced with the task of putting a ten-quaver draught into an eight-quaver pot. West ingeniously suggests (p. 143) two crotchets with a quadruplet plus three crotchets with a sextuplet, i.e. four quavers in the time of three, followed by six in the time of five – a prescription which would daunt (I think) a skilled orchestral percussionist, let alone an amateur singer in an ancient Greek *choros*. If asked to say what happened in practice, I would reply that I have reached a stage of my scholarly career when I am at liberty to put forward heretical views, and I would suggest that, unlike classical scholars, *choros* singers did not regard quantities of syllables as sacred, or song rhythms as an exact science, and simply did a bit of fudging here and there, using false quantities if necessary to fit the words into the basic patterns.

Up to the dochmiac we have been dealing with rhythms which can be analysed without much difficulty into repetitive 'feet' of consistent length, and which seem to have had a pattern of stresses placed more or less regularly on the same part of each 'foot'. It could also be said that these types of line were used fairly consistently in particular contexts – the hexameter in epic, the anapaests in comedy and in certain situations in tragedy, and the Ionics in Dionysiac cult and in drinking songs of a lighter character. We must now look at a number of metrical forms which differ in both these respects. It is possible to analyse some of them into 'feet', particularly into groups of iambics which have been modified by various procedures such as reversal, omission of part of the foot, *catalexis* and so on.

But if we are simply trying to re-create the sounds, I do not believe that it is very helpful to do so: in particular, this would suggest that we have evidence for emphasis by stress on particular syllables, which in fact is very doubtful. This means, in turn, that these patterns cannot be accurately represented in musical notation with bar-lines, since they in themselves imply a regular stress. Nor was the choice of these rhythms related in any obvious way to the content of the words; they do not apparently match any particular 'mood' (ethos), even in the *choros* songs of tragedy. This is strange, in view of the fact that there was such a clear relationship between ethos and musical setting, as determined by the *harmonia* used (see p. 100).[7]

It is also necessary at this point to abandon the concept of lines of verse. The more elaborate structures of Greek song consisted not of regular repeated lines, but of metrical units of varying length, grouped together to form stanzas. These metrical units are referred to by the Greek term *colon* (meaning 'limb' or 'section', plural *cola*) and the process of determining where one ends and the next begins is called colometry. Here again, as in lines of verse which are made up by 'feet', the last syllable of a colon is normally long, but a short one may sometimes be substituted. This may be explained by the supposition that there was a breath-pause for the singer at this point, and where the last syllable was short he had a slightly longer breathing-space. It must be said, however, that it is not at all uncommon for both the sense and the syntax of the words to run over to the following line, and if the singer automatically took a breath, it must have meant that the words were divided up in an artificial way very different from that of normal speech.

Some of the more important patterns of colon must now be examined, and it will become clear that there is a marked difference between the types of stanza used in 'personal' or monodic lyric, written for a solo singer, and those used in 'choral' lyric (for an account of these genres, see pp. 11–12). The simpler and more straightforward nature of the personal lyric required a simple metrical structure, and the two best-known forms of stanza were named Sapphic and Alkaic, after the two best-known poets. Each is a four-colon stanza, with only two or three different types of colon. The following example will illustrate the Sapphic stanza.

— ⏑ — ⏑ — ⏑ ⏑ — ⏑ — ⏑
Poikil- othron' a-than-at' Aph- rod- it- a
Aphro- di- te, splendid- ly robed, im- mor-tal,

— ⏑ — ⏑ — ⏑ ⏑ — ⏑ — ⏑
pai Di- os dol- op-lok-e, liss- omai se
Child of Zeus, the weav- er of wiles, I pray you

—   ∪—   ∪ —   ∪∪ — ∪   — —
may m'as-ais-   i   mayd' on- i- ais- i   dam-na
crush me not with angu- ish at heart and sor- row

— ∪∪ —   —
Pot-ni- a, thum- on
Lad-y   Al-might-y.

The surviving remains of monodic lyric poems (which are for the most part fragmentary and incomplete) suggest that they were quite short, and had one repeating type of line or stanza throughout. But choral lyric, intended to be sung and danced, had a much more complicated structure. It was composed in pairs of stanzas, made up from a wide variety of different types of colon. The first stanza of each pair was called the *strophē* and the second, which repeated exactly the same rhythmic pattern, the *antistrophē*. This exact correspondence of rhythm is called 'strophic responsion'. Attempts have been made to link these terms with dance-movements – *strophē* means 'turn' and *antistrophē* 'counter-turn'. This is a reasonable idea, but can be pressed to rather absurd conclusions, such as the hypothesis that the dance-movements of the *strophē* were performed in the reverse order during the *antistrophē*, or that the dancers moved clockwise around the *orchēstra* for the one, and anti-clockwise for the other. Perhaps the two terms should be interpreted in a very general, non-literal sense; after all, we speak of a 'music-hall turn' without bothering too much about the meaning of the word.

There is another problem which is much more serious and challenging. We have seen that in a number of surviving scores the musical setting follows, to some extent at least, the pattern of rises and falls in pitch indicated by the accents on the words. Since the *antistrophē* follows the rhythmic pattern of the *strophē* very closely, it would be natural to assume that the same musical setting was used for both. But here is the problem. The rises and falls indicated by the pitch-accents on the *antistrophē* do not always correspond to those of the *strophē*. There are three possible solutions:

(a) The *antistrophē* had its own different musical setting.
(b) Its words were sung to the same notes as the *strophē*, with rises and falls of pitch in the 'wrong' places.
(c) Some compromise was made, by delaying or advancing rises and falls of pitch in the *antistrophē*, so that essentially the same melodic outline was adapted to the different words.

There is no certain way of deciding between these answers, though it should be said that the second is not as improbable as it might sound. There are some languages spoken today with pitch-accentuation (including, so I am told, Serbo-Croat) and in some of them it is apparently permissible to ignore the pitch-patterns of speech when setting the words to music. This even occurs when a false rise or fall gives the words a different meaning. Such licence may have been allowed in ancient Greece, but there is evidence to suggest the opposite. There is a well-known and oft-repeated anecdote from the Athenian theatre of the late fifth century BC mentioned by Aristophanes[8] concerning an actor who pronounced a single word with the wrong pitch accent, saying *galen'* →↗↘ instead of *galen'* →↗. As a result, the line of Euripides which he was delivering, instead of meaning 'After the storm I see a calm once more' meant 'After the storm I see a weasel once more'. This caused great merriment, which suggests that the Athenians were sensitive to pitch inflexions. However, it should be remembered that the actor was speaking the line, and had no excuse for his mistake; perhaps singers who were forced by the musical score to distort the pitch-pattern enjoyed more indulgence.

(I well remember when we were in Greece some years ago noticing that the Greeks of today, who use a stress accent, were careful always to put it on the correct syllable, and when I made mistakes in this matter, they patiently helped me to recognize and correct them.)

To illustrate some of these points, and to exemplify some of the patterns of colon, here are two pairs of stanzas from Sophocles' *Antigone*. They form the *choros* song after the scene in which the action begins: a sentry has told how he and his companions have discovered that some unknown person has given burial rites to the traitor Polyneikes, an action strictly forbidden by the newly-appointed king, Kreon. The substance of the song is as follows (I have not tried to provide a translation which follows the rhythm of the Greek words).

Strophē A: There are many awesome things in the world [the word *deinos* has all the nuances of 'strange', 'terrifying', 'clever', 'skilled' and some more], and none more awesome than Man; he can traverse the storm-rent sea amid the gales, driven on in his course by towering waves; and he can wear down Earth, immortal, unwearying, the greatest of the deities, as his mule-drawn ploughs go back and forth year after year.

Antistrophē A: And the meshes of his nets he casts around the carefree flocks of birds, the beasts of the wild, and fishes of the sea, ingenious Man; and by his devices tames the wild creatures of the hillside, and puts his yoke on the necks and shaggy manes of horses, and on the tireless mountain oxen.

Strophē B: And language he has taught himself, and thought swift as the wind, and sense of community: how to escape from frost and piercing rain – Man, the all-resourceful. He can contrive to meet all things that come his way, save only Death; from that he cannot find escape, though for crippling disease he can find remedies.

Antistrophē B: This subtlety that can contrive skills beyond all expectation steals sometimes into evil paths, sometimes to noble ends. He who respects the earthly laws and the justice of the gods by whom men take their oaths shall have a city that is exalted; but the audacious one who allies himself with wickedness shall be an outcast. May he who would do such things never be a guest in my house, and may I never have thoughts like his!

In the following layout the *strophē* runs down the left-hand side of the page, and the corresponding *antistrophē*, which follows it in performance, down the right, so as to facilitate a close comparison between the corresponding lines. I have tried to make the sounds and rhythms as clear as possible to the non-Greek reader, but there are some very difficult problems involved. The English phonetic version is bound to be inaccurate. I have marked the long and short syllables as clearly as I can; the rises of pitch within the words as normally spoken are indicated by arrows (♪) before the syllables on a higher pitch, and where the circumflex accent occurs the rise and fall is marked as ♪♪.

STROPHE A

332 Polla ta deina k'ooden an-

333 -thropoo dein- oteron pelei //

334 too- to kai po-li- oo peran

335 pontoo kheimer- i- o noto **

336 kho- rei peri- bry- khi- oisin

337 per-on hyp'oidmas- in; // the- on

338 te tan hyper- tat an, Gan

339 aphthiton, a- kamat- an apotru-etai

ANTISTROPHE A

342 koopho- no-on te phy- lon orn-

343 -ithon amphi- ba-lon agrei //

344 kai thayron ag-ri- on eth-ne

345 pontoo t'einal- i- an physin **

346 speirais- i dikty-o-klostois

347 periph-radays anayr;// krat- ei

348 de maykhan- ais agraul- oo

349 thayros oress-ib- ata, lasi- aukhen- a t'

— ∪⏑∪ — ∪⏑∪ —⏑∪∪ —⏑∪∪　　⏑—∪∪ —⏑∪∪ —⏑∪∪ — ∪⏑—

340 illomen-on ar- otron etos eis etos, 350 hippon hypax-emen amphilophon zygon,

—⏑— —⏑∪ — ∪ ⏑— —　　⏑——⏑— ∪⏑—⏑∪ ⏑—⏑ ∪

341 hipp-ei- o genei pol- eu- on.　　351 oor-ei- on t'akmay- ta taur- on.

STROPHE B　　　　　　ANTISTROPHE B

— ⏑ — ∪ ∪ —∪⏑∪ —　　∪ ⏑—∪∪ — ∪⏑∪ —

352 kai phthegma kay-an- em- o-en **　362 sophon ti to maykhan-o- en **

⏑∪ — ∪∪ —∪⏑∪ —　　⏑∪ — ∪∪ —⏑∪⏑∪ —

353 Phronema ka-yasty- nomoos　363 tekhnas hyper el- pid' ekhon

— — ∪∪⏑—∪∪ — ∪⏑— —　　∪∪ — ∪⏑∪ —∪∪ — ∪⏑— —

354 orgas edi- daxato kai dysaul- on　364 tote men kakon, allot' ep' esthlon herpei

⏑∪—∪⏑— — ∪ —　　⏑∪— ∪⏑— — ∪ —

355 pagon hyp- aithrei-a, kai **　365 nomoos ger- airon kthonos**

⏑ ∪ — ∪ ⏑— — ⏑∪ —　　∪⏑—⏑⏑∪ — — ⏑∪ —

356 dys-ombra pheugein belay**　366 the- on t'enorkon dikan**
—∪⏑∪∪⏑∪∪∪∪ —∪⏑— ∪—　　—⏑∪∪∪ ⏑∪∪∪⏑∪—∪ — ∪ —

357 panto- poros:// aporos ep'ooden erkhetai 367 hypsi- polis:// apolis ho-to to may kalon

∪⏑—∪ ⏑— —⏑∪ —　　⏑∪—∪⏑— —⏑∪—

358 to mellon: Hai-da monon　368 syn- esti tolmas kharin.

⏑—⏑∪ — ∪⏑—∪ —　　⏑ — ∪ — ∪⏑—∪ —

359 pheux- in ook ep-ax- et-ai**　369 mayt' em-oi par- hesti- os**

⏑∪—∪— ⏑ ∪— ∪ —　　⏑∪—∪ — ⏑∪ — ∪⏑—⏑

360 noson t'amayk-hanon phygas　370 genoi- to mayt' is-on phron-on

— ⏑ ∪ — —　　—⏑∪⏑— —

361 sym-peph-ras-tai　371 hos tad' er-dei

A few comments on these four stanzas, and the features which they illustrate, may perhaps be helpful.

First, the 'strophic responsion'. From a comparison between the corresponding lines in *strophē* and *antistrophē* it will be seen that the patterns of long and short syllables are almost exactly the same, apart from the final syllable of each line and a few which are optionally long or short in the pattern of the colon. These differences are really very trivial, and it is doubtful whether an ancient Greek audience would have been aware of them.

Another striking point of correspondence is in the phrasing and sense-pauses. In *strophē* A and *antistrophē* A there is a clear pause (marked //) at the end of the second line. In fact, the first two lines as printed form a single musical phrase (note that a word runs over in each case) and would surely be sung as such. There is another clear pause before the final word in 337 and 347, with a change of subject matter in each; the final word in each case runs closely on to the next line (337 *theōn te*, 347 *kratei de*), and leads via a short colon to a pair of cola in a markedly different rhythm, with a pause at the end of both 340 and 350. The last colon in each stanza is a 'supplementary comment'.

In *strophē* B and *antistrophē* B the correspondence is not quite so close, but still noticeable. Each has a strong pause after a 4-syllable word (*pantoporos* in 357, *hypsipolis* in 367, followed by a word of three short syllables, starting with a negative prefix (*aporos* 357, *apolis* 367). If the musical setting was the same, this 'echo' must have been very striking. From then on the correspondence is not close; in the *strophē* there are three phrases on the same theme as before, while in the *antistrophē* there are only two, each striking a moral note.

The correspondence of pitch-patterns between *strophē* and *antistrophē* is less obvious than that of the rhythms, but it is there none the less. Bearing in mind that a syllable with an acute accent should be on the highest pitch that occurs during a word, but that other syllables could be on the same pitch, it would be quite easy to devise a musical setting for eleven of the lines in the *strophēs* which would be compatible with the corresponding lines in the *antistrophēs*. In fact, there are no less than five pairs of lines (marked **) in which the pitch-accent pattern is exactly the same.

There may also be some explanation for the non-correspondence in at least two of the other pairs. The last line of *antistrophē* A, 351, seems almost to reverse the pitch-pattern of 341; this could be explained by the supposition that the musical setting for the second pair of stanzas had a different tonal centre, or a different 'musical colour', and that 351 might have been the 'bridge passage' in which the 'modulation' took place. Similarly 371, the last line of the second *antistrophē*, forms the 'coda' to the song as a whole, and leads into a passage of anapaests announcing the arrival of Antigone under guard. It might well have had its own independent melodic line.

Of the remaining seven pairs of lines there are several which could possibly have been sung to the same melody provided that (as I firmly believe) some licence was allowed, and an exact note-for-accent correspondence was not demanded.

These stanzas also illustrate very graphically the great variety of rhythms used in Greek choral song. In the twenty pairs of lines there are no less than twelve different patterns, even if minor variations of some patterns are ignored. This contrasts strongly with the most famous 'reproductions' of Classical tragedy in English literature. In *Samson Agonistes* Milton used the same iambic rhythms for the chorus 'songs' as are used in the spoken dialogue scenes, the only difference being in the length of the lines. In *Atalanta in Calydon* Swinburne used a variety of simple rhythms, but each choral 'song' has a single, fixed line pattern which is repeated:

Before the beginning of years
There came to the making of man
Time with a gift of tears,
Grief with a glass that ran . . .

The same pattern of three stresses, with one or two unstressed syllables between, continues throughout the 48 lines of the 'song'.

I hope that this very detailed analysis of a typical *choros* song will not be regarded as an end in itself, but merely a fact-finding exercise, after which the various features which have been treated in isolation can be put back together again, and the work viewed as a whole. It will then be seen that there is a great deal of artistry in its composition and construction. But Sophocles, like all great poets, has used his art to conceal the art, and created a work which would have been totally accessible, and totally comprehensible to his audience. And of the 15,000 or more who heard it at the first performance, there must have been many who would remember it, and whistle, hum or perhaps even sing it, for a long time afterwards.

5

MUSIC AND ACOUSTICAL SCIENCE

There are two threads running through the history of Greek acoustical science; one, which begins earlier, is the study of musical pitch and the relationships between notes of different pitch. The philosophers who drew this thread (if one may so put it) were mostly mathematicians at heart, with an interest in applying mathematics to music. The second thread was the study of the physical phenomena of sound, which on the whole did not involve mathematical analysis, and was the topic of interest for physicists or, as they would call themselves, Natural Philosophers (*Physikoi*).

The first thread originated from a chance discovery which influenced the Pythagorean school of philosophers. They were in the habit of attributing all important discoveries to the Founder himself, Pythagoras; but the influence of this discovery pervades their thought so thoroughly, and from such an early date, that here for once the attribution may have been correct. Pythagoras' discovery was that there is a mathematical relationship between lengths of vibrating string which produce pairs of notes which sound harmonious when played together. This can be observed when a vibrating string is shortened by stopping, in such a way as to keep the tension constant. If its length is shortened by half, it will sound an octave higher; if by one-third, a fifth higher, and if by a quarter, a fourth higher (Figure 5.1).

As they themselves put it, the ratio (*logos*) of the octave is $^2/_1$, that of the fifth is $^3/_2$ and that of the fourth $^4/_3$. At the same time they saw that, musically, a fifth (doh–soh) and a fourth (soh–doh') added together make up an octave; but mathematically, the two ratios have to be multiplied, not added, to give this result ($^3/_2 \times ^4/_3 = ^{12}/_6 = ^2/_1$). Similarly, the difference between two intervals is the larger ratio divided by the smaller; for example, the difference between a fourth and a fifth (a tone) has the ratio $^3/_2$ divided by $^4/_3$ (i.e. multiplied by $^3/_4$) = $^9/_8$. Finally, if a note is required which is exactly half-way between two others, it is necessary to find the square root (not the half) of each of the numbers in their ratio; and the Pythagoreans were well aware of the difficulty involved in using the square root of 2, which is an 'irrational' number.

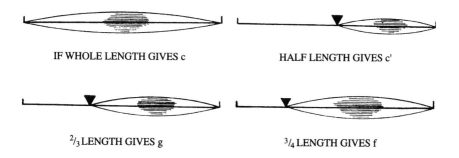

IF WHOLE LENGTH GIVES c

HALF LENGTH GIVES c'

$^2/_3$ LENGTH GIVES g

$^3/_4$ LENGTH GIVES f

Figure 5.1 Pythagoras' discovery

It is not known how Pythagoras made this discovery, and any attempt to reconstruct the process raises difficult problems. In the ancient world there were a number of apocryphal stories about it, most of which are palpably untrue, such as the version in which he heard harmonious notes coming from various anvils in a blacksmith's shop, and found that the weights of the hammers being used were in certain ratios to each other. This is of course nonsense; the pitch of the resonance would depend on the dimension and shape of the anvils, not those of the hammers. Nor can we give any credence to stories of his having tied various weights on to lengths of string. In fact, ancient acousticians never solved the riddle of the relationship between tension and pitch. They were aware that the thickness and density of the string were both factors influencing the pitch; they knew that a thick, heavy string would give a lower note than a thinner and lighter one of the same length and under the same tension, and in Ptolemy's very accurate experiments with a monochord he specifies that the strings must be of an exactly constant thickness along their length. He even prescribes a special test to check this, and if the string fails this test, he demands that it should be replaced. But they seem not to have attempted to assign a numerical value to the tension (in terms of units of weight), or to relate such a numerical value to the pitch. In fairness it should be said that the true formula, by which the pitch varies according to the square of the tension, is not one that would easily be arrived at by chance.

The most likely situation in which Pythagoras' original discovery was made would have been the sight of a musician playing an instrument of the lute type, and stopping the string against the fingerboard in various places. It would be obvious that the octave note was heard when the string was stopped at its mid-point, and the fifth when it was stopped one-third of the way up. The problem is that instruments of this type, though well known in Egypt from an early date, were not apparently a familiar sight in Greece until the fourth century BC, long after Pythagoras' time (see

Chapter 2, p. 77). The ancient tradition that he found the ratios by experimenting with a monochord is not very credible either; whoever constructed the first monochord (probably some centuries later) did so in order to test and explore an already established theory, not to look for a new one. Even then, the Pythagoreans do not seem to have been very interested in discovering exactly why there was a relationship between string lengths and the pitches of notes. They contented themselves with forming mathematical theories about musical intervals which started from comparative physical measurements of string lengths.

These measurements, however, formed a very important feature of their acoustical theory. They regarded musical pitches as magnitudes which, though they could not be measured physically (as is possible nowadays with a pulse-counter) could stand in a numerical ratio to each other; and they believed, as axiomatic, that these magnitudes were related, directly and exactly, to lengths of string which could be measured physically, and whose ratio could be determined in this way.[1] This is in contrast to the 'musical' school of thought, best represented by Aristoxenos, which held that the notes were, so to speak, points with no magnitude, and that the intervals between them were the measurable quantities. Members of this school pretended, by the use of fractions and additions and subtractions, that they were making scientific measurements, but in fact they were merely judging the 'quantities' of the intervals by ear and by guesswork. The Pythagoreans did their measuring with a ruler; they called the monochord *kanon*, which means a measuring-rod.

We have a description of a sophisticated version of this instrument in Ptolemy's treatise.[2] He begins by making the claim that this is the only accurate means of measuring intervals. The measurement of resonant lengths in woodwind instruments, he says, is unreliable; the points from which the measurements should be taken are uncertain (for example, should one measure from the top or from the centre of a fingerhole on the aulos?) and in all wind instruments an element of 'disorder' (*ataxia*) arises from variations in the force of the airstream. He adds, with a hint of despair, that experiments which involve suspending weights from strings, like those with auloi, do not give accurate results, but are more likely to give rise to slanging-matches between their practitioners. One practical problem he mentions is the difficulty of obtaining sets of strings (for the various weights) which are exactly uniform in length, thickness and density, so as to make the tension the only variable factor.

So we are left with the single string of the *monochordos kanon*, stretched along a rigid board. We do not know how the tension was achieved or adjusted. As no mention is made of any weights (the method used on modern versions of the apparatus) we must assume that something like the tuning mechanism of the lyre or kithara was used (the *kollopes*; see pp. 51–3). Two 'rollers' of equal diameter were placed under the string to define

132

the limits of the total vibrating length, and between them 'little bridges' (*hypagōgia*) which, he says, should be 'narrow and smooth', and very slightly higher than the rollers, so as to cut off portions (*apopsalmata*) of the total length. (The word 'narrow' seems to mean that they make contact with the string at one sharply-defined point, unlike the bridge of a lyre or kithara, which probably had a gentle curvature; see p. 51). Then a ruler is placed along the string, and calibrated so as to make it easy to mark off any required length, or pair of related lengths (Figure 5.2).

This raises some interesting problems. Was the ruler marked in any sort of fixed unit? This is most unlikely. The smallest standard Greek unit of length was the *daktylos* ('finger', actually meaning the last joint) which was about $^3/_4$ inch or just under 20 mm, and this would have to be subdivided for any measurement to be accurate. In fact, because it was a matter of measuring ratios between lengths, and not the lengths *per se*, the exact size of the unit did not matter, provided it was small enough. It is likely, therefore, that the total length of the string was arbitrarily chosen and then bisected successively into halves, quarters, eighths and so on, until there were perhaps 512 units, or (better still) 1,024, which on a string of just over 1 m long would give divisions of about 1 mm.

There is a further problem, however. When the theorists who are working out a series of ratios try to set them in tables of numbers, they tend to calculate a number of units for the maximum length which is derived from the lowest common multiple of all the numbers involved in the ratios. For example, Ptolemy sets out Archytas' ratios for the intervals in the diatonic, chromatic and enharmonic tetrachords in the table on p. 134. It is probable that Ptolemy himself has supplied the numbers –

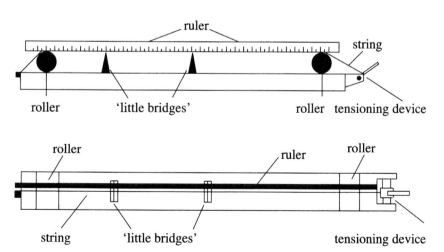

roller   'little bridges'   roller   tensioning device

roller   ruler   roller

string   'little bridges'   tensioning device

Figure 5.2 Monochord, side and plan view

Enharmonic		Chromatic		Diatonic	
Length (units)	Ratio	Length (units)	Ratio	Length (units)	Ratio
1,512	5:4	1,512	32:27	1,512	9:8
1,890	36:35	1,792	243:224	1,701	8:7
1,944	28:27	1,944	28:27	1,944	28:27
2,016		2,016		2,016	

they are unlikely to have been in Archytas' original work.

These large numbers are obviously derived from pure arithmetic, without any consideration of the difficulties of calibrating a ruler to measure them. Other tables go up to completely impracticable numbers of units[3] while others seem to have been kept within reasonable limits – in one chart the number is 672, an entirely suitable number for marking on a ruler. It should also be borne in mind that Ptolemy is expounding mathematics to a highly critical audience, who would pounce on any errors, however trivial. In the table above, if the figure 1,701 were rounded down to 1,700 (which nobody using a monochord would ever notice), all the numbers could be halved, and when it came to the ruler on the string, the 2,016 units could be halved to 1,008.

This almost certainly explains why the 'rollers' were used to fix the maximum vibrating length of the string. The ruler could be made slightly longer than the maximum available between them, and could be simply marked by repeated bisection (which could be done in the early stages with a set-square and dividers) until the units were as small as possible – say about 1 mm. If the vibrating length of string were a little over 1 m this could give 1,024 units of length, from which a length of 1,008 units could be set with the rollers, and the intervening lengths (each of them half the number of units in the table above) marked for the 'little bridges'.

Was the monochord ever played as a musical instrument? Ptolemy suggests that on occasion it was regarded as intermediate between an instrument and a piece of scientific equipment.[4] He stresses its serious limitations in comparison with the kithara and lyre – it cannot sound two different notes together, as they can, nor 'jump' accurately from one pitch to another. Apparently there were marks on the string (measured accurately by the ruler), to which the 'little bridges' were moved as required; but, as one can easily guess, it is very difficult to avoid a slight glissando between notes, especially if the tempo is fast, and also the movement of the 'bridges' along the taut string makes a squeaking noise. (On my own reconstruction of the monochord I got over this by fixing a number of 'little bridges' just clear of the string, and pressing it down on to them as on the frets of a guitar.) The only remedy Ptolemy suggests is that the monochord should not be played solo, but to the accompaniment of an aulos or pan-pipe (*syrinx*), instruments which disguise its faults.

The deficiency in the monochord was no doubt one reason for the development of another instrument – the 'multichord measurer' (*polychordos kanon*). This is described by Ptolemy,[5] together with an additional feature called the *helikon*, a movable bridge (or, to be more exact, *capotasto*) which swings about a pivot at its right-hand end. This enables the whole instrument, which has eight strings, to be retuned very easily to any required key, without changing the intervals between the notes (Figure 5.3).

The eight strings were chosen to be as nearly uniform as possible, of the same total vibrating length and all tuned to the same pitch. If the scale was to be an octave in extent, the bottom string AC was exactly twice as far away from the pivot E as the top string BD. This meant that the ratio EC:ED (i.e. 2:1) would be the same as that between YC and ZD, the portions of the strings AC and BD which are cut off below the swinging bridge. The length ZD would therefore sound an octave above YC. Moreover, this would apply whatever the position of the lever: if it were swung down from A so as to cross AC at X and BD at O, the ratio between XC and OD would still be 2:1, and the two notes, though both higher in pitch, would still be an octave apart.[6] It would, however, be very difficult to calibrate a scale on the segment over which the lever swung; in fact, Ptolemy suggests that the key should be set by adjusting the lever so as to tune the lowest string to the equivalent pitch on another instrument (e.g. the lowest string of a kithara or lyre).

To get the remaining notes of the scale (which in practice consist of two disjunct tetrachords) it is necessary to space out the strings at distances from E which reflect the ratios between the various notes. For the top note of the lower tetrachord, a fourth higher than the note from YC, the string must be $^3/_4$ of the distance along from E towards C; similarly, the string for the lowest note of the upper tetrachord must be placed so that CE/FE = $^3/_2$. These are the 'fixed' notes of the scale; the intervening notes would not, unfortunately, be 'movable' in the Greek sense – they would be set to predetermined fixed ratios. In the example in Figure 5.3 I have used the ratios used by the mathematicians including Euclid and, incidentally, Plato.

The great advantage of this instrument over the monochord is obvious. Most of the tricks and resources of the kithara-player, such as strumming, damping, and harmonics, would be available and, above all, the con‐secutive notes in a sequence could all be heard together, while on the monochord each note had to be 'killed' before the next could be sounded.

I have pursued the history of pitch-measurement through to its later stages in order to make the account continuous. We must now return to the fourth century BC, and examine the development of theories on the nature and causes of sound, and on differences in sound quality.

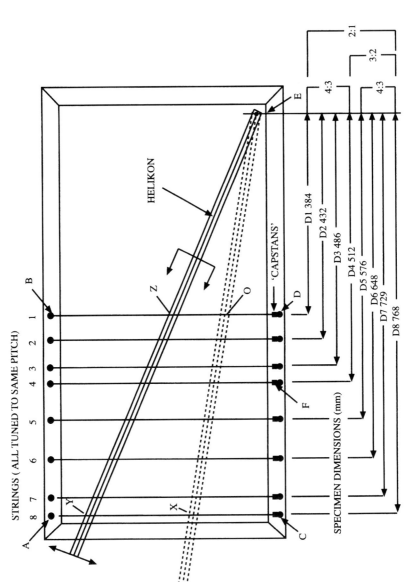

Figure 5.3 'Multichord Measurer with Helikon'

As I have said, the Pythagoreans were content to base their theories on measurements of string lengths, without making any serious attempt to show how or why the string length determined the pitch. This is in a way odd, because there are a few visible clues which might have been followed up. They seem to have done some experiments which involved suspending weights from lengths of string; and though these experiments did not give the answers they were looking for, they might have given some hint about the way in which a string vibrates. For example, the weights must sometimes have swung to and fro on the strings in the manner of pendulums, and it could have been seen that they took the same time to swing to and fro, regardless of whether the swing was a slight one or a big one. That would have explained why a string swings back and forth at the same frequency, and so gives a note of the same pitch, whether it is plucked firmly or lightly, and why its pitch is independent of loudness, or volume. This phenomenon could be observed with the naked eye in the case of a long, thick string at low tension.

Unfortunately, when the philosophers of the fourth century BC began to investigate acoustics, they chose for their observations other sources of sound, in which changes of pitch and changes of volume are combined in a confusing way. In only one of the surviving treatises, whose author was more closely allied to the Pythagorean tradition, are the two variables clearly distinguished.

The principal sources with which we shall be concerned are three passages: two of them are incomplete fragments, and the third is a very short treatise which contains in its introduction a clear and unequivocal statement of the true cause of pitch differences.

The first is a fragment from a work by Archytas,[7] a philosopher in the Pythagorean tradition who 'flourished' (as the older books used to say) in the first half of the fourth century BC, and whom we have already encountered in connection with the ratios of intervals. He was acquainted with, and a contemporary of Plato.

Archytas begins by explaining the apparently mysterious nature of sound. He points out that there can be no sound unless there is an 'impact' between one body and another, both of them being in motion. If they are travelling in opposite directions, they meet and slow each other down, thus causing a sound, and if they are going in the same direction but at different speeds, the faster-moving ones may overtake the slower and strike them, again producing a sound. (If Archytas were alive today, he would have a ready-made analogy on any trunk road!) Sound is created by every impact, but is not always audible; the impact may be too weak, or it may take place too far away from us. He also says, surprisingly, that a sound may be too loud for us to hear. He quotes the analogy of a great quantity of water being poured into a vessel with a small opening – it splashes over, and none goes inside. The massive but inaudible sound which he may have had in mind was that which, according to Pythagorean theory, was produced by the heavenly bodies going around in their orbits.

Archytas next tries to explain differences of pitch between sounds; he does not apparently concern himself (at least, not in the fragment preserved here) with the question of transmission of sound through the air. Various remarks suggest that he assumed that a 'lump' of air actually passed from the sound source to the ear, and that its velocity of transit determined its pitch. This invites comparison with a missile travelling through the air, and that analogy bedevilled the efforts of later thinkers. The ancients never really grasped the concepts of momentum or kinetic energy, and made various ridiculous suggestions to explain why a missile continues to move after it has left the hand of the thrower, and no more force is being applied. They were aware that the missile slows down as it travels. If this were applied to a sound, it should mean that its pitch gets lower as it gets further from its source; this clearly does not happen, but Archytas none the less asserts that: 'Of the various sounds which strike our (organ of) perception, those which arrive from the impact swiftly and strongly seem to be high in pitch, while those which arrive slowly and weakly sound low in pitch.' He goes on to give a number of illustrations which, he believes, prove the truth of this theory.

1) If we wish to speak or sing loudly and at a high pitch (note that the two notions are confused) we expel the air from our lungs more forcibly. This means that the force and speed of the impact makes the sound both louder and higher in pitch.

2) When an aulos is played, air is blown through the mouthpiece by the player. If it 'goes into' (we would rather say 'escapes from') a fingerhole high up on the instrument, it has still got a lot of pressure behind it and is travelling fast, and so produces a high note, but if it has to travel further down the instrument before reaching the air outside, it has lost its force, and so sounds a weaker note of lower pitch. (Being unable to see any kind of 'impact' in this situation, he seems to have thought of the rapid dispersion of the air, caused by the sudden release of pressure, as an alternative explanation for the origin of sound. See below, p. 142).

3) Worshippers in mystery-cults used an instrument called a *rhombos* – a diamond-shaped piece of hard leather on the end of a length of string, which they whirled around through the air; Archytas points out that the faster it is whirled, the louder the sound and the higher the pitch.

He quotes two other analogies, but they are rather confused and confusing. The view that high pitch is related to velocity had a strong influence on later thinkers; most of them, however, drew a distinction (which Archytas apparently did not) between the velocity of the bodies

138

involved in the original impact, and the velocity of transit from that point to the ear. (The idea that higher-pitched sounds travel faster is one that dies hard; Sir Thomas Beecham is said to have maintained it against overwhelming scientific evidence.)

The second passage which gives more insight into ancient theories of acoustics is also quoted by Porphyrios in his commentary on Ptolemy; according to Porphyrios it comes from a work by Aristotle, which would date it somewhere around the middle of the fourth century BC. However, there is some argument among scholars as to whether this is correct, and some of them prefer to attribute it to Strato of Lampsacus, a philosopher of the Aristotelian school whose life spanned the last quarter of the fourth century and the first quarter of the third.[8]

In this work the concept of 'impacts' as the sources of sound is developed and explored, and the author tries to explain the transmission of sound through the medium of air. If it was Strato this is not surprising, because he is known to have been interested in the nature of air, and to have made some experiments or demonstrations to show that air has 'body', and is compressible and elastic. A passage in the introduction to the *Pneumatika* of Hero of Alexandria is thought to have been derived from him.[9]

The author begins by restating that sounds are caused by 'impacts' (*plegai* in Greek). He is particularly concerned with those which are caused by the breath emerging from a woodwind instrument or by a vibrating string. The repeated 'impacts' of a vibrating string on the adjacent air could be seen if the string were thick enough, and vibrating slowly enough, but the author does not seem to be aware that the aulos also produced a series of impacts, one each time the reed-tongues opened and allowed a small quantity of air to pass through – at least, he says nothing about it. He does, however, explain why the successive impacts from a string are heard as a continuous note; we shall return to this shortly. In the aulos the impacts which were the origin of the sound, but which obviously could never be seen, were thought to occur at the highest open fingerhole when the air escaped from the confined space of the instrument into the open air.

He describes the transmission of sound as follows. The initial impact imparts a certain movement to the air immediately in contact with the source, and this air passes on a 'parallel' movement to the adjacent air, and so on. As a result, the pitch and tone quality remain the same, irrespective of the distance over which it has travelled. The four ways in which the air transmits the movements are described as 'contracting and extension' (i.e. by compression and rarefaction) and also as 'catching up and colliding' with the adjacent air. The first two of these represent a very accurate perception of what actually happens; the author is in effect describing a pressure wave passing through the air as a medium. The process is shown diagrammatically in Figure 5.4.

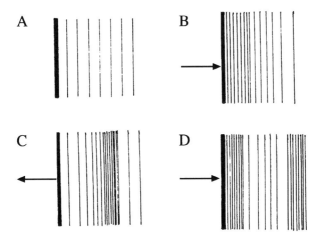

Figure 5.4 Air compressed by impacts

So far his account is accurate; but when he speaks of 'catching up' and 'colliding', he is reverting to terms which Archytas had used, and which derive from the older erroneous theories of 'sound particles' travelling through the air at different speeds according to their pitch. Here we have a phenomenon which we sometimes encounter in Greek technical writings; it is very difficult to judge whether the author simply did not realize that he was putting forward a false and discredited theory along with the correct one, or whether some busybody copying out the manuscript many years later remembered the other theory from a different text, and showed his cleverness by interpolating it.[10]

After this initial statement, the author expands his description: 'For when the *pneuma* strikes against the neighbouring air (*aër*), this air is immediately carried along by force (*bia*), thrusting forward the air beyond that again, so that the same sound (i.e. sound of the same pitch and timbre) extends in all directions, as far as the movement of the air persists.'

There are two significant terms used here: *pneuma* means air under pressure and in movement, as opposed to *aër* which is air in its natural (static) state. *Bia* is used by most scientific writers to describe movements which are not due to natural forces such as gravity, but to the application of a mechanical force; in fact, such movements are sometimes described as 'contrary to nature'. In his account of air, Strato speaks of it being compressed 'by force' (*bia*) by a piston in a closed cylinder and, when released, expanding to its 'natural' volume.[11]

The final remark in the previous paragraph ('as far as the movement of the air persists') is then explained: sound does not go on travelling indefinitely, because the motive force of the air is spread out over an ever-increasing area, and so becomes dissipated, 'like the winds (*pneumata*) which blow from rivers and from the land'. This illustration is rather mysterious. Perhaps it refers to winds which blow with great force down a river valley, but become gentle breezes when freed from confinement at the river mouth; the 'winds which blow from the land' could be off-shore evening breezes, which are troublesome near the shore, but cease to be so further out to sea. A little later he compares the dispersion of air (not sound this time) when it escapes from a long thin tube to the dispersion of water which has been flowing along a narrow ditch, and is allowed to spread out over a field.[12]

The remainder of the passage quoted by Porphyrios is largely taken up with observations on the different qualities of sound, in most cases the sounds of human speech and animal noises; this part is much more reminiscent of Aristotle, and there are frequent parallels with his *Researches into Animals* and other biological works. For the most part they are rather trite statements of the obvious, connecting a quality of sound with the quality of the source (e.g. that a rough throat causes a rough sound, and a long windpipe causes a constricted and throaty sound, etc.). Incidentally, in describing sound qualities, he sometimes uses colour terms, such as 'bright', 'dark' and even 'grey' and 'white' (though that last does not bear the technical sense it has nowadays). It is interesting that some of these terms, translated into Latin as *clarus* (bright) *fuscus* (dark) and *candidus* (white) were used by Roman writers on oratory to describe voice qualities.

However, among the various phenomena described there are half a dozen or so which have some bearing on musical instruments, and which deserve mention. One concerns the reeds of the aulos, and will be instantly recognized by any woodwind player. The author says that they must be 'dense, smooth and consistent' (i.e. with fine, not coarse fibres, a polished interior surface and without variations in diameter) 'so that the player's breath may pass through them smoothly and without being fragmented; this is why those which are moistened and soaked with saliva give a more pleasant sound, while dry ones sound unpleasant (*kakophona*)'. Moreover, he says, moisture in the breath also helps, by enabling it to pass through the instrument more smoothly and with less fragmentation. He also applies the same theory to the voice.[13]

There are also some remarks about the quality of gut strings. Those which sound best are 'the smoothest and most even in every part (i.e. with no variations in thickness) and whose manufacture is the same from every angle, and the joinings (*symbolai*) of the fibres hard to discern'. This is a little difficult to interpret; the 'manufacture' clearly refers to the crafts-manship of the string-maker (it was a recognized specialist craft) and 'the same from every angle' (*pantothen homoian*) seems to mean that if the string were twisted around between the fingers its appearance would not change as it revolved, because there were no discoloured or misshapen strands, and they were evenly twisted throughout. The number of strands may have varied according to the thickness of the string and the pitch to which it was designed to be tuned, but the ideal was clearly to make a smooth string which looked like a single unity, in which it was difficult to see the individual strands. This may be the meaning of the word 'joinings', but there is another possible interpretation. He uses the word *neuron* for the strands, which could mean animal sinew, as used in the springs of ancient catapults.[14] This was available only in short lengths of a few inches, and had to be 'joined' end to end to make a rope, whereas gut was available in lengths sufficient for most stringed instruments. Elsewhere he speaks of strings being 'stranded' or 'side-stranded',[15] which may mean badly made, or perhaps frayed; the effect is compared with that of a horn with a crack in it – the vibration travels so far along it, but is 'fragmented' when it reaches the fault.

One other phenomenon connected with strings has been mentioned before (p. 56). The author says[16] that tightly twisted strings make a harsh sound, and so do strings which are plucked elsewhere than at the middle, i.e. near the crossbar or the tailpiece of a lyre or kithara. This is due, he thinks, to their being under greater tension there than at the centre. This is of course an error, but it is easy to see how it arose. The force needed to displace the string over a given distance from its normal position is greater near the ends, because the same amount of movement causes a much greater increase in the tension, and therefore requires a greater force. In fact, the tension is equal throughout the string.

Another passage has caused a lot of controversy.[17] The author speaks of the effect of the dispersion of air, which is to make sounds weaker and less clear. He says that auloi provide a clear example, 'for those which have their mouthpieces at right-angles to the [unintelligible word here] give out a softer sound, which is not so clear; for the air in its motion falls suddenly into a much broader channel, and no longer travels under tension, but is scattered.' He contrasts this with auloi which have reeds which beat together (if that is the correct emendation of the text). Most scholars have taken this to refer to a kind of aulos which had its reed inserted in the side of the pipe near one end (emending the unintelligible word to mean 'bore'); but the very phenomenon which is being explained makes this virtually impossible. A reed cannot operate unless the pressure can build up to a high level in its stem, so as to force open the reed-tongues. This requires a bore of the same diameter as the reed-stem, or very nearly the same; in a pipe of much wider bore it cannot happen.[18] There is, in fact, no such instrument, and the 'maenad pipes' (see p. 71) should not have been interpreted as such. If we look closely at the phenomenon described, it seems clear that he is talking about a flute, where the air under compression in the player's mouth is suddenly released into the much wider bore of the instrument, which gives the flute a softer and less incisive tone than a reed instrument. The only problem is the word 'mouthpieces', which seems to be used in a very vague sense.[19]

One final remark is of concern to those who attempt to reconstruct ancient auloi. The author has spoken earlier of animal horns used as musical instruments (exactly how is not clear) and remarks that those which have been baked are harder in substance, and therefore produce a 'harder' sound. But, he says, instruments made of fennel stalks (*narthēkina*) have gentler sounds, 'because the sounds, falling on a softer material, do not rebound with the same force'. The instruments in question were presumably pan-pipes (see pp. 69–71) but the same criticism applies nowadays to replicas of auloi made from plastics such as polythene; they tend to have a rather dull tone. Past and present makers of oboes and clarinets have always tended to use the hardest materials available to them, even though they are more difficult to work in.

These remarks about the qualities of materials and sounds do not form the basis for any general theory of acoustics – they have only the status of anecdotal evidence. But among them there is a brief discussion of harmony and discord, and an attempt to explain why some pairs of notes 'blend' with each other, and others do not. This offers a very interesting comparison with the Pythagorean explanation of the same phenomenon.

The basic idea is that 'impacts' which reach the ear at exactly the same time blend with each other and form, in effect, a single sound. The followers of Aristotle were well aware that a musical note could consist of a series of separate impacts (the proof could be seen in a string vibrating at a low pitch); the reason why it seems to us to be continuous is that the gaps between impacts are so short that we miss them.[20] Once again, a visual analogy is given: if a series of coloured spots pass rapidly in front of the eye, they appear as a continuous line, because the eye does not have time to spot the blank spaces between them. This, of course, is the phenomenon on which cinematography (and television) depend. The ancients do not seem to have been aware that the aulos also creates a series of impacts; but, to be fair, they had no possible means of knowing that the air oscillates back and forth in the pipe – as far as they could tell, it travelled in one direction only.

Although we cannot distinguish the individual 'impacts' of a sound, we can distinguish between a pleasant sound and an unpleasant one. The prime example of the latter is the noise of a file being drawn across a piece of hard metal.[21] The impacts fall on the ear as a chaotic mass, 'so that one is fading away while another is gaining strength', and the effect is a fragmented sound; the corresponding effect using the sense of touch is a rough, spiky surface. At the opposite extreme, a single pure musical note sends impacts to the ear which are each in one piece, and arrive at regular intervals.

The gist of this theory is that impacts which coincide on their arrival at the ear seem to 'lose themselves in each other' (our author uses a splendid triple-compound word, *peri-syn-kata-lambanesthai*) and we hear them as a single, pure and unfragmented note. This of course can only happen between two notes that are at the same pitch; if there is any difference of pitch, there are bound to be non-synchronous impacts, which detract from the purity and pleasant quality of the combined notes. It is easy to see that the greater the number of these 'stray' impacts, the less pleasant the sound will be, until we eventually arrive at the noise of the file, with hundreds of impacts, none of which is synchronized with any other.

In describing this effect, the author comes very close to recognizing that the pitch of a note depends on the frequency of its 'impacts', a conception which is spelt out by only one ancient author – Euclid, in his *Division of the Monochord* (see p. 145). Our author says: 'In all concords the impacts on the air caused by the higher-pitched note occur *more often* owing to the speed of the movement: so it comes about that the last of the sounds strikes our ear at the same time as the one from the slower-movement.' I take 'the speed' to mean the speed of the movement which generates the impacts, i.e. the speed of movement of a vibrating string or of the air passing through an aulos, but there is much scholarly controversy over this.[22]

However, for the 'synchronized impact' theory to be credible, we must assume that all sounds travel through the air at the same speed. Thus, if we have two notes an octave apart, the higher one will create twice as many impacts in a given time as the lower one; so every alternate impact from the higher note will merge with one from the lower, so that only one in every three will be 'unpartnered'. This gives the nearest thing we can get to a perfect concord (Figure 5.5).

Figure 5.5 Harmony from synchronous impacts

The Pythagorean interpretation of this effect turns out to be a description of the same phenomena expressed in mathematical terms. Having worked out the ratios of the various intervals (the octave 2:1, the fifth 3:2 and the fourth 4:3), the Pythagoreans realized that the smaller the numbers involved in the ratio, the more concordant the interval would be. Their method of assessing the degree of discord is based on this. Though it may sound odd to a mathematician, it seems to make good sense in terms of acoustics.

They took what they called the 'foundations' of each ratio (i.e. they divided the two numbers by the highest common factor)[23] and subtracted 1 from each of them. The sum of the two remainders then gave an index of the degree of discord, which I have chosen to call the 'PDF' (Pythagorean Discord Factor). We are told that the units which they subtracted from each number were called 'the same' and the remainders 'different', and it is easy to see from Figure 5.5 that the number of 'sames' is equal to that of the synchronous impacts, and the number of 'differents' is equal to that of the unpartnered ones. In other words, they were simply counting the latter. If the notes are a fifth apart, every third impact from the higher will coincide with every other one from the lower note, and we have three 'differents' – a less harmonious interval than the octave, which has only one. The least concordant of all those intervals which the Greeks recognized as such is the fourth, with five 'differents'. Any interval with more than that was considered discordant. Porphyrios, the source of our information,[24] sets out the theory 'as Archytas and Didymos record it', implying that it was in circulation before Archytas' time, i.e. before the end of the fifth century BC. It is also probable that Archytas had it in mind when making some of his calculations of the intervals in the tetrachord. For instance, the two very small intervals in his enharmonic (28:27 and 36:35) combine to give a ratio 16:15, a much less discordant interval than the usual one given by the Pythagoreans for that interval, which was 256:243, with a PDF of 497, compared with Archytas' ratio of 16:15, with a PDF of only 29. The remaining interval in Archytas' tetrachord is 5:4 with a PDF of 7, only a little more discordant than the fourth. More on this topic will be found in Appendix 1.

The third text concerned with acoustics is a short treatise entitled *Division of the Monochord*, attributed to the greatest of the geometricians, Euclid. There is some dispute as to whether it was really written by him, and it has been suggested that here once more we have parts of more than one work patched together, or at least that there is more than one author involved.[25] If Euclid was indeed the author, the work would date from somewhere around 300 BC.

The work follows a plan common to many other scientific treatises of the period;[26] it begins with a number of propositions about sound which are 'axiomatic' – meaning that the reader is asked to accept, without proof, certain assumptions and definitions. Then the implications of these axioms are explored and demonstrated.

The first two statements are very reminiscent of Archytas' work. Sound, he says, depends on 'impacts', and impacts presuppose movement. But then comes the real advance on Archytas' notion of 'rapid' and 'slow' movements which determine the pitch. This author says: 'Some movements are more closely-packed (*pyknoterai*) and others more widely spaced (*araioterai*), and those which are more closely spaced cause notes of higher pitch, and those which are more widely spaced cause notes of lower pitch.' Here, at last, we have got away from the cruder equation of 'high speed (itself an ill-defined term) = high pitch', and arrived at the true explanation, which is 'higher frequency = higher pitch'. The terms *pyknos* and *araios* had been in use for many years to describe different conditions of air, 'compressed' and 'rarefied',[27] and of course the first term, used as a noun, *pyknon*, denoted the three 'close-packed' notes at the bottom of an enharmonic tetrachord (see p. 94).

Next comes another step forward. The Pythagoreans were content to accept that there was some relationship between the length of a string and/or the tension applied to it and the pitch of the note it gave; but they did not explore the reasons. This author makes an attempt to do so, at least in the case of tension. He says that if a note is higher in pitch than it ought to be, it is 'slackened by the subtraction of movement' until it reaches the correct pitch, and a note which is flat is 'tightened by the addition of movement'. The words translated as 'slackened' and 'tightened' were applied literally to strings, but could be extended to notes, meaning 'flattened' and 'sharpened' respectively. In this context the 'addition of movement' clearly means 'increasing the number of vibrations per second'.

This in turn leads to another very important conceptual advance. If notes can be made to reach the correct pitch by addition or subtraction, he says, they must be composed of parts, and these parts must have numbers assigned to them which can stand in various ratios to one another. Moreover, the numbers assigned to the parts will be whole numbers, since if two quantities are to be compared, or if the ratio between them has to be found, they must be divided into 'parts' of the same size. In the latter part of the treatise he uses diagrams to illustrate the quantities. These are not geometrical constructions, but merely graphic illustrations of the numbers in the form of straight lines. For example, in proposition 6 he shows[28] that a fifth, in the ratio $^3/_2$ added to a fourth in the ratio $^4/_3$ make up an octave. It is highly significant that the lines in Figure 5.6 represent the 'quantities of movement' of three notes; they obviously do not represent lengths of string, since the longest line represents the highest pitch. Nor do they involve any direct measurement of those quantities, but only the ratios between them, for which purpose all three of them must be divided into 'parts' of the same size.

This is really the culmination of the Pythagorean understanding of pitch and intervals: the quantification of pitch (if only in a relative sense). It makes a strong contrast with the more naive Aristoxenian quantification of intervals, as though they were the magnitudes and the notes, or pitches, were points.

The first nine propositions which follow the introduction are strictly mathematical ones, but they have important implications for music. The author uses the terms 'multiple', 'epimorial' and 'epimeric' to describe various sorts of ratio. 'Multiple' obviously means that the larger number

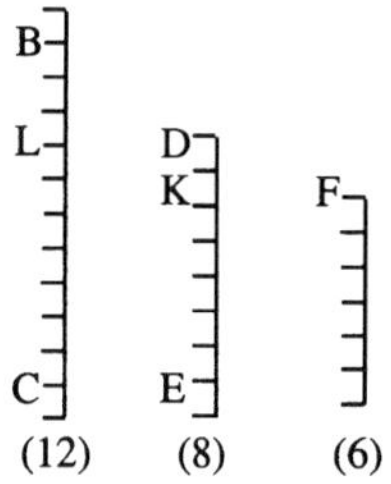

```
B                    (Euclid's Proof)
                     BC = 1½  DE, DE = 4/3F
L       D            LC = DE, BL = 1/3 BC = ½ DE
        K    F       KE = F, DK = ¼ DE, = 1/3 F
                     DK = ¼ DE, and BL = ½ DE,
                     so DK = ½ BL. BL = 1/3 BC,
                     so DK = 1/6 BC. But DK = 1/3 F
C       E            So BC = 2 x F
(12)   (8)   (6)
```

Figure 5.6 Euclid's 'graph' representing intervals

can be divided by the smaller, e.g. $^2/_1$, $^3/_1$ (an octave and a fifth), $^4/_1$ (double octave), etc. 'Epimorial' means a ratio in which the larger number is one greater than the smaller, e.g. $^4/_3$, $^9/_8$, $^{28}/_{27}$, etc.; and 'epimeric' is used if the two numbers are not related in either of those two ways (e.g. 81/64, etc.). He states in the introduction as an 'axiom' that notes which are in a multiple or epimorial ratio are more harmonious than those which are not.

There are several other propositions which have an important bearing on music. One is no. 9, which states that six tones (i.e. six successive intervals in the ratio $^9/_8$) add up to more than an octave. The proof is a simple arithmetical one; he takes as a starting-point the number 262,144, and multiplies it six times by $^9/_8$, giving the following:

$262,144 \times {}^9/_8 = 294,912$
$294,912 \times {}^9/_8 = 331,776$
$331,776 \times {}^9/_8 = 373,248$
$373,248 \times {}^9/_8 = 419,904$
$419,904 \times {}^9/_8 = 472,392$ But an octave above 262,144
$472,392 \times {}^9/_8 = 531,441$ $(262,144 \times 2) = 524,288$

In fact, this has no direct bearing on ancient Greek music, since the Greeks did not employ octave scales of six whole tones; but it does anticipate the problem which was solved many centuries later on keyboard instruments by the device of equal temperament (see Appendix 1).

A number of other points are raised on which this analysis differs from that of Aristoxenos. Proposition 16 shows that a tone cannot be divided into two or more equal parts,[29] whereas Aristoxenos did not hesitate to do so. Euclid also shows that the central note of a *pyknon* does not divide it into two equal halves; musicians may have thought that they were doing so by the judgement of the ear, but in strict scientific terms they were not.

All in all, this short treatise relating science and music is one of the best-informed and most interesting of those which have come down to us from ancient Greece.

147

6

MUSIC AND MYTH

Myths played a vitally important part in the formation of Greek attitudes, thought and belief, and given the Greeks' intense interest in music, it is not surprising that a number of their myths related to music and musicians.

It has long been recognized that myths can be divided into various categories.[1] Some (the 'aetiological' myths) were stories invented to explain why the world is the way it is, or to explain why rituals in honour of the gods are carried out in certain ways. The classic example of the latter is the story of the sons of Helios, the sun-god, who wanted desperately to be the first to sacrifice to Athena on the island of Rhodes when it first rose up out of the sea. They climbed to the top of the island, only to find that they had forgotten to bring with them the means of making fire; that is why, said the Greeks, ever since then offerings in that shrine have not been burnt, as was the usual convention.[2] Another class of myth is in the nature of an Awful Warning; it tells of terrible punishments visited on those who do not accept the superiority of the gods in all things. Perhaps the most horrifying of these was the story of Niobe, who boasted that she was more prolific than the goddess Leto, having twelve children as compared with Leto's two (Apollo and Artemis). These two deities responded by killing all Niobe's children, and Niobe herself was transformed into a rocky cliff, and her tears into a spring of water which ran from it. The story was a very popular subject in poetry and in art. The core of the most important of the musical myths, that of Marsyas, is a cautionary tale of this kind.

Yet another type of myth is that which describes the skill and achievements of a divine or semi-divine figure (i.e. the offspring of a god or goddess and a mortal); these stories involve skills which a human might possess, but which the hero has in a superhuman degree; he is usually not only the son of a deity, but is also helped and guided by a superhuman protector. The story of Perseus and the Gorgon is of this type; it is set in a world of fantastic monsters, while that of Orpheus, with which we shall be concerned, takes us through the mythical realms of nymphs, the abode of the dead, and a wild region of northern Greece.

There is some disagreement as to whether stories which may have some kind of historical basis (e.g. the Trojan War) should be called myths; they may acquire in the telling a great deal of superhuman achievement and divine intervention, as in Homer's poems, but in older textbooks they were generally classed as saga, not myth. There is, of course, a considerable grey area between the two.

Before dealing with the musical mythology, a word of warning must be given to those unfamiliar with this area of study. The Greek myths were not codified in holy writ or carved on stone. Wherever we possess several versions by different authors, we are likely to find variations in the details, and sometimes even in the basic form of the story; and the differences may go so deep as to render the variant versions completely incompatible with one another. In my career as a university lecturer I was often asked by students, 'But which is the true version?' The answer is, of course, that these are myths (the Greek word means 'tales told') and there is no factual or historical truth known to us with which they may or may not conform. The 'truth' is what has been chosen and determined by the poet or artist himself, and we have to accept it as such for the duration of the play, or poem, or whatever. We may even find the same author using two incompatible versions of the same story. As an example, Euripides in his *Women of Troy* makes Helen a vain woman whose irresponsible and immoral behaviour has caused the Trojan War; but in his *Helen*, he takes a version of the story in which she was taken to Egypt and remained there in innocence throughout the war, and the 'Helen' who was taken to Troy by Paris was a phantasm which resembled her exactly.

The popularity and influence of a myth often depends on the skill and fame of a poet or dramatist who has written the 'classic' version of it. As a result, a myth which has not been particularly well known in earlier times may assume much greater importance as a direct result of a great drama or epic poem. This seems to be true of the first of our myths – the story of Orpheus. He is not mentioned in Homer or Hesiod, whose works, dating from the late eighth or early seventh century BC, are a vast repository of tales, including the great majority of the significant ones, even if some of them are merely summarised in a few lines. During the fifth century BC the awakening of interest in Orpheus' story probably dates from the production of a tragedy by Aeschylus called the *Bassarai* or *Bassarides*. This was the second play of a trilogy (see p. 21) known as the *Lykourgeia* after Lykourgos, the central figure in at least one of the other plays, which seem to have dealt with the tragic fate of those who opposed the worship of Dionysos.[3] They are all set in Thrace, a region to the north-east of Greece.[4] This is consistently regarded as the birthplace of Orpheus and the scene of his death, with which Aeschylus' play was concerned. Unfortunately, hardly any of the text has survived, and we have no idea of how he was characterized. We know that he was torn to pieces by the

Bassarids, who were maenads (female worshippers of Dionysos) and we can reasonably infer that he had in some way offended Dionysos or his followers, since that was the reason why Lykourgos was punished. But how, or why would he have done so? We shall have to return to this problem.

The two other themes in his story are, of course, his supreme musical skill and his love for Eurydike. (That is how the name was spelt in Greek; we tend to say 'Eur-iddisy', or after Gluck, 'Eury-deechay', but in Greek and Latin Poetry it was 'Eur-iddy-kay'.)

The origin or cause of his musical skill is something of a mystery; he is said to have been the son of the Muse Kalliope, but the earliest reference to this is apparently in Timotheus, a poet/composer at the very end of the the fifth century BC. Of course, there may have been other earlier indications now lost to us. One reason for the obscurity may be that his birthplace was a semi-barbarous region outside the strict limits of the Greek world (Thrace remained so for many centuries). This is also in keeping with some elements in his story which belong not to the world of the Olympian gods and their protégés, but to the more primitive world of folk-tale and magic. Certainly his powers are magic; he was a singer and player of the lyre (not, as a rule, the kithara, which may be significant) and he would charm birds and animals with his music, and even inanimate objects such as rocks and trees. The tradition that he sailed in the Argo with Jason goes back quite a long way, and his services to that expedition are described much later by Apollonios of Rhodes (third century BC; see Chapter 7). They included settling quarrels, giving the tempo to the oarsmen, and outsinging the Sirens, who were daughters of the Muses.

Eurydike is rather an enigmatic figure. She was a nymph, and married to Orpheus; but she is hardly mentioned in the literature surviving from the Classical period, though there are other females with the same name, e.g. Kreon's wife in Sophocles' *Antigone*. The earliest version of the full story we possess is in a Roman poet, Virgil;[5] by his time (late first century BC) it had been worked on by Alexandrian scholars, whose highly sophisticated thought-processes may have given their own colouring to it.

The outline is this: after they had been married for a short time Eurydike, while running away from a pursuer, was bitten by a poisonous snake, and departed to the realm of the dead. Orpheus mourned her loss, and after vainly trying to console himself with music, journeyed to that dark and terrifying realm and persuaded its King and Queen (Dis and Proserpina in the Latin version) to allow Eurydike to return to life with him, on condition that she should walk behind him, and that he should not look back until they came out into the daylight. When they were almost there, a sudden madness came over Orpheus, and he looked back; then Eurydike had to return to the dead, and there was no second chance – he had lost her for ever.

It would be quite in accordance with the conventions of myth for the gods of the underworld to require some act of atonement, or sacrifice, to be offered in return for the privilege he had been granted; but the condition that he should not look behind him is strange. The reason, I believe, is that we are not in the realm of thought where the laws of Greek heroic myth apply, but in that of magic. The connection between magic and the dead is well established in Greek literature – Hekate, the patron goddess of witches and sorcerers, is a an 'earth' deity (*chthonian* in Greek), associated with the world of the dead, and likely to be encountered in graveyards and at crossroads, where magic rites were performed at night.[6] These included the burial of certain objects, and it was the usual practice to walk away after such rites without looking back. There is logic of sorts at work here. For the magic to succeed, it is necessary to have implicit faith in its efficacy; to walk away without looking back is a declaration of this faith, whereas taking a sly peep afterwards to see what is happening is virtually an admission that one's faith is not total. This is one possible explanation of the dire results of Orpheus' failure to keep to the condition. His foolish act could be explained as a sudden madness, but the suggestion has been made[7] that he was expecting to see her shadow as they emerged into the light, and as she was still a ghost she did not cast one. This led him to think that he had been deceived, and so he turned round.

There is one piece of evidence which might be taken to reflect an alternative version of the story, with a happy ending. It is a relief sculpture now in the National Museum in Naples, which is thought to be a copy of a relief which was placed near the Altar of the Twelve Gods in the Athenian market-place (*Agora*) in the late fifth century BC.[8] It shows Orpheus, Eurydike and Hermes (all named); Orpheus stands on the right, wearing a strange pointed Thracian cap, and holding a lyre, while Eurydike, her left hand on his shoulder, has partly pulled aside the robe which has been covering her head. They are gazing soulfully into each others' eyes, with a expression which is enigmatic, but not obviously one of despair or sadness. Hermes, on the left, is carrying his 'travelling hat' (*petasos*) behind his shoulder, indicating that he has made, or is about to make, a long journey. He was the deity who escorted the souls of the dead from this world to the next, and one possible interpretation of this picture is that he has just made the return journey, bringing Eurydike with him to be reunited with Orpheus (this 'happy ending' version was adopted by Gluck for his opera). On the other hand, the relief sculpture could mean the exact opposite – that Hermes is to take her back to the underworld – but this seems less likely.

In the more usual version Orpheus then returned to his native Thrace, and for seven whole months languished on a high mountain above the river Strymon mourning his loss, composing sad melodies which 'tamed tigers and made oak trees come to him'. Eventually he met his death at the hands of maenads – female worshippers of Dionysos. Virgil tells how they tore his limbs apart 'during the sacred nocturnal rites', which does not imply drunken or erotic revels, but a ritual of dancing and animal sacrifice, very occasionally replaced by human sacrifice. Why did they do that to Orpheus?

Aeschylus apparently followed the older tradition in representing Lykourgos as a mortal who offended against Dionysos by attacking the Maenads and the god himself, who jumped into the sea to escape; Lykourgos was punished by blindness and death.[9] There is a problem here, in that the *Lykourgos* is said to have been the satyr-drama at the end of the trilogy and this story hardly seems to match the mood of such a play. It would be out of character for Orpheus to behave in the kind of way that Lykourgos did; but there is some evidence that he offended Dionysos in a different way. It comes from a work called *Katasterismoi* (meaning 'myths and constellations'), attributed to the great scholar Eratosthenes, who worked in Alexandria in the third century BC, though the text we have may be a later version by somebody else. He tells us[10] that 'according to Aeschylus the poet', Orpheus did not honour Dionysos, but considered the Sun (Helios) to be the greatest of the gods, and addressed him as Apollo; he used to wake up before daybreak and climb to the top of Mount Pangaios, so as to see the first of the sun at sunrise (a rather tactless move, as the mountain itself was sacred to Dionysos). As a result, Dionysos became angry with him, and sent the Bassarides (his maenads) against him; they tore him apart limb from limb, and the Muses collected his remains and buried them. This is in marked contrast to their treatment of another minstrel who, like Orpheus, came from Thrace. His name was Thamyris (sometimes spelt Thamyras) and he was punished for his presumption in challenging the Muses to a contest – an action similar to that of Marsyas, to whose story we shall be coming shortly. The Muses punished him in deadly fashion, by causing him to lose his gift of song and his memory.[11]

Virgil does not mention this reason for Dionysos' anger or the maenads' actions. He remarks that Orpheus had no thought of any other love or another bride, and hints very vaguely that this may have offended the maenads, who saw him as a misogynist. Ovid, for reasons of his own, says[12] that he resorted to homosexual affairs, and this was the cause of their hatred of him; we need not take this seriously. Virgil also glosses over the manner of his death in one line, suggesting that it was an unimportant epilogue to the main story, which was what really interested him.

I have confined this account strictly to those aspects of the myth which are musically interesting, and have avoided any mention of the cult which grew up around Orpheus from fairly early times, with a body of sacred writings supposed (by the faithful, at least) to have been composed by Orpheus himself, and a set of beliefs about the origins of the gods and the world, and about the immortality of the soul and the after-life. Such 'Orphic' writings as do survive are mostly of poor quality (unlikely to have moved any oak trees) and palpably derived from other Greek poets, in particular from Hesiod. This is a vast subject, with an extensive scholarly literature, but it belongs to the history of philosophy and religion rather than that of music. Here we should rather remember Orpheus as the supreme musician, whose story over the centuries has inspired what is perhaps the finest piece of poetry ever written in Latin and, centuries later, one of the most moving works in the repertoire of opera.

The second of the two most important musical myths presents a strong contrast. Marsyas is consistently represented in art, and spoken of in literature, as a satyr – a non-human creature, brash, noisy and boastful, whose music was in keeping with his personality. And though Orpheus, despite his birthplace, was entirely Greek, Marsyas hailed from a 'barbarian' land (meaning one where Greek was not spoken) – namely central Asia Minor, now Turkey but then called Phrygia.

In this myth we have a very complicated story, with two strands which may originally have been separate, but which have been interwoven to such an extent that it is difficult to sort them out. The first strand involves three characters on the borderline between myth and dimly remembered history – Hyagnis, Marsyas and Olympos. Hyagnis is a very shadowy figure – a Phrygian, in some versions the father of Marsyas, the inventor of the aulos and the composer of the oldest known piece for that instrument, the 'Great Mother's aulos tune' (*Mētrōon aulēma*).[13] He lived in Celaenae, a town in Phrygia where there was a cult of the Great Mother (Cybele) whose worship was of an orgiastic character, accompanied by aulos music. It is quite possible that this version preserves a distant folk-memory; the instrument is often said to have originated in Asia Minor, and to have been brought to Greece along with the cult of Cybele and that of Dionysos, which was closely linked with it. But the natives of the area attributed the composition of the *Mētrōon aulēma* to Marsyas.[14]

The ancient historians of music obviously did not have any clear evidence of these matters, and gave free rein to guesswork. They do agree generally, however, on the claim that Marsyas taught Olympos to play the aulos, and that certain tunes still preserved in the oral tradition in Classical times were believed to be genuine compositions by Olympos or by his teacher. They were highly regarded – Plato says that they were 'charming', even when played by an unskilled aulos-player.[15] From this it appears that Olympos was regarded as an historical figure, while Marsyas was from the realm of mythology. Characteristically, just as Hyagnis and Marsyas were linked as father and son, so Marsyas and Olympos were linked as teacher and boy-favourite.

Another point of general agreement is that they were all Phrygians, and that the 'Phrygian style' of composition and of aulos-playing originated with them. Aristoxenos, a very reputable historian of music, asserted that they had invented the Phrygian *harmonia* (see p. 100) which is to say the same thing in musicologists' language.[16]

All this is quite straightforward; but now enter Athena, bringing with her a whole lot of problems. Most of these arise from the fact that there were two different and contradictory traditions regarding the invention of the aulos and its music, which were not successfully blended together. According to the other tradition, Athena was the first performer on the instrument, and the first outstanding composer: but for reasons which were regarded with some scepticism even in antiquity, she discarded the instrument, and Marsyas (literally) took it up and developed his own skill and style.

The first problem is – did Athena invent the aulos? There is an inherent difficulty here, in that the same Greek word is used for 'find' and 'invent'. Pindar describes the goddess's achievement in *Pythian* 12, 18–27 (my translation is a prosaic paraphrase of the Greek, which destroys the sublimity but makes the meaning at the prose level clearer):

> But when she had rescued the man so dear to her (Perseus) from these toils, the maiden goddess fashioned the all-sounding music (*pamphōnon melos*) of auloi, in order that she might imitate with her instruments the shrieking cry forced from the jaws of the Gorgon Medusa. Having found (or invented) it, the goddess gave it to mortal men to possess, and she named it 'the *nomos* of many heads', a competition-piece that brings renown in the contests that excite the people, passing often through the delicate bronze and the reeds which dwell beside the city of the Graces where the dancing-places are delightful, in the precinct of (the river) Kephisos, reeds which are faithful supporters of the dancers.

A number of matters require comment. First, it is not explicitly stated that she invented the aulos. She is said by a later writer (Telestes, at the end of the fifth century) to have found the instruments in a thicket; this would seem to be a very unlikely answer to a problem which Pindar may have perceived, but wisely chose to veil in ambiguity. In his poem she is credited with a composition, the '*nomos* of many heads', which was clearly in the same genre as the Pythian *nomos* (see p. 5), being a piece of programme music for solo aulos, which narrated the story of Perseus slaying the Gorgon, complete with the monster's death-cries. This, I believe, is the explanation of the adjective 'maker of all sounds' (*pamphōnos*) which Pindar used elsewhere of the aulos, meaning that it had a wide range of different timbres, and was capable of producing various sound-effects (e.g. the songs of birds; see p. 19). It also had a much greater dynamic range (from *pp* to *ff*) than the kithara.[17] As for the 'many heads', this could refer to the snakes on Medusa's head, or to 'movements' in the composition.

The latter part of the extract seems merely to say that Athena's composition has been preserved for posterity, and is used as a test-piece for aulos-players. It is said to be frequently performed in Boeotia, near the river Kephisos, where the reed-beds supplied the raw material for the aulos reed makers (see pp. 28–9). This may be an allusive compliment to Pindar's home territory, and to the aulos player whose victory he is celebrating. The 'delicate bronze' is best interpreted as the metal fittings on the *phorbeia* (the mouth-band worn by players in competitions; see p. 31); the poem is a bit too early (about 490 BC) to refer to bronze casing on the body of the instrument. He calls the aulos reeds 'faithful supporters' (*pistoi martyres*) of singers and dancers in a *choros*, which I think is a general statement, not specific to the performance of a *nomos*. But all this concerns performers in Pindar's own day, and tells us nothing about Athena.

One explanation for the introduction of Athena into the story which immediately springs to mind is that the Greeks were reluctant to admit that their most popular musical instrument, acceptable in almost every musical context, and seen in vase paintings being played by the Muses, was of foreign origin. Accordingly, it might be thought, they invented a story which gave priority to the Greek goddess, and then tried to account for the aulos having 'emigrated' to Asia Minor and subsequently 'come home' again, bringing with it the Phrygian musical tradition. There is a curious parallel here with the god Dionysos. Historically, his cult almost certainly originated in Asia Minor, and was imported into Greece; but the Greeks claimed that his mother had been a daughter of Kadmos, the Greek king of Thebes, and that by a series of bizarre events he had been born a second time, taken to Asia Minor to be brought up by the nymphs there, and eventually 'come home' to Thebes.[18]

Stories regarding the reason for Athena's rejection of the aulos are consistent; the fullest account is in Plutarch's essay *On the Restraint of Anger*, written in the late first century AD.[19] He attributes the story to 'the jokers' (*paizontes*), which would normally mean comic poets, but might refer to writers of satyr-plays, in which Marsyas would be entirely at home. Athena, it seems, was playing the aulos, and caught sight of her reflection in 'some river or other' and, being shocked by the distortion of her features which the effort caused, threw the instrument away and vowed never to touch it again. Plutarch quotes a couple of lines of unknown authorship[20] in which someone (presumably Marsyas) says to Athena: 'Your appearance is unseemly; let go of the auloi, take up your equipment (*hopla*) and make your cheeks decent.' He also quotes an early poet (perhaps Simonides) as saying that Marsyas invented the *phorbeia* to solve this problem: 'With shining gold (not, please note, common bronze!) he strapped up his hairy head and his boisterous mouth, with thongs tied behind.' It is not clear whether he offered it to Athena (*hopla* would normally mean her shield and spear, but could just possibly mean the *phorbeia*). If he did, she apparently did not take up the offer – women are not seen wearing the *phorbeia* (see p. 32). She was in any case displeased with Marsyas for picking up the aulos, and was shown in some works of art smacking him for doing so.[21]

It is surely significant that no place-names are mentioned, either for her finding of the aulos or for this episode; nor is there any explanation for Marsyas' presence in it. This is strange: the land of mythology does not have latitudes or longitudes, but the great majority of myths are located by a geographical name, whether real or invented. Moreover, the next episode in the story – the contest between Apollo and Marsyas – is firmly located at Celaenae in Phrygia, and may therefore have some historical basis, whereas the Athena story certainly does not.

The story of the contest itself is told fairly consistently. Marsyas claimed to be a better musician than Apollo, and challenged him to a contest; note that it was between Apollo, who sang and played the kithara, and Marsyas, who played strictly instrumental music on the aulos. They agreed that whoever won could 'do what he liked' with the loser – a typical Greek euphemism for the infliction of any punishment, including torture or death. (What, if anything, Marsyas could have done to Apollo is a matter of doubt.) The contest was to be judged by the Muses, who must have travelled to Phrygia for the occasion, as did Apollo, which is surprising. One of the best representations in art is the relief on the Mantinea Base, dating from the late fourth century BC, which shows Apollo seated in a sedate pose with his kithara, and Marsyas swaying about and posturing with his aulos.[22] Between them stands a slave holding a knife with which Marsyas was to be flayed – not without the suggestion that the result was prejudged. The posture of Marsyas is slightly reminiscent of another statue, much earlier, by the famous sculptor Myron, which shows him gazing in surprise and wonderment at the aulos which Athena has thrown away.

The normally accepted version was that Apollo was judged to be the victor, presumably on the tasteful and impartial verdict of the Muses; but Apollodoros, another of the scholars who worked for a time in Alexandria in the second century BC, introduces a very strange variant in his great encyclopaedia of myths. He says[23] that when the conditions had been agreed (as stated above) and the contest began, Apollo 'turned' his kithara before competing, and demanded that Marsyas should do the same. Because he could not, Apollo was declared the victor. What is meant by the Greek word *strepsas*? I have not been able to find a context in which it definitely means 'inverted'; and in any case, if Apollo could play his instrument upside-down, so could Marsyas (by lying on his back, as satyrs often do).[24] If it meant that Marsyas was required to blow the wrong way down his instrument, this reduces the whole story to fatuous nonsense, and robs Apollo of any credit for a victory won by a piece of blatant cheating. However that may be, Marsyas was flayed, his skin being made into a balloon, and hung up in a temple in Celaenae.[25] One related anecdote is worth quoting, because it affords a parallel with the story of Orpheus. Pausanias, in his *Guidebook to Greece* (second century AD) tells of a visit to the Temple of Peitho (Persuasion) in Corinth. There, he was told, Marsyas' auloi had been deposited. After his death they had floated down the river called Marsyas, into the river Maeander, westwards across the Aegean Sea and into a river called Asopos, which flows through southern Boeotia. Then they came (overland, somehow) to the Gulf of Corinth, drifted ashore, and were found by a shepherd. The temple had been destroyed by fire long before Pausanias' time, and the auloi with it.[26] There is a clear parallel in the legend that, when Orpheus was killed, his lyre floated down the river Hebrus (along with his head, still singing in death), and came ashore on the island of Lesbos.[27]

Much has been written about the significance of the contest, and only a very brief treatment is possible here. To begin with, we are dealing with what grew up as a myth, and any interpretation which smacks of rationalism or philosophical subtlety must be regarded as a later refinement. Plato's views come into this category – he held that the contest was between exciting, emotional or even hysterical aulos music without *logos* (punning on the senses of 'without words' and 'without reason') and, on the other side, calm and controlled music, played on an instrument with more accurate pitch, together with words which, instead of arousing wild emotions, conveyed a rational and instructive message. Though he uses the illustration ironically[28] there is a serious point here. But philosophers do not make myths of this kind – they merely use them. What could the conflict between Apollo and Marsyas have originally symbolized in real, possibly historical terms? Very briefly, there are three possibilities, which are not mutually exclusive.

First, as already mentioned in connection with Athena, there may have been a Hellenic nationalist feeling at work – Apollo the Greek against Marsyas the Phrygian. This is not very convincing, in view of the respect with which Marsyas and Olympos were held by the Greeks, and the freedom with which they admitted their debt to the music of other nations.

Second, the conflict may have had a cult significance. Marsyas was portrayed (in the fifth century at least) as a satyr, closely connected with Dionysos, and belonging to the land from which Dionysos came to Greece, whereas Apollo was regarded by the Greeks as the Greek god *par excellence* and had his own cult, centred on Delos and Delphi. A number of myths suggest that there was conflict between the cults in the early stages of Dionysos' settlement in Greece, but that this conflict was settled in time. By the sixth century BC the two deities were sharing the shrine at Delphi, Apollo being 'in residence' during the summer months, and Dionysos for three months during the winter. This reconciliation was later symbolized by a very significant musical occasion. A famous aulos-player called Sakadas from Argos was said to have composed the 'Pythian nomos', an aulos solo celebrating the victory of Apollo over the Python, a snake-like monster, by which he gained possession of the shrine at Delphi. Sakadas was the first aulos-player to perform during the Pythian games at Delphi (in about 586 BC) and the hatred of Apollo for aulos-players, dating from his contest with Marsyas, was thus symbolically brought to an end.[29] As a final comment on the possible cult significance of the contest, it is interesting to see that this story is a counterpart to that of Orpheus: he was undeniably Greek, and played a stringed instrument (though, as we have seen, it was a lyre, and not a kithara) and sang in the manner of Apollo and he, conversely, was brought to a violent death by Dionysos.

Was it a contest at a purely musical level between the kithara and the aulos or, more specifically, between a musical style developed by aulos-players and what the traditionalists regarded as the older, more respectable music for stringed instrument and singer? Two writers of dithyrambs (for this form see p. 4) may afford some clues. Melanippides, about the middle of the fifth century BC, wrote a dithyramb called the *Marsyas*, of which only a fragment remains; it relates how Athena threw away the aulos in disgust, but tells us nothing more. At the end of the century Telestes is said by Athenaeus[30] to have 'hit back' at him. Melanippides had apparently made fun of aulos-players and their music, but Telestes speaks in very complimentary terms about 'the Phrygian king of the sweet-breathing, holy auloi' (probably meaning Olympos, but it could be Marsyas) 'who first constructed the Lydian *nomos* [for 'constructed' he uses the word *harmozein*, which at this date is surely a musical pun on the word *harmonia*] as a rival to the Dorian music, ever-changing in its sound, wickerweaving around with his pipes the wingborne breeze of his breath' (dithyrambic poets were prone to extravagances of diction). Here we have the well-known names of musical styles which were later denoted by the term *harmoniai* in musical theory. There is no great problem about the name Lydian – the Lydians and Phrygians were both non-Greek peoples, living in Asia Minor, whose music was acknowledged to have influenced the Greeks profoundly. The Dorians, however, were Greeks, and their style of music was championed by the traditionalists, being considered noble and respectable.[31] Hence the word 'rival' or 'adversary' (*antipalon*) is highly significant.

Moreover, Telestes seems to have cast doubt on the credibility of Athena's part in the story. According to Athenaeus (who is a very late and not absolutely reliable author) Telestes said he could not believe that

Athena found the aulos in a thicket, and cast it aside, fearful for her beauty, to be the boast of Marsyas, a 'nymph-born, hand-smacked beast'. The second of these adjectives may refer to the tradition that Athena smacked him when he picked up the auloi, but there are other possible meanings.[32] Telestes goes on to say, either with astonishing male naivety or else with heavy irony, that Athena was by destiny and inclination a virgin goddess, and should not have been concerned about her facial appearance.

It must always be remembered that the Greek myths were regarded by writers and artists as 'flexible friends', and were given different inter–pretations according to the aims and purposes of the person using them. The story of Athena's rejection of the aulos was used by the aristocratic Alkibiades in the latter part of the fifth century BC in the cause of educational reform. Up to his time, boys in school were taught to play the lyre, and sometimes (though much less commonly) the aulos. Alkibiades objected strongly to the exercise, and persuaded his teachers to exempt him from it, quoting in his support the fact that Athena had rejected the instrument. But we must suspect that he had personal motives. His biographer Plutarch makes it quite clear in his *Life of Alkibiades* that this young man was fiercely competitive, and a very bad loser.[33] If his aulos playing was not up to much, he might well have argued that it was not a suitable activity for 'better-class chaps' and supported his claim by appealing to the myth.

Just as the Orpheus story had an alternative happy ending, so also, it seems, did the Marsyas story. A fragment of pottery was published in 1956 which shows Marsyas playing a stringed instrument;[34] Boardman suggested that this might be an alternative version of the story, in which Apollo and Marsyas became reconciled, and Marsyas accepted the Apolline musical idiom. The pottery fragment is roughly contemporary with Melanippides' dithyramb 'Marsyas', which may have been the literary source of the story.

The Orpheus myth and the Marsyas myth were the two most important and influential musical myths, but there were a number of others which should be mentioned. Two of them were 'invention' myths, of which the most famous was that of Syrinx (the u in Greek, represented by y in English, was long, so it should strictly be pronounced 'sigh-rinks').

The earliest surviving full version of the story is in Ovid's *Metamorphoses*,[35] written at the end of the first century BC. It goes as follows. Syrinx was a naiad (water-nymph) who lived in Arcadia, in the central region of the Peloponnese, and dedicated herself to hunting and virginity, on the model of Artemis (the Roman Diana), her patroness. The god Pan caught sight of her one day, and tried to woo her, but she ran away from him. After a chase, they came to the river Ladon, a tributary of the Alpheus which runs past Olympia. The water was too deep for Syrinx to cross, so she prayed to her sisters the nymphs to transform her so that she would be safe from Pan, and when he thought he had her in his grasp, he found that he was holding a bundle of reeds of various lengths. He heaved a deep sigh, and his breath, passing over the open tops of the reeds, sounded various different notes; he then fixed a number of reeds together in a row with wax, and made the pan-pipe, which from then onward was his own special instrument. Naturally, Ovid has in his mind's eye the Roman version of the instrument, with graduated pipes (*disparibus calamis*; see p. 176); later writers exploited this motif, likening the unequal pipes to the unequal love between Pan and Syrinx.

Ovid's version is the earliest that we have, but the story of the nymph's transformation is likely to have been made up in Alexandria at least two centuries earlier. The philosopher-poet Lucretius, a generation before Ovid, naturally prefers a rational account of the discovery – that primitive man learned to make and play the pan-pipe from hearing the wind blowing over hollow reeds.[36]

The story of the nymph appears late in the Classical tradition, and seems to have had little influence. The only other significant version is in the Greek novel *Leukippe and Kleitophon* by Achilles Tatius, probably written in the third century AD. It shows a number of interesting changes from the story as told by Ovid. Pan chases Syrinx into a wood, where she disappears into the ground (not into water, which may interest psycho-analytical interpreters) and a clump of reeds appears on the spot. Pan cuts some of them off, but suddenly realizes that Syrinx has been transformed, and kisses the cut ends of the reeds 'as though kissing the wounds of his beloved'. He then binds a number of them together to make the instrument. (The text is doubtful here, and the description odd, but it looks as though there were seven, of various different lengths, i.e. the 'Roman' version). It is clear that two elements – the sensational and the didactic – have been present in the novel from its earliest times.

Then there is another change, almost certainly to enable the author to 'slot in' another story. Instead of keeping the instrument as his own special favourite, Pan hands the prototype over to Artemis, the goddess of chastity, to be hung in a cave near Ephesos, where local girls are taken to undergo a virginity test. If the girl's claim to innocence is truthful, then all is well; but if not, the *syrinx* mysteriously plays itself, and the girl vanishes without trace. We are not told how effective this was in restricting teenage sex in the area.

In later centuries, however, the story acquires considerable importance. Ovid's *Metamorphoses* was translated into English verse by Arthur Golding in 1567, and his version was almost certainly known to Shakespeare. The artist Nicholas Poussin depicted the chase and Syrinx's attempt to escape; he adopted a variant version in which the nymphs are present, but Syrinx appeals for protection to her father, the river Ladon. In his picture the figures are arranged in the form of a half pediment, sloping down from right to left, and by a curious coincidence (it must be, because Poussin could not have seen the sculptures from the temple of Zeus at Olympia) the river-god is in the same reclining position as those on a number of Greek temple pediments – the last in the descending order, near the corner. The story also inspired some fine music, poetry and ballet in the last decade of the nineteenth century and the early part of the twentieth. Debussy wrote a very evocative flute solo which captures the atmosphere of the story, and Benjamin Britten wrote an oboe piece on the same lines. Mallarmé's poem *L'après-midi d'un faune* has frequent allusions to the Syrinx story, for example:

Tâche donc, instrument des fuites, o maligne Syrinx,
De refleurir aux lacs où tu m'attends.

('Try then, instrument of escape, ungenerous Syrinx, to flower once more by the lakes where you are waiting for me'; it is quite impossible to render in English the nuances and multiple meanings of the French.) Debussy's *Prélude à l'après-midi d'un faune* reflects much of Mallarmé's poem in musical terms, including the chase, and Syrinx's plunge into the water. Also, needless to say, the long and elaborate part for the solo flute has many phrases which could have been appropriately composed for the pan-pipe. Finally, Syrinx's flight from Pan is represented in music and dance in Ravel's ballet, *Daphnis et Chloë*.

The last of the myths is another 'invention' story which we have already encountered in Chapter 2. It tells of the appallingly precocious achievements of the god Hermes. His father was Zeus, and his mother Maia, a daughter of Atlas and one of the Pleiades (the group of seven stars eternally chased by Orion). On the day of his birth, or very soon after, he stole the sacred cattle belonging to his half-brother Apollo, and he invented the lyre, inspired by the sight of a tortoise, whose acoustic potential he spotted at once. The episode is told in the 'Homeric' *Hymn to Hermes*, one of a collection of poems in hexameter verse attributed to Homer, but mostly a century or two later than the *Iliad* and *Odyssey*. One or two other details come from a satyr-play by Sophocles called the 'Trackers' (*Ichneutai*), referring to the *choros* of satyrs who are attracted by the sound of the newly-invented lyre, and try to find where the noise is coming from. A fragmentary and very mutilated text of this play has survived. There may be some significance in the fact that this story is consistently set in Arcadia, the central part of the Peloponnese – it may mean that the lyre was, or was thought to be, a native Greek instrument and not, like so many of the stringed instruments, an import from Asia Minor.

Details of the construction of the instrument were set out in Chapter 2 (pp. 61–3); as for the personal consequences, the accounts are fairly consistent. When Apollo came looking for his cattle, Hermes lied to him, denying any knowledge of them. When he was found out (the cattle had been hidden in a cave in some versions) he was cheeky and totally unrepentant, but eventually the two were reconciled. In keeping with this episode, Hermes became the patron god of thieves and tricksters, among many other functions. Though he invented the instrument, he is not often represented in art or described in literature as a player himself – he seems to have handed the lyre over to Amphion, a skilled musician very much in the Orphic mould, and another of Zeus' numerous progeny. Amphion used his musical skill in a most novel way: when the time came for the city of Thebes to be built, he played his lyre, at which the stones moved themselves into place on the walls, a feat which has not yet been achieved even by the most sophisticated modern building technology.

7

THE YEARS BETWEEN –
ALEXANDRIA AND SOUTHERN
ITALY

Alexandria

The period of Athenian military and political dominance in the Greek world effectively came to an end with the conquest of mainland Greece by Philip of Macedon in the latter half of the fourth century BC; her cultural influence lasted for some time after that, but it never regained the dynamic force of the sixth, fifth and early fourth centuries BC, during which the great works of her artists, poets and philosophers were created. With the vast but incredibly short-lived empire of Philip's son, Alexander the Great, Greek culture was spread over a large part of the then known world; but in the process it was diluted almost beyond recognition, except in a number of urban centres which were controlled by Alexander's leading military commanders, known in antiquity as the 'Successors'. The most important of these centres was the great city which he founded not long before his death – Alexandria.

This was a city which differed in almost every possible respect from the earlier city states of Greece, of which Athens had been the greatest. For one thing, it was enormous by their standards; for another, it was not in any sense a democratic city state, being ruled by a hereditary monarch with supreme power. Ptolemy, the first of the dynasty, was the general who took over that portion of the empire after Alexander's death in 323 BC, and declared himself king in 304. He was of course a Macedonian Greek, but his descendants became gradually more and more Egyptianized in their ways, even to the extent of marrying their sisters, which was allowed by Egyptian law. (They were all rather confusingly called Ptolemy, and had to be distinguished from one another by flattering titles such as *Euergetes*, the Doer of Good, or *Philopator*, Dutiful Son.) There may have been a few concessions to democratic principles, but they did not amount to much. And whereas in a Greek city state the citizens had all the rights, and 'resident aliens' had a subordinate status, in Alexandria the Greeks, the Egyptians and other races (notably a considerable Jewish community) were all subjects of the same monarch, though it should be said that the Greeks enjoyed precedence over the others when it came to government appointments. The dynasty ruled for almost three centuries, ending with Ptolemy XIV, the brother of Cleopatra. Only one of them had any personal musical connections – her father, Ptolemy XII, who was known as Ptolemy the aulos-player (*Aulētēs*) on account of his fondness for that instrument. He was reproached in later antiquity[1] for having been so unmindful of his royal dignity as to put on a leather mouthband (*phorbeia*) and have an occasional tootle.

The situation of Alexandria, with a great deal of productive agricultural land in the Nile delta and extensive seaborne trade, ensured an ample revenue from trade and taxation, some of which was used to foster scholarship and the arts. In about 280 BC the first of the Ptolemies founded an institution called the Museum (our Latinized form of the Greek *Mouseion*, or 'sanctuary of the Muses'). This was the nearest thing to a university in the ancient world; scholars were invited to take up residence there, and to pursue both research and creative writing, and the greatest library of the ancient world was assembled in another building nearby. It differed from a modern university, however, in that it was purely a research institution for established scholars, and did not offer teaching to undergraduates.

The literary scholars who enjoyed the royal patronage were mainly involved in collecting and editing the great works of literature from previous centuries; the art of textual criticism really started there, and the manuscripts which survive today (most of them dating from Renaissance times) are ultimately descended, via many copyings, from Alexandrian editions of Homer, the tragedians and many other authors.

There was an official text of the three great tragedians deposited in the Athenian archives from the latter part of the fourth century BC (this is discussed more fully in Chapter 10). The Alexandrian scholars were very anxious to get hold of the best available texts, and Ptolemy II (*Philadelphos*, 'Brotherly Love') was generous in his financial support. He sent to Athens, requesting a loan of the state document, and depositing a large sum of money to guarantee its return; but he then kept it for his library and forfeited his deposit. (Classical scholars throughout the centuries, being for the most part persons of limited means, have always deplored this high-handed action by a very wealthy monarch; but the manuscript was not unique or irreplaceable – the Athenians still had the originals from which it had been copied – nor was it faultless, very probably having some actors' interpolations in it. Perhaps the Athenians would just as soon have had the money.)

The assumption is almost universally made that this document did not contain a musical score of the sung parts of the plays. This may be true, though there is no hard evidence to support it. We do know, however, of a guild of Artists of Dionysos in Alexandria, and they quite probably had a library of their own containing scores of at least some of the music. As for the preposterous story that the great library was destroyed during Julius Caesar's fire-attack on the ships in the Alexandrian naval base in 48 BC, this was a myth which grew up from a simple mistake on the part of the historians of the Civil War. They had learnt from a Greek informant that stocks of corn and papyrus in a dockside warehouse had caught fire from the burning ships alongside the wharf; the word for papyrus (used as writing material and exported in large quantities from Alexandria) was *byblos*, which was not only pronounced the same as the word for book (*biblos*) but was actually spelt the same in Ptolemaic Egypt.[2] Those historians who regarded Caesar as an arrogant tyrant were so ready to believe anything discreditable to him that the bundles of papyrus became 'some valuable books', then 'a lot of valuable books', then '400,000 books' and eventually 'the entire Alexandrian library', reputed to have contained 700,000 volumes (i.e. rolls of papyrus).[3] These supposedly serious writers were evidently prepared to envisage the eminent academics from the Museum clambering over sacks of corn in a dockside warehouse in order to look up their sources and check their references; and it must be said that the myth, with some assistance from George Bernard Shaw (who wrote *Caesar and Cleopatra*), Gabriel Pascal (who made the film) and some Classical scholars (who should know better), is still alive today.

The musical element which was so prominent in so much of the literary output of the Classical period in Athens seems to have been almost eclipsed in Alexandria. The literary genres most in favour were the long narrative or didactic poem, or the short piece written in hexameters or elegiacs, none of which had any musical element. Apollonios of Rhodes, who worked for a time in the Museum (he may have been librarian), wrote an epic poem on the Homeric model, telling the story of Jason and the Argonauts, but the epic had long ago lost its musical connections (see pp. 9–10).

One genre, however, did originate in this period, and had an important influence on later European literature. The main credit for its 'invention' belongs to Theokritos, who came originally from Sicily, but settled in Alexandria for part of his life. His work mostly consists of short poems (up to about 150 lines or so), written in hexameter verse and in a dialect based on the Dorian of his native Syracuse; some of them are set in a pastoral scene, with 'shepherds' (in fact, poets) singing competitively of their loves and their sorrows. Others are in the form of semi-dramatic scenes, the most famous of which is the second poem, known as 'The Sorceresses' (in Greek *Pharmakeutriae*). In it a girl tells in very touching terms of her love affair with a handsome young athlete who has since deserted her, and describes various magic rituals by which she hopes to regain him or, alternatively, to punish him. Another of the dramatic scenes brings us two Alexandrian housewives on their way to a festival, chattering in what a bystander describes as a broad dialect, and then listening to a singer performing a hymn to Adonis. But though this part of the poem (lines 100–144) is ostensibly a song, there is no evidence that it was intended to be the libretto for a musical performance. Theocritos himself called these short poems 'little pictures' (*eidyllia*); in English the word 'idyll' has acquired a lot of nuances which have little to do with the original meaning.

If our study is to be narrowly limited to the purposes of this book, there is hardly anything to be said about the pastoral genre except that it frequently refers to a number of 'pastoral' instruments; the most important one has already been described in Chapter 2 – the *syrinx* (see pp. 69–71). This is the pastoral instrument *par excellence*, and the arch-musician of the pastoral world is not Apollo, but Pan; the most fulsome compliment one 'shepherd' can pay to another is to compare his 'piping' with that of the Master.[4] He is, however, a formidable deity, and must be treated with the deepest respect. In particular, one must not play the *syrinx* at midday, while he is having his siesta.

The use of the name and form of an instrument as a poetic symbol can hardly be described as a step in the history of the instrument itself. But there was a development in Ptolemaic Egypt during the period with which we are concerned which was to bring about a complete change in the method of making the *syrinx* sound.

It is probably true to say that the contribution of Alexandrian writers to later ages was surpassed by that of the scientists and engineers who worked under the sponsorship of the Ptolemies. Their achievements in weapons technology and shipbuilding, in medicine, geography and astronomy and many other fields are well known;[5] but one in particular, in the field of hydraulic engineering, had important musical consequences. It was the work of one of the most distinguished of the Alexandrian engineers.

His name was Ktesibios, and according to ancient tradition he was the inventor of the force-pump, the piston and cylinder, and what was called the 'water-organ' (*hydraulis* in Greek). It had been known for a long time that a *syrinx* could be made to sound by a draught of air from any source, though it took a skilled player to make a good musical sound. What Ktesibios did was to invent a mechanical system to provide a continuous supply of compressed air. It consisted of a single-cylinder pump, operated manually by a rocker-arm, and a hydraulic reservoir which stabilized the pressure. This was done by feeding the output of the pump into a bell-shaped vessel which was submerged in a tank of water; as the pressure built up in the bell, water was displaced from it, and although the input of air and the amount being drawn off were continually fluctuating, the pressure in the bell stayed roughly the same, and the organ was able to play continuously.

The most detailed description of the device, in which it is treated as a hydraulic machine rather than a musical instrument, is in Hero of Alexandria's *Pneumatica*, written some centuries later (late first century AD) but closely based on the inventor's design. The structure is set out in detail in Appendix 2.

A slightly earlier account in Latin by the Roman architect Vitruvius (late first century BC) describes something corresponding to the stops on a modern organ. He mentions a system whereby air could be supplied to, or cut off from, a whole row (or 'rank', as it is called nowadays) of up to eight pipes as required; but it appears that all the pipes were of the same design, and that the 'stops' were used to change the pitch of the instrument (perhaps by the use of '4 ft' or '2 ft' ranks) and not as on a modern organ to modify the tone or volume (the 'voicing'). One development in the design of the organ is obscure. In illustrations of organs from the first century AD onwards, the pipes appear exactly the same as modern 'flue' organ pipes, with a 'throat' at the base which acts as an artificial pair of lips, and directs the stream of air on to a straight edge, and so sets up the oscillations in the pipe (Figure 7.1).

But this design appears suddenly out of the blue, and there is no evidence in the ancient writers as to when, or by whom, it was developed. The reason for this may be that it was carried out by craftsmen and musicians, whose work did not find its way into the textbooks of mechanics or engineering. Hero refers to the pipes as auloi, but this cannot mean that they had reeds; the reeds in a modern organ are metal strips which vibrate at a predetermined rate in a metal slot – i.e. they are 'free' reeds and, unlike the 'beating' reeds of an aulos, can be relied on to sound when air is blown through them.

Another instrument must be mentioned here – the *monaulos*, or 'single aulos', so called to distinguish it from the aulos 'proper' which, as we have seen, was a double pipe. It seems to have been an Egyptian instrument in origin, and almost all the surviving remains of these instruments have been found in Egypt.[6] It was, however, apparently used by the Greeks in

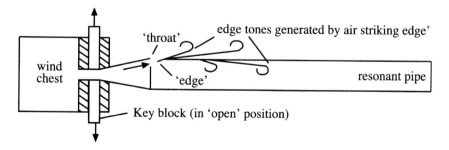

Figure 7.1 'Flue' organ pipe

Alexandria; one of the speakers in Athenaeus' 'Wise men at Dinner' (*Deipnosophistai*), written in Alexandria in the late second century AD, makes fun of 'You Alexandrians' as being fond of this instrument, which 'gives pain rather than pleasure' to the hearers.

It was, in fact, similar to one pipe of an aulos, with a cylindrical bore and a double reed[7] but is distinguishable from the aulos by the fact that it may have up to ten fingerholes without keywork, whereas the aulos is limited to six. This means that it had a much wider range of notes than the aulos, but must have lacked the exciting tone of the two pipes sounding together. This is presumably the main reason for the speaker's disparagement of the instrument.[8]

One other instrument makes its appearance in the period covered by this chapter, occasionally in mainland Greece but more commonly in Southern Italy from the mid-fourth century onwards. It is a variant form of the kithara, which has a rectangular soundbox and plain arms which form a continuation of it, without the elaborate 'fretwork' which characterizes the fifth-century kithara. When viewed from the front, the arms appear straight. One of the earliest illustrations from the Greek mainland is on the Mantinea Base, a set of relief sculptures which are now in the National Museum in Athens. The mode of representation has one peculiar feature; the arm on the right is almost straight, but the one on the left appears to curve away from the body of the instrument. This feature was pointed out in the article on lute-players by Higgins and Winnington-Ingram[9] which has already been referred to in Chapter 2. It represents the sculptor's attempt to show three dimensions in low relief, indicating that the kithara, which is here seen from the back, had a concave front surface, so that if it were held with the soundbox vertical, the crossbar would project forwards and the strings, instead of running roughly parallel to the sounding-board, would slant towards its base. This would mean that the bridge, which was apparently near the centre of the sounding-board, would have to be higher in order to reach them.[10] Like the larger 'classical' kithara, this version had a vertical ridge down the back of the soundbox, looking rather like a ship's keel seen from below. This type of kithara is quite frequently shown in South Italian vase-paintings (mostly in frontal view, with no suggestion of the curvature), and for this reason is referred to as the 'Italiote' kithara, a term denoting something which is essentially Greek, but belongs to the area known as Magna Graecia, or 'greater Greece' – the cities of Southern Italy and Sicily (Figure 7.2).

Another interesting feature of this instrument is that it is shown in some illustrations with more than the usual seven strings. As we have seen (p. 101) the normal kithara used by 'progressive' composers may have had as many as eleven strings by the end of the fifth century BC, but this is not shown in vase-paintings. This may be due to the painters' habit of

Figure 7.2 'Italiote' kithara

adopting 'images' or 'icons' of many different objects, and drawing them to exactly the same pattern over a long period, irrespective of changes which may have taken place in the objects themselves. However, in wall-paintings of Roman date, many of which were based on Greek paintings of the period with which we are concerned, a larger number is quite often shown.

Southern Italy

From the late eighth century BC onwards most of the southern third of Italy and the eastern half of Sicily was colonized by Greeks, and the entire culture of the area was effectively dominated by Greek ideas and values. However, the cultural supremacy of Athens in mainland Greece was not reflected there; almost all of the colonies had been established before Athens became pre-eminent, and most of the colonists were racially distinct from the Athenians, being Dorians from cities of the Peloponnese, whereas the Athenians were Ionians. In the heyday of their imperialist ambitions in 414 BC the Athenians attempted to invade and conquer Sicily, but suffered a disastrous defeat. Politically, too, the Sicilian Greeks were different, being ruled in many cases (particularly in Syracuse) by what they called 'tyrants'. The word was not altogether a pejorative one in this context, merely signifying a powerful, monarchical ruler who had seized power by force, as against one who had inherited it.

The cities of southern Italy and Sicily became very prosperous and wealthy, and were regarded by the mainland Greeks as enviable fleshpots. A number of eminent poets and musicians spent some time at the court of one or other of the 'tyrants'; Pindar speaks appreciatively of the lavish hospitality he received from Hieron the ruler of Syracuse[11] and Aeschylus spent the last few years of his life in Gela as a guest of the same monarch. Early in the next century Plato visited Syracuse to meet some philosopher friends, and later to take part in a political experiment which promised well but turned out in the end to be a disaster. His puritanical soul was deeply offended by the lifestyle of the court, 'eating and drinking to repletion twice a day, and never going to bed alone at night'.[12]

From the very limited evidence available (virtually all of it pictorial) it is clear that the musical and literary culture of the whole area was rich and varied. Many of the larger cities had very large theatres, comparable with the biggest on the Greek mainland (such as Epidauros); and there is also evidence for the role of music in small-scale, mobile theatres.

A number of vase-paintings, many of them from Apulia (the region on the Adriatic coast near the 'heel' of Italy) and dating from the second half of the fourth century BC onwards, show a kind of theatrical performance; we know that the actors who took part in them were called 'twaddlers' (*phlyakes* in Greek), and the vases are known as 'phlyax vases'. They show actors on a stage which looks as though it was temporary, made of wood and designed to be assembled or dismantled quite quickly, and transported on carts from town to town. There are usually three or four pillars supporting the stage across the front, with curtains hung between them to hide the space below. The stage is about 3–4 ft. (90–120 cm) high, and there are sometimes steps leading up to it from ground level. The scenery also consists of curtains which are sometimes looped apart, and there are frames which represent doors.

The actors present us with a curious anachronism. Many of them are dressed in the kind of costume similar to that worn by comic actors in Athens more than a century earlier, with grossly padded stomachs and buttocks, and very large artificial phalluses. Such was the costume of actors in the 'Old Comedy' of Aristophanes and his contemporaries; but there are clear signs in the texts of early fourth-century comedy that the cruder style of costume and speech went out of fashion, and was replaced by a more gentle and sophisticated form, which will be discussed in the next chapter. It is not unusual to find the survival in a colonial culture of fashions which had become obsolete in the homeland, but Athens was not the homeland of these colonies, and it is equally credible that they represent an even older tradition, from which the Athenian comedy itself had developed two centuries earlier. There are references in the historical sources to the Dorian origins of comedy[13] and, as we have seen, many of the Italian and Sicilian cities were colonies from Dorian cities in Greece.

However this may be, the *phlyax* vases show a strange type of performance. A number of mythological stories can be discerned in the scenes shown. One of the most famous of them, reproduced in many textbooks, shows Zeus climbing a ladder up to Alkmena's bedroom window, with Hermes holding a lamp to guide him (the scene would of course have been played out of doors in broad daylight). Sometimes comic scenes of a more general kind are shown – thieves, gluttons and buffoons – without any obvious mythological connection. In some of the pictures there is evidence for the presence of an aulos-player, and there is one extremely interesting scene mentioned by A.D. Trendall in the course of a discussion on the dramatic scenes on these vases.[14]

The scene shows the right-hand side of a typical *phlyax* stage, with its pillars and curtains in front and steps from the ground level. A 'stage-set' tree rises from under the stage (propped up in a pot, presumably) and behind it, actually in full view but supposed to be hidden, is the theatre aulos-player, wearing the typical elaborate dress and the appropriate mouthband, and playing two thin pipes of equal length. On stage in front of the 'tree' is a *phlyax* actor wearing the usual wrinkled tights and short (immodest) tunic; he does not wear a mouthband and is obviously miming on dummy pipes. It seems that we have here an analogy to the scene in Menander's comedy discussed on p. 184, and possibly also the scene in Aristophanes' *Birds* mentioned on p. 18, when an actor on stage mimes the actions of a player while the real player performs out of sight elsewhere. It was clearly an old-established comic routine.

It does, however, establish beyond doubt that the *phlyax* plays had a musical accompaniment, and that the aulos-player (sometimes, at least) mounted the stage among the actors. Whether the Roman tradition (see p. 187) was derived from this, or grew up independently, is a matter of doubt. Another link with early Roman comedy is that it too may well have been performed on a similar, small wooden stage which could be dismantled and moved from town to town. This will be discussed in the next chapter.

8

THE ROMAN MUSICAL
EXPERIENCE

The role of music in Roman life and literature was very limited indeed
compared with its all-pervading influence in Greek culture. This is
reflected in the fact that all the aspects of Greek musical life dealt with in
Chapters 1, 2, 3, 4, and 5 can be covered in the Roman context in the
course of a single chapter, albeit rather a long one. In order to preserve
some sort of historical order it is necessary to shift the focus now and again
from the role and function of music to the design of instruments, and from
instruments to acoustical science, and so on; but I venture to hope that
this will not cause much difficulty to the reader.

In dealing with the role of music in Roman life we shall not be looking
at the emergence of a new and totally different musical culture. It would
be fair to say that the Romans did not attempt to develop a musical
identity of their own. In early times they adopted Etruscan musical
traditions, and employed Etruscan players, especially when they required
musical accompaniment for religious rituals. When their empire
expanded to take in the Greek mainland and the Greek cities of the
Eastern Mediterranean (particularly Alexandria), they adopted Greek
musical theory and its terminology, much of which they simply
transliterated into their own alphabet, and they did not generally (with
one notorious exception, to be dealt with later) aspire to become
competent amateur performing musicians themselves, but were content
to listen to foreign professionals, mostly Greek. It is a strange paradox,
therefore, that in later centuries the nation which became accepted as the
musical nation *par excellence* should be the Italians, descendants of those
not-so-very musical Romans. It is their language, and not Greek, that has
become the international language of music throughout the world.

The Romans themselves do not seem to have been troubled or
embarrassed by their lack of interest and proficiency in music. The reason
may well be that when they encountered the Greek civilization in South
Italy and Sicily in the late third century BC, they themselves were at a very
early stage of their cultural development. Moreover, they were prepared to
admit that when they had come across the Greeks' very sophisticated

tastes and techniques in music they had chosen to be listeners and admirers rather than competitors.

However, the complete story of Roman music starts much earlier – in the fifth century BC. For some time before the Latins (the nucleus of the Roman nation) emerged as an independent and significant political power, they had been dominated by the Etruscans, their neighbours to the north (in the region now called Tuscany). Even after that domination had been thrown off, the Romans still respected the Etruscans as the expert authorities on religious ritual, particularly the arts of divination by augury and by interpretation of omens. Another part of this expertise was concerned with the correct use of music during ritual sacrifices, and for a long time the Romans seem to have employed Etruscan musicians to provide it. Even in the late first century BC, Virgil envisages a contemporary sacrifice with a 'fat Etruscan' playing on an ivory pipe.[1] There is also a delightful story in Livy[2] which illustrates the stranglehold (as a tabloid journalist would term it) exerted in earlier times by the 'State musicians', many of whom were probably Etruscans, though they lived in Rome.

These musicians belonged to a sort of guild or trade union (*collegium*) which was almost certainly a 'closed circle', and may have restricted its membership to those of Etruscan descent. In 311 BC the man who held the office of censor (a very senior magistracy, with powers to regulate public morality and religious practice) was Appius Claudius Caecus, better known to later generations as having built the first 'trunk road' out of Rome and the first aqueduct to bring water supplies in. He was a member of a very aristocratic, not to say arrogant, family, and his behaviour towards the state musicians could be described as grossly insensitive. He deprived them of one of their best 'perks' – the right to dine at the public expense in the Temple of Jupiter after the main religious festivals. The immediate response of the union was 'everybody out', and they meant it literally: they marched *en masse* to Tibur (now Tivoli, about 18 miles up the valley of the river Anio) leaving nobody in Rome able to play for public sacrifices, funerals or performances in the theatre.[3] The people of Tibur were friendly to the Romans, and tried to negotiate with the musicians and persuade them to go back, but without success. Then their town council devised a very clever plot. They invited some of the musicians to a banquet, at which there was 'going to be music later on', and plied them with vast amounts of wine, of which, according to Livy, woodwind players were inordinately fond. When they had all slid under the table in a stupor, they were loaded on to wagons and trundled back to Rome, to wake up next morning in the middle of the Forum with a terrible hangover. A crowd surrounded them and persuaded them to stay, but not without some concessions: they had to be given assurances that they would not be accused of 'blacklegging'[4] and they were to be allowed to parade around the streets in their festival costume for a 'licensed rave-up' for three days in every year, while those who were actually playing at public sacrifices got back their free dinners in the temple.

So the influence of Etruscan music on Roman culture is well documented, but unfortunately there is very little evidence for the nature of that music. Indeed, the Etruscans have always been a bit of a mystery. They may have been indigenous to that part of Italy, but a strong ancient tradition[5] held that they were immigrants from Asia Minor, and some modern scholars support this view. They were themselves in cultural contact with the Greeks as early as the fifth century BC; a large number of the Greek vases now in European museums were found in graves in and around Etruria, having been exported there from Greece. There must have been strong trade links, if nothing more. But the culture of the Etruscans was very different from the Greek. They had their own language, which has not yet been deciphered to the satisfaction of the philologists. The surviving underground tombs, which have been excavated (and robbed!) at intervals over the last two centuries, attest a strong preoccupation with death and the after-life, in the face of which they seem to have tried their best to retain with themselves in the burial chamber as much as possible of life's satisfactions and pleasures. As a result, there are scenes of banqueting and entertainment painted on the tomb walls, in which some instruments are shown and, meagre though this evidence is, it offers an interesting comparison with Greek illustrations of the same period.

One particular example will suffice. It dates from the early fifth century BC and is in the 'Tomb of the Leopards' in Tarquinia (Figures 8.1 and 8.2). The scene is a banquet, and the figures shown here are the two musicians in attendance. We have here the combination of aulos and lyre, whereas the most common Greek duo is aulos and barbitos; the latter instrument does not appear in Etruscan art, nor in Roman until much later. The forms of the instruments are also different. The aulos pipes are shorter and thicker (i.e. of larger bore) than the usual Greek form, and they have a pronounced 'bell' at their ends, which is normal in Etruscan

Figure 8.1 Etruscan aulos

Figure 8.2 Etruscan lyre

pictures but rare in Greek. In fact, they look rather like short clarinets. Like the Greek auloi, they have the two bulbs (*holmoi*; see p. 32) and part of the reed itself can be seen between the top *holmos* and the player's lips. There is a strongly marked black band around the top of the body, which probably represents a silver decoration. On one point, however, they do resemble the Greek auloi – the pipes are equal in length. So far as I am aware, there is no Etruscan illustration which suggests an origin for the 'unequal' pipes which we shall encounter later. The player's fingers are clearly shown in position on the fingerholes, and even the clever trick of putting the little finger under the nearer pipe, to enable the thumbhole to be opened. The fact that the little finger on the other pipe is on top should not, I think, be taken to indicate that the instrument is playing two different notes – it could be licence (or carelessness) on the part of the artist.

The form of the lyre is also slightly different from that which appears in contemporary Greek illustrations. The arms seem to emerge in the same way from the front of the soundbox, but it is almost exactly round, with no sign of the 'shoulders' of the Greek version (see Figure 26.8, p. 63). The player's stance, with the left hand behind the strings and the plectrum in the right hand, is the same as that of the Greek players, except that the right arm is held back, whereas the Greek artists favour a position across the front of the strings. Perhaps the Etruscan artist is concerned to show that the player is plucking the strings with his fingers, and not using the plectrum. The picture should show the band passing around the player's left wrist and the far arm of the instrument; either the artist has ignored this, or else the pigment used to paint it was less enduring than the others, and has faded away.

These are two instruments which can be studied in comparison with the Greek versions; but there is evidence from a slightly earlier period that the Etruscans used other instruments, some of which do not appear in

Greek art at all, and others which appear very rarely.

One artefact of Etruscan manufacture which has been found widely distributed around the Mediterranean area is the bronze bucket, usually referred to by its Latin name, *situla*. Some of these buckets have relief decoration on them, usually in horizontal bands, containing scenes from everyday life. One of them, dating from the late sixth century BC, is in the *Museo Civico* in Bologna (Figure 8.3).

The relief decoration shows a charming little musical scene, with two players seated at opposite ends of a sofa, and wearing broad-brimmed hats which look remarkably like the Mexican sombreros of old cowboy films. The rest of the details are not shown in Figure 8.3, as they are not very clear. There seem to be two small boys jumping around on the ends of the sofa, and a quiet, admiring listener on the left.

But it is the instruments which are of most interest. There is a lyre of quite different design, and a pan-pipe (*syrinx,* or from now on the Latin name *fistula*). The Greek version of that instrument was discussed in Chapter 2 (pp. 69–71) and it will be remembered that its pipes were all of the same length, giving the instrument a rectangular form. Here, in an Etruscan illustration, we find the 'Roman' version with pipes of graduated length. It is not possible to say whether the pipes were open or closed at their bottom ends; a modern survival of the instrument, the Rumanian *naiu*, has got graduated pipes which are 'stopped', the final tuning being adjusted by pouring molten wax into them. There are, however, a very few late Roman illustrations which show an instrument with two or three much longer pipes at the 'long' end. One suggestion might be that they were open pipes, sounding a note of the same pitch as a stopped pipe of half the length, but with a fuller and rounder tone.[6]

The other interesting feature is the context in which the pan-pipe is being played. In Greek literature almost all the references are to a pastoral environment, closely linked to the myth which named Pan as the inventor of the instrument. But here we see it in an indoor scene (or so it seems, but

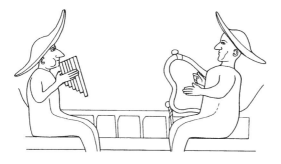

Figure 8.3 Etruscan duet

why are they wearing hats?) which could be some sort of party. The instrument also appears in banqueting scenes on cinerary urns, depicting the hoped-for joys of the after-life.[7] The use of the instrument for domestic entertainment seems to have become a traditional Roman practice, with very few parallels in Greek literature or art.

The design of the lyre shown in this picture is also different from that shown in contemporary Greek illustrations, at least in the upper part which is visible. Instead of the two arms with the crossbar fixed across them, the strings appear to be attached to a continuous rail, perhaps made of bent wood, which curves around at each 'corner', and dips a little at the centre. In fact, it faintly recalls illustrations of Middle Eastern lyres of many centuries earlier. The player's left hand is in the usual position, though the instrument is seen from behind.

There is also abundant evidence that the Etruscans were fond of trumpets of various kinds, all of which later became popular with the Romans. There are four Latin words for this type of instrument, and they can be assigned with some confidence to three types shown in illustrations dating from the late fourth century BC in Etruscan art to the late imperial period (fourth century AD) in Roman reliefs. The words are *tuba, lituus, bucina* and *cornu*. None of the three instruments is like the Greek *salpinx* (see p. 77). The *lituus* appears in early Etruscan and Roman illustrations (Figure 8.4).

It consisted of a long straight tube with a curved bell at its lower end, giving it an appearance slightly suggestive of an alto saxophone without its top bend. One surviving instrument has been found at the Etruscan town of Caere (now Cervetri, about 30 miles north of Rome), and is in the

Figure 8.4 Lituus

177

Museo Etrusco Gregoriano in Rome. The tube is about 63 in. (1.6 m) long, which is quite a lot longer than most instruments shown in illustrations, which are usually about 3 ft (1 m). Its pitch would have been a bit lower than that of a modern bugle, though comparison cannot be exact, as the bugle's bore expands consistently along its length, while the *lituus* has a constant bore for about four-fifths of its length. It had no keys or valves, so it would have played the same series of notes as a bugle – probably not the fundamental, but the second, third, fourth and fifth harmonics, which for an instrument 3 ft long would be roughly f', c", f" and perhaps a". There is no sign of a mouthpiece on this instrument (this is also true of the Greek *salpinx*; see p. 79); the only hint of one is that in one illustration[8] the instrument is painted yellow (to represent gold?) and the mouthpiece red (copper?). However, it seems unlikely that ancient players would not have discovered by experiment the advantage of using a wider opening than that of the tube for a more comfortable and effective embouchure, and in illustrations of another type of trumpet of much later date (e.g. the Trier mosaic; see p. 203) the picture clearly suggests the cup-shaped end of a modern instrument.

There is one more difficulty in interpreting the evidence for the *lituus*. The Etruscans used a staff with a curved end, which looks like a modern walking-stick, for marking out points in the sky when interpreting omens. This was also called a *lituus*, and in some of the more blurred illustrations it is not clear which kind of *lituus* is shown.

A second type of trumpet (or rather, horn) appears in Etruscan art from the fifth century BC and often thereafter in Roman art. This is a longer instrument of lower pitch. It is difficult to assess the resonant length with accuracy, but somewhere between 6 and 7 feet (1.8–2.1 m) would be a reasonable guess. This would give it a pitch about an octave lower than the *lituus*, perhaps f–c'–f'–a' or thereabouts. The problem of handling a tube of this length is solved by curling it around the player's body – the same solution employed nowadays in the (much longer) sousaphone. It also appears that the bore of this instrument expands fairly consistently from the mouthpiece to the outer end. As will be seen from Figure 8.5, the mouthpiece is slightly towards the player's left; the tube curves across in front of him, then upwards and behind his right shoulder, ending above his head with a conical bell, which in some illustrations faces forwards. As the instrument must have been quite heavy, there is a rod fixed diagonally across the loop which rests on the player's right shoulder, and is gripped by the right hand; the left hand holds the mouthpiece end to the mouth.

It is generally held that the names *cornu* and *bucina* both apply to this instrument, but this is not certain. It would be reasonable to suppose that parts of the instrument were originally made from animal horn (*cornu* means that), and the first syllable of *bucina* ('bovine note-player') would suggest that horns of cattle were used. The characteristic shape was later

Figure 8.5 Bucina or *cornu*

reproduced in metal, most probably bronze. Virgil, describing how the Fury Allecto stirred the Latins to war when Aeneas and his followers arrived in Italy, says that she climbed to a rooftop, and 'on a bent-back horn (*cornuque recurvo*) blew a long, hellish note'. A few lines further on he makes it clear that this is a *bucina*.[9]

It appears, then, that the names *cornu* and *bucina* were more or less synonymous and interchangeable. But the fourth name, *tuba*, is explicitly distinguished from both of these, and from *lituus*. This instrument, though it is mentioned by the earliest Latin authors (Ennius has a splendid line: *'The trumpet with its terrible sound said "taratantara"* ') does not figure prominently in art until the last century BC. It was a straight trumpet, similar in appearance to the post-horn which hangs on the walls of pseudo-ancient inns in England. The main difference is that the flare of the bell is more gradual than that of most post-horns. The range of this instrument would have been a little higher than the *lituus*, but not much, and its tone would have been more strident and penetrating. The *salpinx* in Greek authors and the *tuba* in Latin authors are both given the adjective 'Tyrrhenian' or 'Etruscan', in accordance with the ancient tradition that it had been invented by the Etruscans. (Tyrrhenos was the name of the supposed leader of the emigration from Asia Minor to Italy.) The Greeks dated the invention later than the Trojan War (see p. 80).

The Greek *salpinx* was used almost exclusively in military contexts, and was not considered to be a musical instrument in the strict sense; most of the illustrations show a solo player in military costume (see Figure 2(c).9 on p. 79). In Etruscan and Roman art, however, the various kinds of trumpet and horn are shown playing in small ensembles and, in contrast to the Greek pictures, playing with other instruments such as the tibia and kithara. Figure 8.6 shows the musicians at the head of a rather grand funeral procession (the dead man, not shown, is laid on a couch carried on a litter by eight bearers, and surrounded by his family and other mourners). To do musical justice to the occasion there is a *lituus*-player

Figure 8.6 Early Roman funeral

(top right) two horn-players (*bucinatores* or *cornicines*) and no less than four tibia-players.

Naturally, the Romans also used the trumpet in military situations and for sounding alarms of all kinds. This 'multiple function' leads to a very amusing climax in an episode of Petronius' novel the *Satyrikon*, known as 'Trimalchio's Dinner-Party'. (It was written in the time of Nero, mid-first century AD.) The host at this party, when he and the guests are becoming maudlin with much drink, insists that they rehearse his funeral procession. One of the guests happens to be an undertaker who has come there straight from a funeral, bringing with him his assistants, including the trumpeters. When they strike up the Roman equivalent of the Funeral March, *fortissimo*, the local fire-brigade mistake it for an alarm call, and burst into the dining-room with axes and a fire-engine, and everybody gets extremely wet.

However, the trumpets and horns were not confined to the grim needs of war or public safety, or to the solemn ritual of a funeral. An Etruscan stone sarcophagus (again from Caere) dating from the mid-fifth century BC shows that the Etruscans used these instruments to accompany a wedding procession[10] from the bride's home to her husband's, and there is no reason to doubt that the Romans did too. The carving shows a *bucina* or *cornu*, a man holding (but not playing) a *lituus*, a kithara-player whose instrument has a round base, and a tibia-player, followed by the happy couple, the bride carefully showing off a pearl necklace.

The one feature common to all these occasions is that they were outdoor events – processions through public streets, when it was necessary to call attention to the proceedings, to attract spectators and, possibly, to achieve some measure of crowd and traffic control. Needless to say, there was also an element of ostentation involved, and for the Etruscan gossips after a wedding the burning question would be 'How many trumpeters did they have?'

One other instrument was certainly used by the Etruscans from very early times, but appears hardly at all in Greek literature or art until the late fourth century BC, and then in cosmopolitan Alexandria (see Chapter 7). This is the transverse flute, *plagiaulos* in Greek and *obliqua tibia* in Latin. It has already been discussed in Chapter 2c (pp. 71–2); to recapitulate briefly, it was a flute quite similar to the modern instrument, with an embouchure-hole, across which the player blows, close to one end. In illustrations of the first century BC and later it is apparently about 2 ft (60 cm) long, with the pitch of a modern flute (lowest note around middle c). It is illustrated on an Etruscan cinerary urn found at Perugia, dating from the late second century BC, where it appears to be shorter, but this may be due to the restricted space of the artist's 'frame' (Figure 8.7).

The embouchure hole is clearly visible, and the player's fingers (the index and little fingers of his left hand have been damaged) apparently show a cross-fingering technique, with the right index finger raised and the two holes below stopped. The player's facial expression is exactly that of a flautist, with a faintly haughty protrusion of the upper lip. Virgil, in the passage quoted on p. 173 speaks of the fat Etruscan 'blowing on to the ivory' (*inflavit ebur*), which suits a flute much better than any other wind instrument. It remains a popular subject in Roman art down to the third century AD and beyond.[11]

Figure 8.7 Etruscan transverse flute

181

The early history of Roman literature (to sum up an enormous subject in a few sentences) shows a fairly predictable series of stages. To begin with the Roman writers translated or imitated existing Greek works, and then gradually developed the power and scope of their language until they were able to establish a literary tradition of their own, guided by Roman moral and aesthetic values and attitudes. They never broke free entirely from their Greek models and Greek inspiration, nor did they consciously try to do so. Throughout most of the period of Roman greatness those who received a formal education (a small minority of the population as a whole, but a minority which included virtually all the writers and poets) made themselves sufficiently fluent in Greek to read any of the surviving literature; and that was a large corpus, of which the works that have come down to us are only a small fraction. One has only to look at the recommended reading list for a trainee orator in Quintilian's great work[12] to see a Roman expert's admiration for the Greek writers and his pride (strong, but not uncritical) in his own.

When they first encountered Greek literature in its developed form, they found all the poetic *genres* defined and formulated. They chose four as the most significant and challenging, and regarded them as the ones they most sought to emulate. They were epic, tragedy, comedy and lyric.

Unfortunately, there is little that can be said of the musical element in the Roman versions of the first two or the last. Even in Greece in the fifth century BC the epic had probably lost its musical accompaniment (see pp. 9–10) and to the Romans it was a purely literary form, designed for reading aloud, not by a professional reciter (rhapsode) but by the poet himself. The earliest writers adapted some Greek tragedies to their own language and style, but only fragments of their work remain. These include some passages which reflect the sung *choros* parts of the Greek originals, but they do not apparently follow the Greek metres. Nor have we any clear evidence to show whether or not there was any music composed for the performance of these tragedies, and if so, by whom. The only clue we have is that music was definitely composed for the comedies which were adapted from Greek originals at about the same time, and it would seem rather a strange option to accord this honour to comedy and deny it to tragedy.[13] The only complete tragedies we have, which do contain 'songs' for the *choros*, were written by Seneca and his associates much later, and were probably not intended for stage performance; nor are they likely to have been sung in any circumstances. We must return to them later.

With comedy, however, the situation is quite different. The two great writers, Plautus (Titus Maccius Plautus, about 250–184 BC) and Terence (Publius Terentius Afer, about 195–159 BC) were separated by a generation. They also differed in status, and in the milieu in which they worked.

Very little is known about Plautus' life. The few facts known in antiquity were padded out by ancient commentators, largely on the ridiculous assumption that incidents in his plays must reflect real-life occurrences. We do know that he was a professional actor-manager with, for a time at least, his own troupe of players. He earned his living (and hence was later accused of commercialism) by writing and staging comedies which were sponsored for the most part by Roman magistrates in charge of the public festivals. As a result of this practical experience his plays are eminently actable, and exploit most of the resources of the comic stage.

The plays he chose as his models were Greek comedies of the fourth century BC, and to understand their nature we must now go back in time to the Theatre of Dionysos in Athens at the end of Aristophanes' life.

A number of changes took place in the style and nature of comedy, starting at the end of the fifth century; to treat them in detail would be far beyond the scope of this book, and we must confine ourselves strictly to those with musical significance. We have seen that Aristophanes had a number of musical elements in his plays – songs by the *choros* as they made their entrance, the *parabasis* in which they came forward and addressed the audience directly, short songs between the later episodes, and in some plays a sort of musical extravaganza at the end. But in his last two surviving plays, written in the early years of the next century (*Women in Parliament* in 391 BC and *Wealth* in 388) the part of the *choros* has been much reduced. There is no *parabasis*, and towards the end of the earlier play instead of the words for a song we find the one word 'KHOROU' in the text, meaning, apparently, 'song by the *choros* here'. Whatever they sang (and we have no idea what it was) neither the lyrics nor the music were written by the poet. Aristotle, writing half a century later, complains of a similar trend in tragedy whereby 'interludes' (*embolima*) which had no relevance to the plot were inserted between the acts.[14] One clear implication of this was that the playwright was merely required to write dialogue and not, as in the previous century, to be composer and lyricist.

As the fourth century advanced, these trends became more firmly established, and in the one complete surviving play by Menander (the *Dyskolos*, or 'Old Cantankerous' as he is called in Norma Miller's Penguin translation) which was produced in 316 BC, the entire performance of the *choros* is represented by the word KHOROU, which occurs four times between the five acts. This, however, does not represent the whole of the musical content of the play. Towards the end there is a scene in which the title character is trying to recuperate from a nasty accident, but is dragged out of his house and made to join in the merrymaking and dancing by two slaves, who are thus getting their own back on him. At line 879 there is a stage direction 'the aulos-player plays' and the rhythm of the words changes from the usual six-foot iambic line, which has been used for dialogue throughout the play so far, to the eight-foot line with 'fade-away' so it sounds like this:

'Why play your pipe, you silly twit? I haven't time for music. . . .'

The player presumably stops, but starts up again when the action gets more lively a few minutes later (though there is no indication of this in the text).[15] The eight-foot iambic rhythm is kept for the rest of the play; the natural assumption is that the lines were shouted, or perhaps chanted in some way (so as not to be drowned out by the aulos) while the knockabout action, probably with a lot of pseudo-dance movements, went on.

It is generally assumed that the player addressed here was the accompanist who played for the *choros* during their interludes, and who stood in his usual position in the *orchestra*, probably to one side of the stage. This way of ending a play represents a faint survival of the riotous romp at the end of an Aristophanic comedy. There is, however, an earlier reference to an aulos-player in this play.

In the third act, which begins at line 427, a well-to-do lady enters with a party of servants to make a sacrifice in the shrine of Pan, which is represented by the central door of the three in the stage-set. Somebody (it is not clear who) tells a girl called Parthenis to 'play the Pan Tune', as it was 'not appropriate to approach the shrine in silence'. What are we to make of this? It is unlikely that the male 'extra' who played this non-speaking part would be able to play an aulos competently, and it would be unthinkable for a real-life female player to appear on the Athenian stage at this date. Much the most likely explanation is that the theatre piper, who had just finished playing for an interlude a few minutes earlier, would nip behind the scenery and play the appropriate tune (it would be a traditional one) while the actor mimed the movements of an aulos-player. We have already seen a parallel from a slightly earlier date on a South Italian vase (see p. 171). The device has of course survived over the centuries: in many productions of *The Magic Flute* Papageno plays a dummy instrument, and the notes come from the flautist in the orchestra.

Returning to the Roman scene, we find that Plautus and Terence both chose to adapt comedies of this type by Menander and his contemporaries. Until fairly recent times it was generally thought (especially by philhellenes who dislike the Romans) that this was a process of slavish translation, with little originality. This attitude was tenable because no significant passage of Greek text survived which could be confidently identified as the original of any of the extant Roman comedies. But in 1967 a short passage came to light from the *Double-Deceiver* of Menander, the play from which Plautus adapted his 'Bacchis Sisters' (*Bacchides*). The corresponding passages were examined in detail by E.W. Handley.[16] From this it became clear that Plautus had been much more free and original than had been thought previously, changing the names of characters (though keeping, as was his custom, Greek ones and a Greek setting), changing the divisions of scenes, introducing his own jokes and generally livening up the play. But what concerns us here is the change he made in the musical element, along with an important change in the staging arrangements.

To begin with, Menander's plays were staged in the great stone-built theatre of Dionysos in Athens, with its wide but shallow stage, and the circular dancing-platform (*orchestra*) where the *choros* performed their interludes. Though we have no direct evidence, it seems pretty clear that Plautus' stage was very like the ones shown on the Phlyax vases (see p. 170) – a small wooden structure which could be dismantled and moved to different sites as required. There was no permanent stone-built theatre in Rome until two centuries later. There was certainly no *orchestra*, and there was no *choros* to sing interludes. In one play, 'The Rope' (*Rudens*) a group of fishermen come on, singing a song about the hardships of their life; but this is not an interlude between acts – they probably came on stage (perhaps no more than two or three of them), and left again after answering a brief enquiry from another character.

There is occasionally something to mark the divisions between acts in Plautus' plays. There are occasional asides from the last actor to leave the stage to the effect that someone will keep the audience entertained for a few minutes. It must be remembered that the playwright had to compete for their attention with rival attractions at the festival – Terence complains bitterly about an occasion when a false report of the arrival of a tightrope-walker caused the performance of his *Mother-in-Law* to be abandoned. In some plays an extra character, unrelated to the plot, gives a short semi-topical monologue (for example, in 'Willie the Weevil' (*Curculio*) 461–86, between acts 3 and 4) and in the 'Little Liar' (*Pseudolus*) 573ff. the slave leaves the stage for a short time to 'cook up some trickery', and tells the audience that the tibia-player will entertain them while he is off-stage. But these are exceptions; most plays have no indication of any sort of interlude.

Another change is in the metres used. Menander used the longer iambic line with 'fade-out' only in the final scene of his play, and his aulos-player did not accompany the spoken dialogue in the earlier scenes. This was clearly a special effect reserved for the climax of the action. Plautus used the longer lines – this iambic one and the trochaic equivalent ('in the spring a young man's fancy lightly turns to thoughts of love') – much more extensively, and not only in the closing scenes; in fact, somewhere between two-thirds and three-quarters of his plays are written in the longer lines, and there is good reason to believe that the tibia-player played throughout those scenes. The ancient commentators divided the text into 'speech' (*diverbium*) when the metre was six-foot iambic, and 'sung' (*canticum*) when it was any other. There is a curious passage which makes this almost certain in Plautus' *Stichus* in the final scene of the play, which is in a 'long line' metre. The play ends with a rumbustious and rather lewd celebration by three slaves, two male and one female (all played by male actors, of course), with music provided by the tibia-player. In order to enhance his performance they offer him a drink, and for seven lines (762–8) while he is actually drinking the metre changes to the 'speech mode' (six-foot iambic), then back to the longer lines when he starts playing again.

But these changes – the great increase in the amount of *canticum* and the great extension of the tibia-player's part – were not the only ones made by Plautus. He also introduced scenes which are usually called 'sung in mixed metres', and which do not correspond to anything in the Greek comedy exemplars. As a single example, which will serve to illustrate them all, there is a scene in the *Curculio* in which the young lover visits the bawdy-house in which his girlfriend is lodged, armed with a bowl of wine with which to bribe the old lady who acts as chaperone and doorkeeper.[17] A complete analysis of the scene would take too long, but the following elements can be clearly observed:

- A kind of 'recitative' by the old lady – 'I can smell wine. . . .'
  metre — » »Ω— —Ω— » »Ω etc.
- An 'aria' in which she compares the smell of wine with expensive perfumes
  metre — » » » Ω— — »Ω— » —Ωetc. ($^5/_8$ time)
- Chanted (?) dialogue with tibia music between the young man and his slave
  metre 'long iambic'
  » — Ω » — Ω » — Ω » — Ω» — Ω » — Ω» — Ω — Ω
- Sung dialogue between the old woman and the young man
  various metres
- A 'serenade' sung by the young man to the bolts on the back door, through which his girlfriend is about to emerge
  metre as for 'aria' but probably faster tempo

The scene contains much more rhythmic variety than any we know of from Menander, and apparently a musical element which brings it a little way towards the style and sound of eighteenth-century *opera buffa*. The question is – where did the musical inspiration come from?

We are given the name of the musician who composed the tibia parts for Terence's plays, but we know nothing of Plautus' 'musical director'. Perhaps his tibia-player (there would be at least one in any troupe of actors) more or less improvised the whole score, and nobody thought to record his name. For that matter, we do not know the names of any of his actors, whereas we do know some of those who played the lead parts in Terence's plays. It seems to me highly probable (though this is entirely speculative and without any evidence) that Plautus' musicians would introduce elements of native Italian folk music; he himself came from Sarsina, not far from modern Rimini, in a district which had been called Umbria for many centuries. It covered most of northern Italy to the east of the Apennines.[18] It is perfectly credible that the people of that region had a culture which was distinctive (they spoke a language which was distinct from Latin), and a tradition of folk music.

There is another possible source for the music in Plautine comedy, as well as certain features of its style. There was a kind of theatrical performance called 'Atellan play' (*Fabula Atellana*), which was very popular in southern Italy, especially in the area of Campania, inland from the Bay of Naples. It seems to have been an improvised (i.e. unscripted) performance by actors who wore masks, and the dialogue was originally in the Oscan language, which was the standard language of that area until it was superseded by Latin in the late second/early first century BC. Even then, that language was still spoken by country folk, and there is evidence that it was still in use in Pompeii at the time of the eruption of Vesuvius in 79 AD. The 'Atellan play' was a crude and unsophisticated entertainment, with masked actors playing a number of stock characters such as the glutton, the 'old codger', the clown and so on; it can immediately be recognized as the ancestor of the Renaissance *Commedia dell' Arte*. As there was no written script,[19] there are no texts to tell us whether or not there was music involved, but on balance it seems probable, and if so, a folk-music tradition of the area might have been its inspiration. Plautus was certainly well acquainted with the art form; in fact, his critics occasionally liken his characters to those of the Atellan plays.[20]

It has also been suggested that there was some link between this form of drama and the 'Phlyax' plays popular in the Greek cities of southern Italy, which were the nearest neighbours of the Campanian region (see Chapter 7, p. 170). There may have been some element of burlesque mythology involved in the Atellan plays, which suggests some contact between them and the 'Phlyakes'.

There is virtually no doubt that in early Roman comedy the tibia-player stood on the stage with the actors during the *canticum* scenes, and engaged in some 'stage business' during rapid interchanges. Cicero speaks of a legal expert who 'crossed over in the manner of a Latin tibia-player', meaning that he gave opinions which supported first one side and then the other.[21] This implies two things – first, that the tibia-player stood near the actor who was speaking, and sometimes had to dash to and fro across the stage to do so, and second, that this was a Roman theatrical practice, not a Greek one. We have some pictorial evidence which is ambivalent. There is a relief from Pompeii in the Naples Museum[22] which shows a very lively comedy scene, with four actors in what looks like a typical Plautine scene, and a tibia-player, centre stage but facing to his left; presumably one of the actors on that side is speaking (it is impossible to tell which because of the masks). This relief is dated to the second half of the second century BC, and therefore could in theory depict a performance of Plautus' or Terence's work, but there is much doubt and dispute about this. One problem is that Pompeii and the surrounding region were not thoroughly 'Romanized' until the next century, and at that date Oscan was probably the most widely spoken language. It is most unfortunate that the relief has been damaged at the crucial point, and we cannot say whether the pipes were of the same length or not. There is some evidence on this question to be drawn from Terence's plays; it promises much but proves rather disappointing.

In the manuscripts of all the six surviving plays, or from ancient commentators, we have what were called 'production data' (*didaskalia*). These include the festival at which the plays were produced, the names of the magistrates in charge, the names of the principal actors, the date of the production, and some details of the music. For all six plays the composer was Flaccus Claudi, a slave or a freedman, Claudius (otherwise unknown) being his master or former master. (Note that he has a Roman name.) The Latin clearly states *modos fecit*, so we can be quite sure that this was new, original music, not derived (as the plots were) from Greek originals. We are also told the kinds of tibia used, as follows:

The Girl from Andros	'Equal pipes, right-hand or left-hand'
The Self-Tormentor	'Unequal pipes for Act I, two right-hand pipes for the rest'
The Eunuch	'Two right-hand pipes'
Phormio	'Unequal pipes throughout'
The Mother-in-Law	'Equal pipes throughout'
The Brothers	'Sarranian pipes throughout'

Terence was himself a freedman, and by contrast with Plautus did not depend for his livelihood on the success of his plays. That was just as well, for his prologues tell of failures and frustrations. He was supported by a patron, a senator called Terentius Lucanus, who was a cultured Roman and member of a literary circle whose members were familiar with the plays of Menander and his contemporaries. For this reason, Terence tends to follow his Greek originals more faithfully than Plautus. He does not use the same metrical variety; we do not find the 'songs in mixed metre' as described on p. 186, so the tibia-player would only be required to play for the 'long-line' scenes, of which there are quite a lot.

The names for the types of tibia are rather puzzling. Clearly, the 'left' and 'right' were two different sizes which played at two different pitches. Where we find 'two right' or 'two left' they were presumably played in the way the standard Greek auloi were played – in unison, with perhaps occasional concords of a fifth or octave. From the very scanty pictorial evidence of unequal pipes it is difficult to say which played the higher and which the lower pitch, but that was presumably the only difference between them. Where the pipes are unequal, they must have played different notes, perhaps in octaves, or in one of the ways described on pp. 43–6, or in some other way. Varro[23] speaks of the two pipes as being *incentiva* and *succentiva* – one playing the melody and the other an 'accompaniment' (the prefix sub- corresponds to the Greek *hypo-*, and that can indicate an accompaniment; for example, *hypaulein*, to accompany on the aulos, etc.). A number of remarks in the commentaries on Virgil (most of them written in the second century AD and later) suggest that the 'unequal' pipes were to be equated with the Phrygian, but this is doubtful. The only pictures which show pipes clearly identifiable as Phrygian are much later reliefs depicting Bacchanalian revels, without any obvious theatrical connections (see p. 198). As for *Sarranae*, this is just a mystery. The word may be a variant form of Tyrian, which would mean that they came from the area now called Lebanon, then called Phoenicia, and might have come from a totally different musical tradition, possibly Semitic. We can only speculate. There have also been some attempts to discern differences of tone or spirit between the plays, which might in some way correspond to the type of tibia chosen; some of the plays have quiet, reflective scenes, bordering on the tragic (for example, Demea's speech in *The Brothers*, lines 855–881) and others, such as the *Phormio*, have more incident and intrigue; but no convincing links can be established.

The plays of Plautus and Terence rapidly became 'classics', and were regularly performed in Rome at least down to the end of the last century BC. Whether the original music was preserved in some way, or whether new scores were written for revivals, we do not know. Cicero was a personal friend of a famous actor called Roscius, and saw him play 'star parts' in both tragedy and comedy; it is rather surprising to learn that one of his favourite roles was that of Ballio, the rumbustious and villainous brothel-keeper in Plautus' *Pseudolus*.

The Romans did not make any significant contribution to acoustical theory, but they were very interested in the practical application of that science. This is particularly shown in the work of Vitruvius, whose book represents a praiseworthy attempt to make available to his fellow-Romans, in their own language, the writings of Greek architects and engineers, together with a considerable amount of sound practical advice derived from his own experience as an architect and military engineer, from his knowledge of Roman law and administration, and from his understanding of what are nowadays called 'management skills'.

His work is called '*De Architectura*', often translated as 'architecture'; in fact it covers a much wider range of topics than that word suggests. It includes draughtsmanship, mathematics, historical knowledge, medicine and public health, astronomy, music, building materials and quantity surveying, and knowledge of those aspects of the law which affect such things as leases and contracts.

His excursion into the subject of music comes at the beginning of the section on theatre buildings (Book V chapter 3), and is closely related to the acoustical science which underlies their design. His treatment of the buildings is historical, and largely taken up with Greek theatres which had been built long before his time; this is hardly surprising, since the first stone theatre in Rome had been built in his own lifetime.

Vitruvius' understanding of the principles of acoustics is impressive. He draws on several authors of slightly later date than those discussed in Chapter 5, whose works have not survived. They belonged to the Stoic school of philosophy, whose followers were not in fact deeply interested in science for its own sake, but who entertained some interesting scientific ideas.[24]

The significant advance which they made in acoustical science, of which Vitruvius makes such effective use, is the wave analogy. As we have seen, the Aristotelian author discussed in Chapter 5 was in fact describing something which we would call a pressure-wave, but he did not visualize it as such. The Stoic authors[25] used the analogy of a stone thrown into a pool of still water, causing concentric waves to spread over the surface. This is a much more informative analogy than the 'branching and dispersion' one,[26] in that it illustrates the spread of sound in all directions from the origin, and also the gradual loss of amplitude (i.e. height) of the waves as they extend over an ever-increasing circumference. Moreover, two other phenomena are accounted for: the wave may, like sound, carry across the surface with gradually diminishing strength until it becomes so slight that it is imperceptible. But if it encounters some obstacle in its path, it 'bounces back' or is deflected, and the new waves which result from that have a different centre of origin, and therefore cross over and interfere with the original one (Figure 8.8). In terms of sound, this means that a deflected or reflected sound-wave may interfere with the original one, and make it less clearly audible.

Vitruvius calls the reflection or deflection of sounds *resonantia,* which does not mean exactly what we mean by resonance – for us that term normally implies that the sound is 'bounced back and forth' repeatedly at a specific pitch.

It might be advisable at this point to make a clear distinction, in the Roman context, between a theatre and an amphitheatre; the Roman theatre was, like its Greek predecessor, a semicircular auditorium, while the amphitheatre was a complete oval with tiers of seats all round. It was designed as a stadium, for public displays such as gladiatorial fights, wild beast shows and such like, not for theatrical performances.

Vitruvius applies this principle to the design of a theatre auditorium, with its rising tiers of seats arranged around an acoustical centre. This

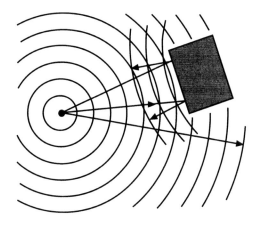

Figure 8.8 Sound-waves deflected by an obstacle

ensures that the sound-waves travel from the actor or singer to each of the listeners by a single direct path, whereas (for instance) in a rectangular room it can travel by several different paths of various lengths, so that several 'copies' of the sound arrive at slightly later times, and interfere with the first one. Vitruvius points out that in an inflected language like Latin it is vitally important to hear the final syllables of words, and if other syllables arrive at the same time (via a longer path), this can cause a lot of confusion.

But Vitruvius is able to advance beyond the 'pebble in a pool' analogy. He points out that sound-waves do not only spread out in a horizontal plane; they also spread upwards and outwards wherever there is free air to allow them through. In modern terminology, they have a spherical wave-front. So if we take a section through the theatre auditorium, the sound can be represented by a series of circles in a vertical plane. For the sound to travel evenly up the rows of seats, it is necessary to provide an uninterrupted path; this can be achieved, says Vitruvius, if a line drawn along the front edges of the seats from the lowest row to the top is roughly straight. Ancient theatres usually had horizontal gangways which ran around the circuit of the auditorium, and since they were for audience access, they had to be considerably wider than the seats. Therefore, he points out, the height of the vertical wall behind the gangway should be the same as the width of the gangway. If it is higher than that, the sound-waves will be 'thrown out into the upper air', and the audience in the tiers of seats beyond will not hear properly (Figure 8.9).

The shape of the Greek theatre auditorium was not based on any kind of scientific understanding. It was found by accident and confirmed by experience that a site on the side of a hill which had a hollow recess and which sloped down at something like 45 degrees gave a good acoustic

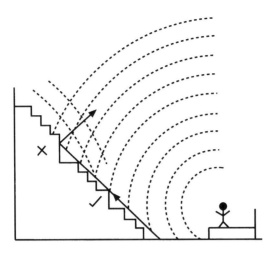

Figure 8.9 Acoustics of theatre with raked seats

response. It was a matter of chance whether the city in which one lived had such a site – Athens was lucky in this respect as in many others. All that was then required was to 'tidy up' the curvature and to excavate steps for the rows of seats. The Romans, being much more ambitious and competent construction engineers, built a number of theatres on level sites, putting in foundations, very high retaining walls and a massive in-fill of rubble and soil to form the auditorium. A good example of this can be seen at Pompeii. They also made a significant change with acoustical implications. In many Greek theatres the ground sloped away behind the stage, leaving an open space and a broad view beyond it. In Roman theatres there was often a straight wall right across the 'mouth' of the auditorium, as high as the highest tiers of seats. Examples of this can be found at Orange, in southern France, and at Aspendos in Turkey, but the one most familiar to Mediterranean travellers is the theatre of Herodes Atticus in Athens, near the foot of the ascent to the Acropolis. Though built in Athens and endowed by a wealthy Athenian, it has the essential Roman design, being built in the second century AD. The wall behind the stage was usually decorated with an elaborate stage set up to its full height, with carved statues, pilasters and arches. It has been suggested that this was really designed for musical performances rather than ordinary drama, and for that reason such a theatre is sometimes called a 'concert-hall' (*odeion*); but there is no good evidence to show that plays were not staged in them.

The section in which Vitruvius ventures into Greek musical theory is that in which he describes a system of resonators (in the modern sense of that word), used to counteract 'dryness' in the acoustics.[27]

As a preliminary to this, he gives a fairly detailed account of Greek scale-structure, explicitly based on Aristoxenos' work. He apologizes for the lack of Latin equivalents for many of the technical terms – for example, the note names such as *hypatē*, *paranē tē*, etc., and the tetrachord names such as *synhemmenon* and *diezeugmenon*. (In fact, he describes the last two as *conjunctum* and *disjunctum* respectively, and we ourselves have adopted these terms in preference to the Greek.) It has become fashionable in recent years to speak disparagingly of Roman writers on scientific and technical subjects; but Vitruvius' version of the musical theory is a perfectly sound and reasonably clear translation, especially if allowances are made for a badly corrupted, and not very well edited Latin text.[28]

He gives the complete list of notes for the Greater Perfect Non-modulating System, as set out on p. 90. They are then divided into three different selections, one containing the 'fixed' notes of all the tetrachords, without *proslambanomenos*. If we take the keynote (*mesē*) to be d′ – the Lydian key – these notes are e–a–d′–g′–e′–a′–d″. Vitruvius calls this the *harmonia*, in accordance with the Greek practice of his day; the word was no longer used as an abbreviation for 'enharmonic'. If the system was to be used in a small theatre, there was just one row of thirteen resonators, two for each of the notes except the lowest. They were in the form of bronze jars with fairly wide mouths, which were placed upside-down on small platforms with cubicles built around them, with open arches at the front (the side facing the stage) and the sides. The jars were apparently propped up on wedges under their front edges so as to collect the maximum sound from the stage. They would have to be specially made for the purpose, and tuned accurately to the required pitches. We are not sure how this was done; perhaps molten wax was poured in to get the correct tuning or, as with modern organ pipes, small strips were bent up or down from the lip.

For the smaller system, the jars were placed in a semicircle around the auditorium seats about half-way up the slope, with the two highest (d″) at the outer ends, and the one lowest (e) at the centre, and the others ranged between them (Figure 8.10). Their effect would be to pick up and

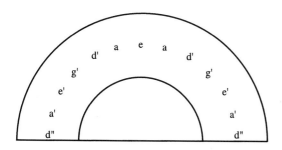

Figure 8.10 Set of resonators for smaller theatres

reinforce the various notes, so that the higher ones would seem to be echoing from the sides of the auditorium and the lower notes from nearer the centre.

If a larger system is to be used, there are three horizontal rows of jars, $^1/_4$, $^1/_2$ and $^3/_4$ of the way up the slope. The resonators for the 'fixed' notes are then placed in the lowest row, while in the central row are a series tuned to the characteristically chromatic notes in the system; these are the notes $1^1/_2$ tones below the top note of each tetrachord, which in the key of d would be f#–b–e'–f'#–b'. For reasons which are not quite clear, another pair were tuned to *paramesē* which, if the normal tuning was used, would be e', the same pitch as the third pair. There is no resonator at the centre of this row, as there is no other 'truly chromatic' note.

The top row contained the diatonic notes, each of them one tone below the top note of the tetrachord – g–c'–f'–g'–c''; next to the centre are a pair tuned to *proslambanomenos* (d) and in the centre a single one tuned to the keynote (d'). The arrangement is shown in Figure 8.11.

The effect of these resonators, which would only be felt in a musical performance, would be to give a response to a singer's voice, and reassure him that the sound is indeed going out to the audience; in the ancient Greek theatre, without a high wall behind the stage, owing to the lack of reverberations, this would have to be taken on trust. Vitruvius has a further intelligent comment on the materials used. When using the wave analogy and speaking of obstructions which divert or reflect the waves on the water, the nature or texture of the obstruction is irrelevant, but when sound-waves are reflected, it is very important. A wooden surface, such as a structure of joists and planks (which the Romans called a *tabulatio*) is set in motion by the sound-waves falling on it, and its vibrations throw the sound back, whereas a dense, solid surface such as marble or concrete does not vibrate in sympathy, and the only 'throw-back' is due to the momentum and elasticity of the air. Vitruvius speaks of theatres built of

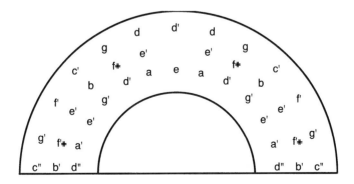

Figure 8.11 Complete set of resonators for larger theatres

wood (no doubt much cheaper than stone ones) which have enough resonance in their structure; the added resonance of the bronze jars is necessary only in a stone-built auditorium.[29] Even in that environment, he says that kithara-singers 'turn towards the wooden doors in the stage-set and gain helpful reinforcement for the voice from them'.

As a final helpful suggestion, Vitruvius says that in smaller towns with limited resources architects have used earthenware jars instead of bronze ones.[30] A copy of his *De Architectura* was to be found in many mediaeval English monasteries, and a number of early churches in England had earthenware jars inserted in the walls of the nave, to enhance the music.

Music in the early Roman empire

We have spoken at length about the theatre and drama, and their musical element. What became of the lyric genre, which was so prominent in the Greek musical world? Sadly it seems, quite literally, to have lost its music. The most outstanding writers of Latin lyric, Catullus and Horace, have plenty of musical allusions in their verses, but most of them derive not from their immediate experience or from the reality of contemporary performance, but from the Greek lyric writers, especially Sappho and Alkaios, whom they took as their models and inspiration.

As an example of this, Horace has a short, witty poem[31] in which he claims to have been a great success with the girls, and to have 'fought the good fight' with signal victories; but now, like a retired soldier, he is hanging up his weapons 'and his battle-scarred barbitos'. The name would sound exotic to the Roman reader, being deliberately chosen to add a Greek flavour to the poetry, and the instrument would be unfamiliar. The word *lyra* and the instrument it denotes were much more familiar, but *lyra* is more commonly used to refer to the poet's art or style than to the instrument itself.

There is, in fact, only one poem of Horace which is thought to have been set to music – the *Carmen Saeculare*, which was commissioned by the Emperor Augustus for the 'Centennial Games' of 17 BC. These games were held once every hundred years (or thereabouts – there was a bit of juggling of the dates) and we have evidence that Horace's poem was sung twice by a choir of twenty-seven girls and twenty-seven boys, once on the Palatine Hill and once on the Capitol. It is a comparatively short work (eighteen stanzas in the Sapphic metre) and there is no suggestion in the words of any dancing; the theme, in fact, is a very 'public' one – the gods' concern for Rome – despite the fact that it is composed in a metre originally designed for 'personal' lyric. We have no evidence whatever about the identity of the composer who wrote the score. Nor should we take too seriously Horace's remark in a poem written about four years later[32] when he is clearly referring to that great occasion: he tells the boys and girls to 'keep strictly to the Sapphic metre and to the stroke of my thumb' (*pollex*, equivalent to the Greek *hypatē*, meaning either the thumb or the string of a kithara that was played with the thumb). We are not meant to envisage Horace himself playing a kithara, as a Greek choral lyric poet might have done.

Much the same applies to the tragedies which were written in the late Republic (the last century BC) and the early empire. The only remains we have of the texts are the ten tragedies attributed to Seneca, about which there is much controversy. One, the *Octavia*, is a historical tragedy concerning the death of Nero's wife, which could hardly have been in circulation before Nero's death in 68 AD, Seneca having been forced to commit suicide three years previously. The rest contain a number of scenes in which a wise old counsellor gives advice to a headstrong young tyrant, which may or may not reflect some real-life scenes between Seneca and his tutee Nero.

The tragedies are written in the classic formula of the Greek dramatists, with entrance songs for a '*choros*' and choral interludes between the episodes of the play; but it is very doubtful whether they formed the libretto for a musical performance. Their metres are quite monotonous, usually based on a single repeating metrical line, and it is difficult to imagine a performance which involved dance. In fact, the generally accepted view is that the plays were intended for private reading, and not for stage performance at all.[33]

The instruments in general use in Roman music seem to be mostly those of the previous two centuries, with certain developments in their design which could be expected. The kithara tends to be a little larger and more ornate,[34] and the 'Italiote' version (see p. 168) is quite often shown. There is, however, a difficulty which arises from the chance occurrence which has given us a large proportion of the surviving illustrations. This was the eruption of Vesuvius in AD 79, which buried Pompeii and so preserved a number of wall-paintings with musical scenes. The trouble is that these paintings are not all contemporary. It was fashionable to have copies made of 'classic' pictures (just as in England sixty or seventy years ago there were copies of Constable and Turner to be seen on many a sitting-room wall) with the result that most of the evidence we have may not depict the instruments in use in the mid-first century AD, but those of the Hellenistic period (the 'years between') two or three centuries earlier.

There is one impressive picture of a lyre, which shows how its shape and size had developed (Figure 8.12).

In order to concentrate on the detail of the instrument, the very large figure of Chiron the centaur has been eliminated from the picture, except for his right hand holding the plectrum. It can be seen that the soundbox is proportionately larger than the 'classic' Greek version, and has virtually lost all pretence at being a tortoiseshell. The arms have reverted to the

Figure 8.12 Achilles being taught to play the lyre

form of elegantly curved animal horns found on some very early lyres, and the whole instrument has been broadened out to take the ten strings. The bridge and tailpiece seem to have been merged into one (which is not acoustically correct, but may reflect the outward appearance), and the crossbar has acquired a flat strip of some material which conceals the tuning mechanism – a pity. Nor is there any clear sign of the sling around the player's wrist which supports the instrument. One final detail – the crossbar has the discs on its ends which formerly belonged only to the kithara.

Pictures of the tibia have changed little from the fifth-century Greek vase-paintings, except that short levers are sometimes shown above the fingerholes, which presumably helped to turn the key-mechanism (see p. 37). The pairs of pipes are almost all 'equal', and the few exceptions may be apparent rather than real. There is, however, a variant version which is shown in a number of relief sculptures, almost all of which depict Bacchanalian revels, with maenads and satyrs. This is, I believe, the genuine 'Phrygian' pipe, with one pipe straight and the other slightly longer, with an upward-turning bell (Figure 8.13).

At first sight this pipe might seem to be the answer to the problem of 'unequal pipes' in the dramas of Terence, but this can hardly be maintained. The earliest surviving representations of this instrument date from the second century AD, and are not, as far as I am aware, ever shown in a theatrical context. A clue to their origin may lie in a passage from Virgil's *Aeneid* in which Numanus, one of the native Latins who regard the

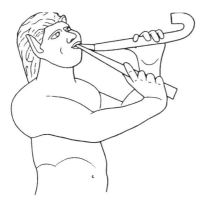

Figure 8.13 Hornpipe or 'Phrygian' tibia

exiled Trojans as invaders, throws taunts at them.[35] He calls them effeminate (by contrast with his own people) and tells them to 'climb the high peaks of Dindyma, where the twin-bored tibia plays its familiar tune; the hand-drums (*tympana*) of the Great Mother of Ida are calling you . . .'. The allusion is to the ecstatic worship of Kybele, closely similar in form to that of Dionysos, with women (maenads) playing *tympana* and satyrs playing auloi. But Virgil, who was very knowledgeable on matters antiquarian, specifies the form of aulos which was native to Phrygia, and therefore familiar to the Trojans. He describes its sound as a 'song from two mouths' (*biforem cantum*), and Servius, an ancient commentator on his work, explains the expression as '*bisonum, imparem*', meaning that the pipes were of unequal length, and played two different notes. I am inclined to think that the instrument was genuinely Phrygian, associated closely with the cult of Kybele, and was brought to Rome directly from the Near East, not via Greece. In Rome its use was still confined to the context of orgiastic worship of Kybele and Dionysos; their cults were closely associated from very early times.

The Pompeian illustrations show some forms of the tibia which do not appear in earlier art, but which we know to have been in general use as early as the fourth century BC. One of these is the 'bass tibia/aulos', which is mentioned by Aristoxenos as one of the five sizes of the instrument (see p. 40). A wall-painting from Herculaneum shows a charming musical scene, with a woman seated on the left holding a score in her hand and preparing to sing, and another on the right playing a kithara of the 'Italiote' type (it was used as the basis of the illustration on p. 169). Between them sits a man with swarthy skin and staring eyes playing (obviously with great effort) a pair of pipes which appear to be about 1 m long (Figure 8.14).

This instrument has already been discussed on p. 41. Its lowest note

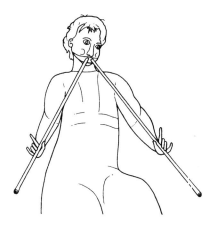

Figure 8.14 The 'super-complete' or bass aulos/tibia

(*bombyx*), produced from the full length of each pipe, would have been in the region of low G, which corresponds to the lowest of the original instrumental symbols in the notation. We are told elsewhere[36] that it takes a lot of breath to fill the entire cavity of a long instrument, and the player here certainly gives that impression. Unfortunately, the wall-painting has been quite badly damaged, and though there may have been signs of fingerholes, they have been almost obliterated, and any attempt at restoration would be based on guesswork.

A number of trends can be observed affecting the musical culture of Rome during the first century and a half of the Empire – that is, between Augustus' establishment of the imperial constitution in the last three decades of the last century BC and the death of Hadrian in AD 138.

One, which can also be discerned at various times in Greek culture, is the growth of professionalism. Music became more and more sophisticated, and amateurs became discouraged both by the difficulty of performing it, and by the unfavourable comparisons which could be made between their own performances and those of the skilled professionals. (A similar trend, though from different causes, took place in England in the 1920s and 1930s with the advent of the gramophone and radio.) The only Romans who had to take a semi-professional interest in music were the orators who, if they were wise, realized that the orator may learn useful lessons from the singer.[37]

In Rome there was another factor which discouraged amateur musicianship; it was a kind of xenophilia, which led Romans to believe that foreigners (especially Greeks) were 'better at that sort of thing than we are'. By way of compensation for this admission of inferiority, they cherished the thought that foreign musicians were all effeminate, 'camp' and generally disreputable. Juvenal speaks of this (as of most other topics) with much bitterness, describing how wealthy Roman ladies were infatuated with 'pop stars', and stole mementos of their performances (a plectrum, for example), and on occasion seduced the singers themselves. The one he particularly envied was called 'Mister Sweetsong' (*Hedymeles*); Juvenal hits back at him by describing him as *mollis* – 'a bit of a poof'.

We know of only one Roman who thought fit to defy this social attitude; and he was able to do so because he was no less a personage than the Emperor himself. He was at the same time willing and eager to do so because he was a vain, eccentric and outrageous character.

A vast amount has been written about Nero, and his name has become a byword for sexual perversion, matricide and appalling cruelty. In this context we are concerned only with his musical exploits, but even in those words lie the seeds of disparagement. Most of our information on the subject comes from the biographer of the first twelve Roman emperors, Suetonius. As with the other emperors, he follows a set sequence in telling Nero's life-story. He begins with his ancestry and family background, and his praiseworthy acts during the first few months of his coming to power, but then comes the standard formula: 'So much for his merits; now we must pass on to his disgraceful actions and his dreadful crimes. He was very fond of music from his early days. . . .'

In fairness it should be said that Nero was only seventeen years old when he acceded to the supreme power over the Roman world and the immense wealth which went with it, and there can be few young men of that age with the moral strength to withstand the temptations he was offered. In fact, he seems to have been kept in check by his two older advisors, Seneca and Burrus, for several years; but Suetonius tends to gather his information under headings (on one of the cards in his index, perhaps) and he gives us all the entries under 'music, disreputable' in a lump,[38] though they probably cover the period from his accession in AD 47 to at least thirteen years later. Moreover, the entries are not in strict chronological order, which makes them quite difficult to sort out.

However, he is quite clear on one point, that as soon as Nero came to power (which suggests that he had not been allowed to do so earlier) he summoned an outstanding virtuoso kithara-singer called Terpnos ('Mister Joy') to attend his evening meal and sing to him afterwards 'until late in the night, for several nights running', and then began to learn the skills himself. He was enthusiastic enough to undergo the rigours of training his voice; he would lie on his back with a sheet of lead on his chest (presumably raising and lowering it to strengthen and expand the chest and lung muscles), and he tried to avoid obesity, which would have caused breathing difficulties, by using emetics and enemas. He also avoided eating anything which was thought to be damaging to the vocal cords – apples are specifically named, but presumably any fruit with acid juice or fibrous skin would be banned. He apparently did not go to the ultimate sacrifice made by some singers – that of infibulation to prevent himself from sexual indulgence, which was thought to be detrimental to the voice. One can hardly be surprised at that.

Apparently he was not endowed with a powerful or clear voice. It is described in two interesting words as 'small' (*exiguus*) and 'dark' (*fuscus*); a Greek writer[39] uses the corresponding words *brachys* ('short') and *melas* ('black'). It is quite difficult to discover exactly what these words mean. The first could mean a voice of only moderate strength; but in at least one context the orator Quintilian uses it as the opposite extreme to *grandis*, which would suggest a very soft voice. In view of Nero's apparent successes as a singer and as a 'herald' in a competitive situation this seems hardly likely, though it must be said that those who were appointed to judge his performance were not free to express their true opinions. The second term, 'dark' or 'black', seems to refer to a voice quality which could be assumed at will, rather than one which resulted from a natural deficiency. According to Quintilian it was useful for emotional effect, for calming down one's hearers, or for exciting pity. Perhaps we should think of it as the tone used by chairmen of public meetings when preparing to read out the year's obituary notices. Suetonius implies that in Nero's case it was a permanent feature, unless we assume that he liked the effect, and usually chose compositions which enabled him to use it; but to translate the words as 'weak and husky'[40] is hardly correct.

What kind of compositions did he perform? Suetonius may have used the word *nomos* in one context (the text is doubtful), and goes on to describe a performance of one such piece called *Niobe* – obviously a dramatic narrative poem sung to kithara accompaniment. Suetonius says that it took a long time to perform as it did not end until 'two hours before dusk' which, as we are not told the time of year or the time at which it started, is not very informative. The timing, however, did prevent any other singers from competing until the following year which was, no doubt, the object of the exercise. It is quite incredible that Nero should have sung continuously for more than about an hour (he was very keen always to conserve his voice) so he must have had some long intervals. As for the stories about his recitals at Olympia, these can mostly be discounted. Suetonius tells of a captive audience (nobody was allowed to leave the theatre, 'even for the most necessary purposes' while he was on stage): expectant mothers went into labour during the performance, and men were lowered down the outside wall of the theatre by their friends, or pretended to be dead and were carried out on stretchers. On being declared the winner, Nero is said to have ordered the busts of previous winners to be dragged from their pedestals and thrown into the privies. All very scandalous and amusing, but scarcely a word is true. There was no theatre at Olympia, and if there had been, it would have been a Greek theatre without any outside walls down which anybody could be lowered.

Suetonius had previously said that Nero held musical contests for the first time ever at Olympia; who then were the previous winners? As for the pregnant women and the ingenious escapers, these were stock anecdotes attached to plenty of other performances.[41]

Suetonius also mentions performances in which Nero appeared on the public stage along with professional actors, in 'tragedies' that were sponsored by the Roman magistrates. We do not know how much music was involved in them, but it would hardly be reasonable to suppose that Nero would enjoy a mere speaking part. One story suggests that he wore a mask and the appropriate costume for the part he was playing; the play happened to be *Hercules Enslaved to Omphale*, for which he wore a ragged costume and chains on his feet. One of the imperial bodyguards, seeing him in the wings and thinking that there had been a *coup d'état*, rushed to the rescue.

Another incident involved a man described as a *hypokritēs* who was on stage with him and reassured him over a slip in his performance. *Hypokritēs* was the standard Greek word for an actor, but here it seems to mean someone in a supporting role. It can hardly mean the tibia-player who accompanied the singing parts – in a performance of a tragedy in the Greek manner (which is surely in question here) he would not be on the stage. Incidentally, we are not told whether the works which Nero sang were in Latin or Greek; he was certainly able to speak Greek fluently, and when in Greece he regularly addressed the populace in their own language.

Nero also claimed to be a very versatile musician. Most of the stories about him relate to 'kithara-singing' – the most prestigious kind of musical performance in classical Greece. But he was also interested in other instruments, particularly the organ. One anecdote relates to the crisis which arose when the governor of Gaul, Julius Vindex, defied Nero's authority and threatened to raise a revolt against him. Nero returned from Naples to Rome, and tried to pass the matter off as a 'minor inconvenience'. Instead of calling an emergency meeting of the Senate, or issuing a public pronouncement to the people, he summoned a number of distinguished persons to his palace and, after a brief reference to the revolt, gave a demonstration of a new type of water-organ, and described its mechanism in detail. It is difficult to be sure whether this was a display of eccentric indifference, or a screen for hysteria, or a subtle exercise in what we now call crisis management. He told his audience that he proposed to install one of these organs in the theatre 'unless Vindex forbids it' – an ambiguous phrase which could equally well mean 'unless Vindex (his name means 'the avenger') prevents me'.

The invention of the water-organ (essentially a mechanically-blown *syrinx*, see p. 166) was ascribed to Ktesibios, who worked in Alexandria in the third century BC, but its earliest appearances in literature as a popular instrument date from the Neronian period. There is evidence from some of the early Christian fathers that it was used in Christian worship, but that evidence is later; the theatre-organ in fact antedates the church organ. No doubt the design was improved so as to make its sound output very loud, suitable for use in the amphitheatre amid the general noise and hubbub. In the work of Petronius already mentioned (p. 180) there is a description of a meal which the host believes (quite wrongly) to have the elegances of a Greek banquet, including a lot of tibia-players, who 'pipe in' the various courses. The butler dances around with much panache while carving the meat. 'You would think', says the narrator, 'that you were watching an *essedarius* (a gladiator who fought from a moving chariot) fighting to the accompaniment of an organist.'

The most graphic illustration of this instrument, shown in the context of an amphitheatre, is the mosaic which was found in a Roman villa at Nennig, near Trier in Germany (Figure 8.15).

This mosaic picture dates from the middle of the third century AD, and has a number of interesting features. The organ has a base 'in the shape of an altar' as Hero prescribes (see Appendix 2) and the pipes are set in a board across the top. There are perhaps twenty-nine of them (if the lines at each end of the row are taken to be part of a supporting frame); unfortunately the keyboard and the player's hands are hidden behind the instrument. It has two cylinders, one on each side; it is difficult to be sure whether the oblique lines below them are meant to represent the rocker-arms or their connecting rods, or whether they are the supporting brackets

Figure 8.15 Organist and horn-player in the amphitheatre

203

for the cylinders. There is no sign of a blower, and it would be very difficult for the organist to operate the pumps with his feet, which probably simply means that the artist has tidied up the picture and left out much of the detail. The lengths of the pipes are not shown accurately to scale, the shorter ones (on the right of the picture) being much too long in proportion to the longer ones unless, that is, they were 'stopped' – filled up with wax to various heights and then inverted. Their number suggests that the instrument could play a complete two-octave scale in several different keys.

The horn shows certain features which could be expected of an instrument which had been in use, and was continually developed, over a long period. It appears quite a lot longer than the early Etruscan ones (compare Figure 8.5 on p. 179) and has a narrower bore, only flaring out quite near the end. The player holds the support bar on his left shoulder instead of his right, perhaps to spare the mosaic artist the problem of showing the lower bend passing in front of his body. Also, there seems to be some attempt to show a cup-shaped mouthpiece, which would improve the tone and range of the instrument; with the additional harmonics available it could play something approaching a diatonic scale, though the player could not, as with the 'natural' French horn, sharpen notes by inserting his hand in the bell.

Nero seems also to have attempted to play woodwind instruments. In the last hours of his life, when the forces of his enemies were closing in on him, he made a vow that if he survived and retained his throne he would celebrate with a music festival, in the course of which he would give three performances, one as organist, the second as tibia-player (*choraulēs*, which normally meant the player who accompanied a *choros* of singers and dancers) and the third as a player on the bagpipes; this is one of the comparatively rare occurrences of the word *utricularius*. Apart from the word itself, and its Greek equivalent *askaulēs*, which means 'bag-piper', we have virtually no information on the instrument: how many drones it had (if any), or what type of reeds were used or any other detail; nor are there any reliably dated illustrations.

In the event, Nero committed suicide, and the Roman people were denied this musical treat; but they probably thought it a small price to pay for getting rid of him.

His death was followed by a period of violence and instability, and none of the succeeding emperors seems to have had any interest in music until Hadrian, who came to power in AD 117, at the age of 41. Though he had been brought up as the protégé of the emperor Trajan (whom he eventually succeeded) and had a long military training involving much austerity and hardship, he was a very cultured man, personally interested in almost all the arts – poetry, music, architecture and the pictorial arts. His reign witnessed an artistic renaissance (heavily influenced by Greek ideals) which made it one of the most interesting to the art historian.

In keeping with this attitude, Hadrian employed a Greek court musician called Mesomedes, who came originally from Crete. He would have been a quite insignificant figure but for the strange quirk of fate by which some of his music has survived in manuscript, copied out many times at various dates; no other scores from the ancient world have come down to us in this way. Some examples of his music are given in Chapter 10.

9

NOTATION AND PITCH

The Greeks evolved two systems of musical notation, of which the earlier one may have been in use by the middle of the fifth century BC. It is unlikely, however, that these systems were generally known outside the circle of professional musicians and singers. There was a very large amount of music which was familiar, through an oral tradition, to a great many people, but this was a matter of listening to a tragedy or comedy, perhaps only once, and remembering the tunes, and singing or whistling them afterwards. There is a famous story which shows that this in fact happened.[1] It appears that Euripides' music was popular throughout the Greek world, and especially in Sicily, but only small bits and snatches of it were known there, picked up from travellers and traders. After the disastrous defeat of the Athenian expedition in 413 BC, many of the prisoners of war were sold as slaves, but managed to gain their freedom by singing what they could remember of Euripides' music to their masters; others went begging for food and water, which were given to them in return for the same service. These were of course common soldiers without any musical education, but they must have been in the theatre audiences at the original performances. There is a very pleasant touch at the end of the story – some of them went to see Euripides when they got back to Greece, and thanked him personally.

Even professional or semi-professional musicians, such as the members of a *choros* in a theatrical performance, were often taught their parts orally by the poet/composer. There is a very convincing anecdote[2] about Euripides' tribulations in this context. Apparently, while he was teaching the melody of one of his lyrics, a member of the *choros* burst out laughing. This infuriated the poet, who shouted at him: 'If you were not insensitive and ignorant, you would not have laughed while I was singing in the Mixolydian mode!' The authenticity of the story is borne out by the fact that these two insulting words, 'insensitive' (*anaisthētos*) and 'ignorant' (*amathēs*), were 'buzz-words' in late fifth-century Athens. West[3] thinks that the reason for the man's mirth was that Euripides was using a strange or old-fashioned intonation, but I am inclined to think that it was a

206

simple case of someone 'getting the giggles' while rehearsing a deeply tragic moment in the play; his sin was comparable to that of a choirboy who sniggers during a funeral service. It is even possible that the actors were also trained orally without a written script, and there may not have been a written text of a tragedy or comedy, let alone a musical score, until after the original production.

Such complete texts with notation have long disappeared, but a few papyrus fragments, manuscripts, and stone inscriptions do preserve Greek words with notation symbols, and because we have the key to them we are able to re-create the surviving fragments of that music to a degree which is not possible with any other musical tradition of the ancient Mediterranean.

The most important single source of our knowledge of the two systems is a work by Alypios, a writer of unknown but probably late date, perhaps third or fourth century AD. He spent a lot of time (bless his heart!) laboriously copying out the names of the notes and the notation symbols, each with a verbal description, for the two-octave scale, or 'Greater Complete System', in each of the fifteen keys and with each of the three variations (diatonic, chromatic and enharmonic; see pp. 90). Almost all of his work survives, enough to give us all the information we need to interpret the surviving scores, though not without some problems. Among these is the fact that the letters and symbols were not standardized; they were handwritten, and varied from one scribe to another.[4]

Alypios tells us that one set of symbols (the two sets run parallel and correspond exactly to each other) was the 'vocal' set (*tēs lexeōs*) and the other the 'instrumental', or perhaps 'accompaniment' (*tēs krouseōs*). It is generally agreed that the signs of the instrumental notation are older, and had almost certainly been in use for some time previously – perhaps from the mid-fifth century BC. At or near the end of that century the vocal signs were, so to speak, grafted on to them. Some of the instrumental symbols resemble letters of the alphabet, but others do not. They were probably derived from an alphabet locally used in Argos (where there was a strong musical tradition)[5] but nobody has entirely succeeded in finding the intrinsic meaning of the symbols, or explaining the significance of the order in which they are placed, or their relationship to each other.

Owing to a peculiar feature to be seen over much of their range, there are not so many symbols needed for the instrumental notation as for the vocal. This is because most of them are used in three different positions, for example ⊂ ∪ ⊃ . Alypios usually calls the second position 'turned back' (*anestrammenon*) which means in practice rotated anti-clockwise through 90 degrees, and the third position *apestrammenon*, 'turned away' (i.e. reversed), but he is not consistent in his use of these terms. Each of these 'triads' represents a *pyknon* – a group of three notes separated by two

207

small intervals, called *dieses* in Greek, and this suggests that the notation was originally designed for scales in which the three lowest notes of each group of four were arranged in this way, namely the 'chromatic' and 'enharmonic' ones (see Chapter 3, pp. 90–2).

We have already seen (p. 58) that the interpretation of this notation offered by Curt Sachs, as a fingering-guide ('tablature') for a lyre- or kithara-player, is not acceptable. I am therefore putting forward another explanation which I believe fits the evidence much more easily – namely, that it was designed specifically for aulos-players. The 'natural' symbol represented a closed fingerhole, the second position a slight raising of the finger, and the third position (reversed) a further slight lift (see Chapter 2, p. 35). As a result, the intervals between the first-position note and the second, and between the second and third, were not fixed, but could vary within limits from one piece of music to another, or from one player to another. So this notation was not, to begin with at least, an exact pitch-notation as such. The 'natural' symbols probably denoted particular holes on the aulos, which may or may not have had a standard pitch, and the others acted as a fingering guide to the player; he was expected to know from experience and convention how big the intervals should be. This is entirely in keeping with the many references to the instability of the pitch of an aulos (Plato[6] speaks of aulos-players 'taking pot-shots at the pitch of each wandering note in the hope of catching it . . .') and also with the fact that a number of different intonations of the chromatic and enharmonic scales are described in the theoretical treatises. These intonations were probably arrived at through a hit-and-miss process by aulos-players in the first place, and adopted by players of stringed instruments, who on many occasions tuned their strings to the notes of an aulos. However, it is clear from the nomenclature of the three notes forming a *pyknon* (for a full account, see p. 54) that string-players played them on three different strings, and having once tuned them to the preferred intonation of the *pyknon*, they could not then change it during a piece of music, whereas the aulos-player could do so ad lib.

It appears that the instrumental symbols had a fairly limited range to start with, and were expanded upwards and downwards to meet the needs of extended scales and additional 'keys'. There is an interesting piece of evidence on the early stages of this process from an unlikely source – a passage in Aristotle's *Metaphysics*.[7] Aristotle is talking about similarities between numbers or pairs of numbers which he regarded as fortuitous and without significance (e.g. that a lyre had seven strings, there are seven stars in the Pleiades, and Thebes had seven gates). One other example he gives is that 'The interval is the same in the letters (*grammata*) from alpha to omega as it is in auloi between the lowest note the instrument can play (*bombyx*) and the highest (*oxytatē*), of which (interval) the number is equal to that of the totality of the heavens' (skipping the details, this means 24).

This passage has been much discussed, and its difficulties pointed out. First, why the very specific reference to one particular instrument, the aulos, and not to a theoretical musical scale?[8] There is a simple explanation. Owing to the restriction imposed by the span of a player's fingers, most auloi had a range of an octave at the most for any one setting of the keys; as the instruments got longer and reached lower pitches, the range got effectively smaller. It would be easy to imagine the aulos as modified by Pronomos (see pp. 36–8) as having a range of an octave over eight fingerholes, from which three different selections of six could be made by means of the keywork in order to play the old Dorian, Lydian and Phrygian scales. Each fingerhole was capable of sounding three different notes, so an aulos with eight fingerholes and a vent-hole, and the option of a *pyknon* based on all but the highest of them, would potentially be able to play any one of 24 notes.[9]

Returning to the instrumental notation, we can find eight signs, each used in three positions, which cover an octave, as in Figure 9.1. I must ask the reader to take on trust for the moment the modern pitch equivalents which are given. They are the ones which have been conventionally accepted for many years, though we must later call them into question. The numbers used to identify the signs are the ones conventionally accepted by scholars, including Pöhlmann, Barker and West; they start from no.1 (F) and go up to no. 67 which is g″. The 'natural' symbols stand for the pitch shown in the bottom line, while those in the '2nd row' stand for that pitch raised by one *diesis* ('+1d') and those in the 3rd row stand for the same pitch raised by two *dieses*.

To look ahead for a moment, it is surely not a coincidence that when the vocal notation was introduced, and co-ordinated with these symbols, the 24 letters of the alphabet were made to correspond to these eight triads, starting from the highest note and working downwards. Thus each triad was represented in the new vocal notation by three consecutive letters. The cardinal letter A was assigned, not to the highest note of one of the two-octave scales, nor even to one of its principal notes, but to a third-

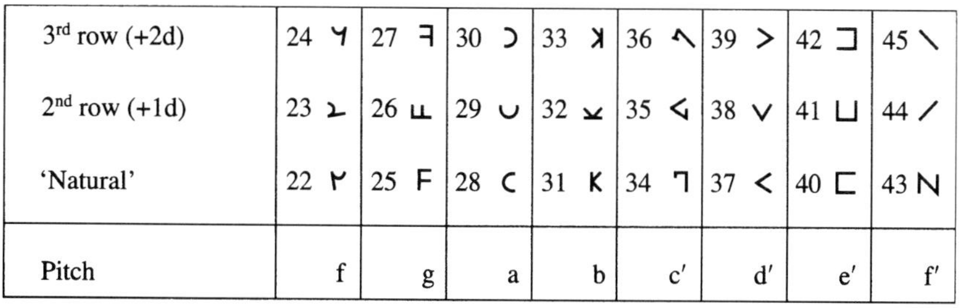

3rd row (+2d)	24 ५	27 ⊣	30 ⊃	33 Ⴍ	36 Ⴝ	39 >	42 ⊐	45 \
2nd row (+1d)	23 ㇄	26 ㄸ	29 ∪	32 ⊻	35 ⊲	38 ∨	41 ⊔	44 /
'Natural'	22 ⱱ	25 F	28 C	31 K	34 ㄱ	37 <	40 ⊏	43 N
Pitch	f	g	a	b	c′	d′	e′	f′

Figure 9.1 Instrumental notation, original octave

position (third-row) symbol, indicating a note raised by two *dieses,* and of variable pitch.

The diagram shown in Figure 9.1 must surely have been the type of thing devised by some early theorists whom Aristoxenos calls the *harmonikoi,* or 'scale-makers', for whom he has a strong contempt. They tried, he says, to understand the basis of scale construction and melodic progression simply by assessing the sizes of all the intervals, and compiling charts of all the available notes; he speaks of them indulging in *katapyknōsis,* or 'packing in the pykna',[10] exactly as I have done in Figure 9.1. He argues, with some justification, that these compilations do not make musical sense; they have no tonal centre, and no structure within or between their parts. In fact, they share some of the characteristics of the twelve-tone (dodekaphonic) system which has come into some prominence in the twentieth century. There is further possible support for this argument in Plato's famous denunciation of 'polychord' instruments.[11] He uses the word *panharmonion* apparently as a synonym for *polychordia;* this has been interpreted as the name of an instrument, but it could equally apply to the 'katapyknotic diagram' above. It contains all the notes needed for all the *harmoniai.*

These eight triads of the instrumental notation covered an octave down to f, but even at a fairly early date we see in illustrations some long auloi, whose pitch must have extended below that. In the notation there are four more definite triads and one more possible one, suggesting that the eventual aulos range which had to be catered for in the aulos notation extended down to A. My guess is that this might have been the lowest note (*bombyx*) of a size of aulos which eventually became the *hyperteleios* or 'bass' (see Chapter 2, p. 40). In my account of the Brauron aulos in Appendix 3, I have suggested that the smaller auloi may have transposed up an octave from the notation; if so, the total pitch range of auloi towards the end of the fifth century BC, when the vocal notation was introduced, could have been from about A to f″, just over two and a half octaves (Figure 9.2). The range of a kithara might not have been so great, even with the use of the octave harmonic (*dialēpsis*), to which we must return shortly.

It was at this stage, late in the fifth century BC, that the vocal notation was introduced. The 24 capital letters of the Greek alphabet, used in one position only, were not sufficient, so the whole sequence was repeated, with each letter modified in some way. Some were reversed, or inverted, but of course a symmetrical letter looks the same back-to-front, and so do some letters when they are inverted. They could be 'turned back' through 90 degrees, as the instrumental signs were, or they could be 'pruned' – bits could be chopped off them. The final awful problem was O, which they solved by drawing a line through its base.[12] The complete set of letters, with their modifications, set out in Figure 9.3. They are given in the

3ʳᵈ row (+2d)	24 Ч	27 Ⅎ	30 Ɔ	33 Ӿ	36 ∧	39 >	42 ⅃	45 \
2ⁿᵈ row (+1d)	23 ⅃	26 ᴜ	29 ∪	32 ⤨	35 ◁	38 V	41 ⊔	44 /
'Natural'	22 Ɽ	25 F	28 C	31 K	34 ⅂	37 <	40 ⊏	43 N
Pitch	f	g	a	b	c'	d'	e'	f'

3ʳᵈ row (+2d)	9 Ꟁ	12 ⊓	15 Ⅎ	18 ⊣	21 ⅂
2ⁿᵈ row (+1d)	8 ⊟	11 ⊥	14 ⋔	17 ⊥	20 L
'Natural'	7 H	10 Ꜧ	13 E	16 ⊢	19 Γ
Pitch	A	B	c	d	e

Figure 9.2 Full range of instrumental notes for aulos

normal alphabetical order, but it must be remembered that the Greeks counted the notes downwards, not upwards as we do, so that in the notation diagrams the order is reversed.

The modified letters from alpha to sigma (that is, all but the last six) were added below the 'normal' series, which took the system down to G, one tone below the lowest instrumental sign. The reason for the choice of sigma as the vocal sign for that pitch lies in the alphabetical sequence of letters, and the fact that it is reversed to act as the instrumental one, and then used in the three positions, suggests that the additional instrumental *pyknon* came with, or after, the vocal system and not before.

Normal forms of letters	A	B	Γ	Δ	E	Z	H	Θ	I	K	Λ	M
Modified forms	Ɐ	Я	⅂	∇	F	7	⊓	ᴓ	—	⤨	V	W
Normal forms of letters	N	Ξ	O	Π	P	C	T	Y	Φ	X	Ψ	Ω
Modified	Ͷ	Ϻ	Q	Ⅱ	b	3						

These six modified signs are used at the top of the scale, above A ⟶	⊥	λ	Ꮎ	✕	♃	ʊ

Figure 9.3 Letters of the Greek alphabet used for the vocal notation

It was clearly necessary to extend the system upwards as well as downwards at this stage, so the remaining six modified letters (tau to omega) were put at the top of the 'normal' alphabet, starting on a'. The instrumental symbols for these two *pykna* are rather confused, and are not written consistently, so it looks as though they were improvised at the time when the vocal signs were added and the range extended upwards.[13] This brings the development of the notation to the stage shown in Figure 9.4. (In each of the 'boxes' I have placed the instrumental symbol on the left and the vocal alphabetical one on the right.)

The notation now extends from G to a', two octaves and a tone. The next and final extension was extremely simple – we may wonder why they did not think of it sooner, though in fairness it should be said that the 'normal' and 'modified' alphabetical symbols did not correspond in octaves. The signs for f' down to b (i.e. alpha to omicron, nos. 45–31) were used with an octave mark, similar to the ones I have been using on our

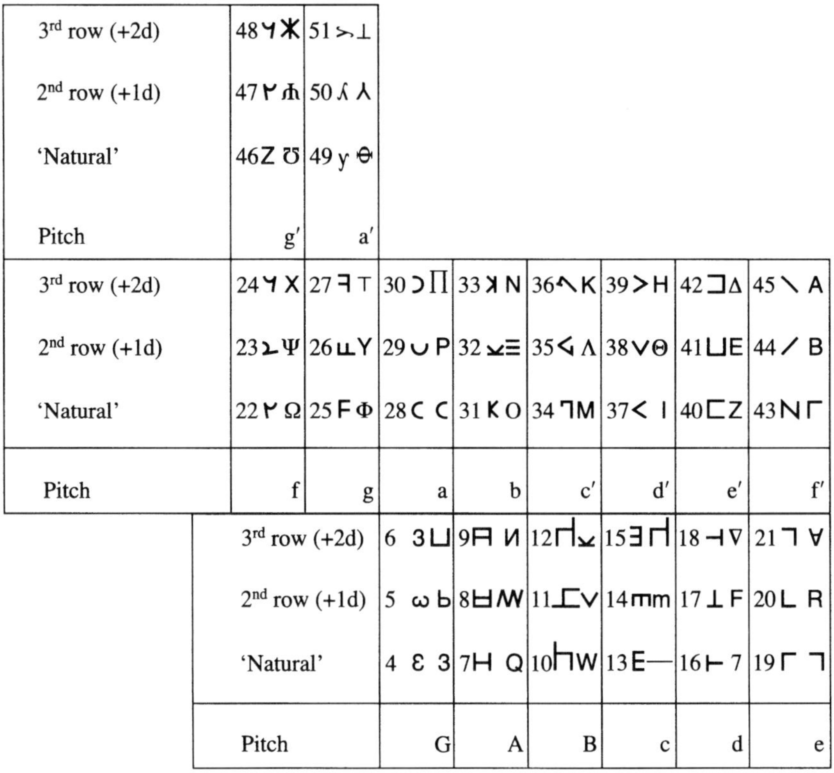

3rd row (+2d)	48 Ч ✱	51 ⅄ ⊥
2nd row (+1d)	47 Ⱶ ⅓	50 ⅄
'Natural'	46 Z ℧	49 γ Ⴀ
Pitch	g′	a′

	f	g	a	b	c′	d′	e′	f′
3rd row (+2d)	24 Ч X	27 ⅄ T	30 Ͻ ∏	33 Ʌ N	36 ∧ K	39 > H	42 ⅃ Δ	45 ∖ A
2nd row (+1d)	23 ⅃ Ψ	26 ⊔ Y	29 ∪ P	32 ⤜ Ξ	35 ⊲ Λ	38 V Θ	41 ⊔ E	44 ∕ B
'Natural'	22 Ⱶ Ω	25 F Φ	28 C C	31 K O	34 ⅂ M	37 < I	40 ⊏ Z	43 N Γ
Pitch	f	g	a	b	c′	d′	e′	f′

	G	A	B	c	d	e
3rd row (+2d)	6 3 ⊔	9 Ⴈ И	12 ⊓ ⤧	15 Ⴆ Ⴈ	18 ⊣ V	21 ⅂ Ɐ
2nd row (+1d)	5 ω b	8 ⊟ Ⱳ	11 ⊏ V	14 m m	17 ⊥ F	20 L R
'Natural'	4 ε Ʒ	7 H Q	10 ⊓ W	13 E —	16 ⊢ 7	19 Γ ⅂
Pitch	G	A	B	c	d	e

Figure 9.4 Notation system with vocal symbols added to the instrumental

letter notation. This took the notation up to f″, and the next higher sign (no. 67, omega inverted, the last of the modified letters) was added, with the equivalent instrumental sign. It is the highest note of the highest of the fifteen 'keys', and does not require notes one or two *dieses* higher (Figure 9.5). I have already suggested that the use of octave marks may well have been associated with the use of the octave harmonic on the kithara; it would be quite logical to suppose that the 'treble' aulos transposed up an octave automatically, but that a kitharist had to be told when to do so.

Having arrived at this stage in the development, with an almost complete list of signs, we can now look at the way in which they were used for the standard two-octave scale, or 'Greater Complete Non-modulating System'. This was set out fully in Chapter 3, but here is a brief summary.

The scale, or system as they called it, was built up from units called tetrachords – groups of four notes covering a fourth. There were three forms of tetrachord; the diatonic (the one most familiar to us) which had intervals in ascending order of semitone, tone and tone, and the chromatic and enharmonic, each of which had two *dieses* followed by a larger interval. The *dieses* varied between a quarter-tone minimum and a semitone maximum, the larger interval above them being whatever was left over from the fourth. The notation indicates *dieses*, without specifying any particular size, recalling once more the origin of the older symbols as an aulos notation.

The tetrachords could be put together in two ways – by conjunction, where the top note of the lower one was the bottom note of the upper one, or by disjunction, where there was a tone between them. The complete scheme of the two-octave scale is shown on p. 214. For purposes of illustration I have set it in the 'Lydian key', with d′ as the 'keynote'. As the Greek names for the tetrachords are a bit of a mouthful, I have called them 'Low', 'Mid', 'Dis', 'Top' and 'Con'.

3ʳᵈ row (+2d)	48 Ⴤჯ	51 λ ⊥	54 Ӿ′N′	57 ⌐K′	60 >′H′	63 ⅃′Δ′	66 ⟍A′	
2ⁿᵈ row (+1d)	47 Ⴠ ɱ	50 ⼊ ⋋	53 ⋈′Ξ′	56 ⟨′Λ′	59 V′Θ′	62 ⊔′E′	65 ⟋B′	
'Natural'	46 Z ʊ	49 Ⴤ Ꙩ	52 K′O′	55 Ⴀ′M′	58 ⟨′ I′	61 ⊏′Z′	64 Ν′Γ′	67 Z′ ʊ′
Pitch	g′	a′	b′	c″	d″	e″	f″	g″

Figure 9.5 Final extension of the notation system

213

The Greater Complete Non-modulating System in the Lydian key

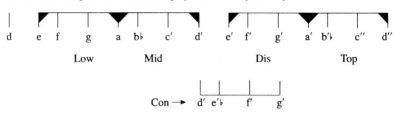

d	e	f	g	a	b♭	c′	d′	e′	f′	g′	a′	b′♭	c″	d″

    Low   Mid   Dis   Top

Con ⟶ d′ e′♭ f′ g′

Just as our stave notation and our standard keyboards have a 'natural key' of c major, so the Greek notation was based on the Lydian key; naturally enough, it comes first in Alypios' tables. All its 'fixed' notes are denoted by 'naturals' (i.e. first-row letters in the vocal notation or first-position symbols in the instrumental), and wherever there is a *pyknon* required there is a group of three consecutive letters, or a triad of first–second–third position symbols. In the fully developed system of keys (see p. 99) there were fifteen, in three groups of five, the Lydian being the highest of the middle group. In the table below they are given in descending order, followed by the pitch (keeping to the traditional pitch equivalents) of the keynote (*mesē*, the central note of the double octave).

Hyperlydian	g′	Lydian	d′	Hypolydian	a
Hyperaeolian	f′#	Aeolian	c′#	Hypoaeolian	g#
Hyperphrygian	f′	Phrygian	c′	Hypophrygian	g
Hyperionian	e′	Ionian	b	Hypoionian	f#
Hyperdorian	d′#	Dorian	a#	Hypodorian	f

I have used only sharps in this table, as all the Greek modifications of symbols were used to raise the pitch, and there is no equivalent of our 'flat' symbol.

This brings us to an odd feature in the notation. Where the bottom note of a tetrachord is a 'natural' (i.e. a first-row letter or a first-position symbol) the next note up is indicated by the next letter above or the second-position symbol, whether the tetrachord is diatonic, chromatic or enharmonic; but according to the musical theorists, the lowest interval was a quarter-tone in the enharmonic, a semitone or slightly less in the chromatic, and a semitone in the diatonic. There are a number of possible interpretations of this. The obvious one is based on the fact that the instrumental symbols were originally an aulos notation. On that instrument, whatever the size of the lowest interval, the note was obtained in the same way, by lifting the finger slightly from the next hole above, and thereby raising the pitch by a *diesis* of the appropriate size. It was not necessary to indicate to an experienced aulos-player what that size was; the

214

notation simply indicated 'one *diesis* up', and it was not necessary to change the symbol when changing from one form of tetrachord to another. Likewise a singer, seeing two adjacent letters of the alphabet, would pitch the higher note at what he knew to be the correct interval above the lower. The problem remains that a string player could not make adjustments of pitch during a piece of music, and must have selected a single pitch for that string (the one next to the lowest in each tetrachord) and used it throughout the piece. This need not have been a problem unless a change in the form of a tetrachord was required during the piece, which is unlikely.

This leads us to the second interpretation. According to this, the pitch of these notes was in fact always the same, and only the upper 'moving' note actually moved. The mathematician Archytas (see pp. 93–4) gave exact ratios for the tuning of the three forms of tetrachord, in all of which the tuning for this note is the same; the lowest interval is about one-third of a tone, and the central interval in the diatonic tetrachord is slightly more than a normal tone.[14] There are, however, difficulties in accepting this explanation. Again and again, the ancient authorities define the 'fixed' and 'moving' notes, and both the central notes are invariably included among the 'moving'. This would be strange, if in musical practice one of them did not move. Also, Ptolemy explicitly criticizes Archytas' figures on this point.[15]

So my explanation is that the earlier instrumental notation was designed specifically for the aulos, and needed only to indicate 'one-*diesis*-up' for that purpose, and that when the alphabetical notation was co-ordinated with it this feature was retained, even though it was inappropriate for string players, and in some contexts misleading. A different procedure was introduced when the range of keys was extended so as to include scales whose 'fixed' notes were not all 'naturals' (i.e. first-row letters or first-position symbols). By this time the aulos had keys for each of the semitones, and they could be set so as to give the 'fixed' notes of the scale in any key (the Pompeian auloi have this facility). Notes one or two *dieses* higher could be obtained by partially uncovering the next higher hole, regardless of what symbol was used for it. In fact, the aulos had virtually become a transposing instrument, which was chromatic in the modern sense of that word.

As an illustration of how the notation works out, Figure 9.6 shows the symbols used for the Greater Perfect Non-modulating System in the Lydian key.

The notation given first is the instrumental, with the accepted numbering scheme. The equivalent vocal symbols are given below.

It will be seen that in each of the five tetrachords the two lowest notes are signalled by the same symbol in the 'natural' position and the 'second row' position. This can easily be recognized from the symbols themselves,

The Greater Complete Non-modulating System in the Lydian key

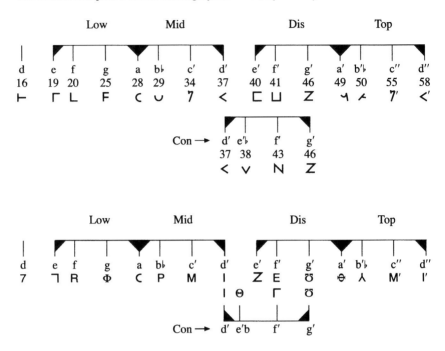

Examples of chromatic or enharmonic tetrachords

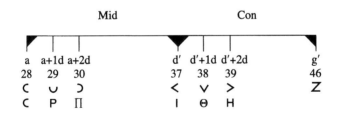

Figure 9.6 Notation for the two-octave system in the Lydian key

and from the fact that they carry successive numbers; similarly in the alphabetical notation they are represented by successive letters. In each system this indicates that the higher note is one *diesis* (a semitone, or sometimes less) above the lower. This is the reason why f' in the 'Dis' tetrachord is denoted by sign 41, one *diesis* above e' (no. 40), whereas in the 'Con' tetrachord it is a 'natural' (no. 43), tuned one tone below g', and played from an open hole on an aulos. It is significant that even when there is a 'natural' available a semitone above the lowest note (for example, b–c′–d′–e′, 31–34–37–40) it is not used – the 'one-*diesis*-up' sign is always used instead. It might be argued that the bottom interval in any tetrachord was always a little smaller than a 'true' semitone.

If any of the tetrachords are chromatic or enharmonic, they have two *dieses* between their three lowest notes, which is indicated by the same sign being used in three different positions; for example, the notes of the 'Mid' tetrachord would have been 28–29–30–37 and in the 'Con' tetrachord 37–38–39–46. This is represented in the vocal notation by three successive letters of the alphabet. As we have seen earlier the notation allows for various different sizes of *diesis*. If the 'tonal chromatic' intonation was used, the intervals between 37 and 39 in the 'Con' tetrachord would add up to exactly a tone, and the pitch of 39 would be exactly the same as that of 40; but if any other intonation was used (e.g. the 'soft chromatic' or the enharmonic) the notation could distinguish between the two different pitches.

For our present purposes, it is not necessary to go more deeply into the problems of the notation system. What clearly happened was that a scheme which was perfectly adequate for the Lydian key and a few others was adapted and tinkered with in order to make it usable for the other keys. This is in itself significant: it means that there must have been some fairly rigid standard of pitch (most probably embodied in the aulos) and that some trouble was taken to make sure that the pitch at which a piece of music was scored was exactly right (within a semitone) for the voices and instruments involved. No doubt on occasion, when a singer had a cold, the accompanist might be expected to transpose the music down a tone or so; but he was expected to do this at sight, and the composer had an exact pitch in mind when he wrote the score.

10

SOME SURVIVING SCORES

We may consider ourselves fortunate in being able to read and interpret the ancient Greek notation signs; but that good fortune does not extend to the preservation of a generous number of scores to which the knowledge could be applied. Of all the great quantity of music composed over the centuries between (say) 600 BC and AD 400, of which a significant fraction might have been written down at some time or other, we have only a miserably small collection of scores, ranging in length from the second Delphic *paian*, which may have lasted about 15 minutes in performance, to some minute fragments containing less than a dozen words, and less than the full complement of notes. Moreover, apart from two small fragments which may have been composed by Euripides we have no remains of the sixth or fifth centuries BC – the great periods of lyric poetry, tragedy and comedy. The two Delphic *paians* are the earliest substantial pieces that we have, and they date from late in the second century BC. (It is true that they show archaizing tendencies, and may preserve something of the flavour of much earlier music, but it is difficult to pinpoint specific features with any certainty.) At the other end of the time-scale we have a Christian hymn which was copied in the third century AD, and probably written not very much earlier.

There is much doubt and dispute about how many musical scores were actually written out in antiquity.[1] The plays of the fifth-century dramatists seem to have been available to the public in written form fairly soon after the original production. It is as well to remember that these texts were copied out laboriously by hand; apparently an editor (or 'corrector', as he was called) would read out from a master text, and a group of copyists would take it down from his dictation; it must have been a very tedious and lengthy process. These texts are very unlikely to have contained musical notation, since only a very small minority of professional musicians would have wanted it, or been able to use it, and only the composer and a few of the musicians would have been able to write it. Most of the melodies of the *choros*-songs and other musical passages would be remembered by those taking part in the production. (I

218

can attest this from personal experience; as 'ASM' in the Cambridge production of the *Agamemnon* in 1953 I was present at about seven performances and a recording session, and after more than forty years I can still remember most of Patrick Hadley's music.)

At least some of the music would be recalled by a considerable number of the very large audience – perhaps as many as fifteen to twenty thousand – who watched it. This oral tradition could have lasted for quite a long time, especially as a number of the more popular fifth-century plays were revived during the following century, when there was an acknowledged dearth of good playwrights, and the Athenian magistrates were prepared to 'give a *choros*' (i.e. authorize payment of the production costs from state funds) to anyone who wished to revive tragedies by the outstanding dramatists. These revivals caused certain problems. The producers and actors sometimes cut or inserted lines in the dialogue, and even rewrote the endings of some plays in order to link them with others which were not originally intended to follow on; for example, the ending of Aeschylus' *Seven against Thebes* may have been altered so that it could be followed by Sophocles' *Antigone*. However, apart from a few minor changes it is likely that the music remained substantially the same, whether or not a score was available. The freedom of producers and actors to alter the text was restricted in 330 BC by the so-called 'Decree of Lykourgos'. An official version of the complete plays of Aeschylus, Sophocles and Euripides was deposited in the Athenian archives, and any producer wishing to revive one of their plays had to get the Chief Clerk to read over this official text to the actors (presumably before they started rehearsing), so that if it had been badly hashed about in an earlier production which they had seen or taken part in, this fact would be made clear to them.[2]

The pressing question is, of course, whether this official version (the document itself ended up in the Ptolemies' library in Alexandria; see p. 164) had a musical score. There is no direct evidence to show that it had, or that it had not, and we have to rely on arguments from probability. In the original production, the poet/composer would have directed the players and trained the *choros* to sing his melodies as he thought fit (witness the story about Euripides discussed on pp. 206–7), and for this he might not have needed a written score. But unless the producer of a fourth-century revival was an accomplished musician, he would probably have employed a chorus-master (*chorodidaskalos*, as he was called in Greek), and that individual must have had, or been able to acquire, an exact knowledge of the complete musical score. Here, it seems to me, the oral tradition must have become inadequate. We can all remember, from listening to a few performances, 'One fine day' from *Madame Butterfly*, or 'Your tiny hand is frozen' from *La Bohème*; but how many of the other melodies from those operas can we remember in detail? Bearing in mind that the amount of sung material in a typical Greek play was anything up to one-third of its running time, the same must have been true then. Only the 'hits' – the catchy, memorable tunes – would be widely known, while the rest of the score might only be remembered by the singers who had taken part, and a few others. If a revival took place within a generation of the original production, this would be no problem; but if a long time had elapsed, are we to imagine the chorus-master touring the Athenian taverns in search of elderly ex-chorus-men who might be able to sing him the tune of one of the less-known songs? Presumably so; and there is good reason to suppose that, in the manner of collectors of folk-songs in recent times, he might have jotted down the notes, and built up over a few years a collection of scores for future reference.

Another development which took place towards the end of the fourth century BC may also have led to the writing and preservation of scores. A group of professional musicians began to assemble in Athens to form a 'college' (*synodos*), and by the beginning of the next century, if not earlier, they were formally organized into a guild – the 'Artists of Dionysos' (*Dionysou Technitai*).

Their connection with the theatre is clear from their choice of patron – the deity whose name was attached to the main drama festival and to the theatre building itself. But they also provided musical performers and directors for any kind of concert or religious occasion. We also know that they were responsible for the training of young professional musicians, and that they negotiated contracts and received privileges (such as tax-exemption) from other states in which they gave performances.[3] It could thus be said that they performed the functions of a performers' agency, an Academy of Music and Drama, and a Musicians' Union.

It is difficult to believe that such an organization did not possess a library of scores. Even if the majority of the works they performed were new compositions which were directed in performance by the composer, they must surely have written down a score for future performances, or just for the archives. Moreover, we have actual evidence which points this way. A similar guild was formed at about the same time in the north-west coastal area of Asia Minor, known as the 'League of Artists of Dionysos in the Ionian and Hellespont Area', which had its centre in Teos, a town on what is now the coast of Turkey, about 36 miles (57 km) south-west of Smyrna (Izmir).[4] An inscription found there gives a list of what appear to have been examination subjects for the younger student members, which include playing the kithara, singing to the kithara and, most significantly, *rhythmographia* and *melographia*. The suffix *-graphia* almost invariably refers to the physical act of writing or drawing with a stylus; though we speak of 'writing a tune', the Greeks did not – they called it 'creating a tune' (*melopoiia*) or 'making a rhythmic pattern' (*rhythmopoiia*). The words *melographia* and *rhythmographia* could only refer to the writing down of melodic and rhythmic notation.

It is therefore reasonable to assume that a library of scores was held by each of the guilds of musicians, but the question is academic, because the sad fact is that none of them has survived. This is perhaps not so surprising. Sections of some literary and philosophical libraries from the same period did survive, albeit through a number of lucky accidents; but they contained books which were of interest to wealthy patrons and collectors, who were able to appreciate their poetic or intellectual value. It is very unlikely that any such person would be likely to want, or be able to use, a collection of scores. What is more, the musicians' guilds would probably be most unwilling to make them available to anyone other than their own members, for fear that their stock-in-trade might get into the hands of a rival guild.[5] So they were lost, and all that we can do is to root around for a few precious scraps which found their way into rubbish-bins.

That is precisely what we have left of fifth-century music – two papyrus fragments, both found in Egypt. One, containing a few lines from Euripides' *Orestes*, dates from about 200 BC,[6] and the other, containing an even smaller fragment of his *Iphigeneia in Aulis*, from a little earlier. Appearances seem to suggest that these are scores for a singer or singers who were performing 'selected arias' from the dramas, and not part of a complete score of either play. There was a group of 'Artists of Dionysos' in Alexandria at this time, when there was very little in the way of creative writing of new drama, but a very intense interest in the 'classics' of the fifth century (see Chapter 7). It may well be that when they were called upon to give recitals, they would copy out their 'sheet music' from the main collection in their guild library. Papyrus was the normal writing material for everything from shopping-lists to scholarly books; the reason why so much of it has been found in Egypt, and so little elsewhere, is that it was home-grown and therefore cheap, and was often thrown away as rubbish, or used as wrapping material. Once buried in the hot, dry sand it can survive remarkably well for many centuries.

However, this is not the way in which the two most important musical scores have been preserved for us. For many years they have been known as the First and Second Delphic Hymns, and the first was thought to date from about ten years before the second; but it has now been established that they both date from an occasion in 128/7 BC (years are given in this form because the Greek calendar year began in June, so that the first half of that Greek year was in our 128 BC and the second half in our 127). The Artists of Dionysos went in a body to Delphi for a celebration in honour of Apollo, and a stone inscription has fortunately survived which records the decree of the Athenian People by which they were commissioned.[7]

The inscription gives some details of the personnel involved – a Principal Delegate and four Assistant Delegates, plus the 'trainer of the Great *Choros*' and no less than forty singers who were sent 'to sing the *paian*', together with various musical entertainers 'to enhance the god's festival days'. These included two aulos-players, seven kithara-players, one aulos-singer (*aulōdos*), two kithara-singers, eight 'comedy-singers' (*kōmoidoi*), three 'tragedy-singers', three chorus-trainers and one comic actor (*kōmikos* – not a singer; did he recite comic monologues?). Their names are all given, and are interesting. One of the forty singers was Athenaios the son of Athenaios, who was almost certainly the composer of the first *paian*, and one of the kithara-players was Limenios the son of Thoinos, definitely the composer of the second. (Another singer, Thoinos the son of Thoinos, was presumably his brother. Yet another singer was called Pindar the son of Aristotle – quite something to live up to!) One of the Assistant Delegates, Philodromos, is specially named as having contributed 'not a little money' towards the costs of the festival – clearly an example of private sponsorship in late Hellenistic Athens.

The two composers were apparently commissioned to compose *paians*, or hymns of thanksgiving, and so proud were they and their patrons that the text and score of each piece was carved on stone slabs, which were set into the outer wall of the Treasury of the Athenians at Delphi. They were found in the ruins of that building by French archaeologists in 1893; the building itself was reconstructed, and the badly broken fragments of the inscriptions were reassembled (not to everybody's satisfaction) on a marble slab which is now in the Delphi Museum.[8]

The first Delphic *Paian*

The text of the first *paian* is carved on two blocks which were found side by side, with one vertical column on each and a heading which ran across both of them at the top. The top left-hand corner of the left slab has been broken off, so that the first words of the heading, which described the nature of the piece, have been lost, and with them the beginnings of the first and second lines of the text. There is also damage at the slab's right-hand side. It was previously thought that there would be room there for about five letters, which formed the composer's name, followed by the word *Athenaios*, 'an Athenian'. But Mme Bélis has now shown that there is only room for one letter, so we must take *Athenaios* as his name, not his nationality. As for the description of the piece, all the surviving text is in the metre of a *paian* (more of this shortly). The second composition is described in its heading as a '*paian* and *prosodion*' and its final section is in a different metre, but we do not know exactly how much of Athenaios' work has been lost, or how it ended. The heading of the second composition explicitly says that it is by Limenios the son of Thoinos, an Athenian; it also is carved in two columns, but the slabs are more badly damaged than those bearing Athenaios' text, and the work is more difficult to interpret or restore.

The form and nature of a *paian* were not clearly defined. The root meaning of the word is 'healer' or 'helper'. It could be used as an alternative name for Apollo (as in Limenios' work, bars D9–10) or as the name of a song of praise or intercession, usually addressed to Apollo but sometimes to other deities, particularly Asklepios, the god of medicine. It might be sung in a moment of crisis or danger, in times of plague or famine, or as a hymn of thanksgiving after escape from any of these misfortunes. In the late Hellenistic period with which we are now concerned, we even find *paians* addressed to mortal men, such as influential rulers with whom the singers wished to ingratiate themselves. A fragment survives of one which was addressed to Titus Quinctius Flamininus, a Roman consul who treated the Greeks with great liberality in the early years of the century, about eighty years before the present occasion.[9]

The favourite rhythm for these compositions was the one used in both the Delphic *paian*s, known as the Cretic or Paeonic (see Chapter 4, pp. 121), but other metres were sometimes used. A *prosodion* was a 'processional', presumably sung while approaching a shrine, during which the singers called on the god by name; the substance of the final section of Limenios' composition is not markedly different from that of the *paian*, but there is a change of rhythm.

During the years when it was thought that the first *paian* (which was then known as 'anonymous') had been composed some ten years before that of Limenios,[10] the similarities between the two were assumed to be due to plagiarism on the part of the later composer. But if we accept that Athenaios and Limenios were commissioned at the same time, we have to assume either that they were given the same fairly detailed briefing, or that there was a traditional form for the *paian*, and a number of themes which were more or less obligatory. Both describe the scene at Delphi where the musicians were performing (almost certainly in the theatre, much as it can be seen today) and both invoke the Muses, mentioning their home on Mount Helikon. Both pay tribute to Apollo's musical skill and to the reliability of his oracles, and both refer to his victory over the Python, by which he gained possession of the site. This is all very much as we would expect anyway, and hardly calls for explanation. There are, however, two other allusions which are not so obviously natural to the context. One is a reference to the *Galatai*, variously translated as 'Gauls', 'Galatians' or 'Celts', and to an episode in which they attacked Delphi, but were defeated by military force, or by a snowstorm, or both. Very little is known of this ethnic group, or where they came from, except that it was somewhere in northern Europe, from where they made a number of incursions into Greece, Italy and the Near East. Most of them were short-lived raids, but one of their expeditions took them to an area of north-west Asia Minor, where some of them settled permanently, and became the 'Galatians' of New Testament times. The attack on Delphi took place in 278 BC, a century and a half before the present occasion, but may have been brought more vividly to the minds of the listeners in 128 BC by the fact that the shrine had been threatened more recently with looting, following hostilities between the local Greek states and the Romans. Less than twenty years before, the city of Corinth (not so far away over the gulf) had been sacked and completely destroyed by the Romans, as punishment for a futile and stupid attempt to drive them out of Greece.

This is the reason for the reference to the Romans in Limenios' final section. The Athenians (who are very fond of mentioning that their territory is 'unconquered') were granted a position of privilege by the Romans; they paid no tribute to Rome, and were allowed almost complete independence when the rest of Greece was virtually a Roman province. The wish expressed in the final words – 'and may the Roman dominion, crowned with mighty force of arms, be ever increased, vigorous and ageless in glorious victory' – is, if one may be permitted to call a spade a spade, a piece of diplomatic creeping, uttered in the hope that the Athenians would be able to keep things as they were.

A close examination of the inscriptions gives a few points of information. Presumably each of the composers wrote out his score on a sheet of papyrus, from which the stonemason worked while carving the letters. It is possible that he was illiterate, and simply copied the letters without understanding them. This need not be a problem – in fact, it may be an advantage, in that it avoids the error of the stonemason carving what he expected to see, or what he thought should be there, instead of what was actually in the text. (I can remember a number of secretaries in Classics departments who, without knowing a word of Greek, were able to copy-type long passages without a single mistake.) He has made a few mistakes: the word which should be OLYMPOS comes out as YLOMPOS, and we can only speculate as to whether he did not notice the mistake, or whether he considered that once made it could not be corrected. The composers may have written on the papyrus exactly what was to go on the stone, with the letters (all capitals) in rows, without word-divisions, accents or punctuation, and with some words running over from one line to the next. We might expect that, for the better appearance of the inscription, the line-endings would be lined up (justified, as we call it) to some extent, but they are not; they do not coincide with word-divisions or sense-pauses, and the lines vary in length from 28 letters to 34.

The notation signs were carved above the syllables of the text, but there was a difference from modern notation in that if a series of syllables were on the same note, the sign was not repeated, but remained in force until the next sign indicated a change of pitch.

If a syllable is divided between two notes (the Greeks called this a *melisma*) the vowel or diphthong is repeated in the text, e.g *Phoibon* becomes *Phoi-oibon*; but sometimes, for no obvious reason, the second occurrence is changed – *ai-thei* (two notes) becomes *ai-ei-thei* (three notes). This writing convention was strictly observed in the *paian*s, but came to be ignored in later musical scores.[11]

The most important difference between the scores of the two compositions is that Athenaios uses the 'vocal' notation, while Limenios uses the 'instrumental' (see Chapter 9, p. 207). Limenios is listed as a kithara-player and, if we accept a plausible restoration of the title lines on his score, accompanied the singers, which could be compared with the practice of 'directing the performance from the keyboard' in Baroque music. There is no such indication on Athenaios' score, and as he is listed among the singers, we should assume that he acted as chorus-trainer (*chorodidaskalos*), or perhaps sang with the others under the direction of somebody else. There is an indication of the role of each composer in the scores themselves. As we have seen, the notation signs are placed above the letters of the text; but in Athenaios' score they are above the vowels in the words, whereas in Limenios' they are usually above the initial consonant of the syllable, if it has one. This is not always meticulously observed, but often enough to be significant. In the following illustration I have separated the words to make things a little clearer, and have underlined the important consonants.

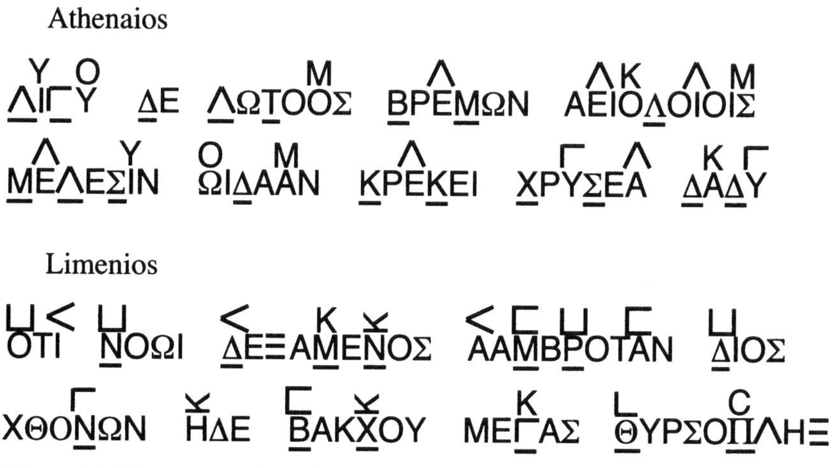

Athenaios

Limenios

Figure 10.1 Scores as written by Athenaios and Limenios

This phenomenon could be explained by the demands of performance. Athenaios wanted to indicate the pitch of each syllable to his singers, and of course only the vowel sounds have a determinate pitch. But Limenios' score, being designed for the accompanist, had to indicate the exact timing of the kithara-notes (the *krousis*, as he would call it) and that falls on the initial consonant. If he had followed Athenaios' placing of the signs, he would have 'come in late on the beat'.

There is one other feature in Limenios' score which may be significant. Athenaios does not anticipate any difficulties of pronunciation for his singers, since he himself or the chorus-trainer would sort them out. But Limenios, in about half-a-dozen places, puts in what seems to be a pronunciation guide. If an *n* was followed by a *k* or *kh* in a Greek word, it was usually nasalized, as it is in English; so *onkos* was pronounced as 'ongkos', and spelt in Greek *ogkos*. The same thing happened if the *n* was at the end of one word, and the *k* or *kh* at the start of the next, but in that situation the spelling was not altered to indicate the nasalization. Limenios repairs this omission in a few places; so in bar 21 *lipōn Kynthian*, which ought to be pronounced 'lipōngkynthian' is spelt *lipōg Kynthian*, and in bar 26 *prōtokarpon klytan* is spelt *prōtokarpog klytan* so that the singers would pronounce it 'prōtokarpongklytan'. For similar reasons, in three other places a final -*n* is changed to -*m* if there is a *p* or an *m* at the start of the next word.

For a musical analysis, it is convenient to divide Athenaios' composition into three sections and treat them in turn. They are all in the same rhythm, represented in the notation by $^5/_8$ time, the possible variations being:

— ∪ —   — ∪∪∪   ∪∪∪ —   and   ∪∪∪∪∪

First, the gamut, or range of notes used. It is pitched in the 'Phrygian key' – that is, the central keynote of the two-octave scale is M in the Greek notation, traditionally thought to correspond to our middle c (c′). The structure of the complete scale is as follows:

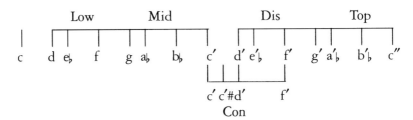

In this composition, three of the five tetrachords ('Low', 'Dis' and 'Top') are diatonic (semitone, tone, tone in ascending order), one ('Mid') is modified diatonic, and the conjunct tetrachord is either chromatic or enharmonic. This last point is made clear to the singers and ourselves by the presence of the three consecutive letters of the alphabetic notation K Λ M (reading downwards, as always). As we have seen (p. 208) the notation does not specify chromatic or enharmonic – it simply indicates a *pyknon* or group of three notes separated by two small intervals called *dieses*, and the musicians were expected to know what size of interval was called for. Musicologists in the fourth century BC tended to regard the quarter-tone enharmonic *diesis* as the intonation which was used in the Good Old Days, which had been replaced in their times by something nearer to the chromatic, which was easier to sing (see p. 94). However, the wording of this *paian* is intended to sound archaic, and the singers may have been told to use the smaller intervals to enhance this effect. The quarter-tones cannot conveniently be represented in ordinary notation. I have treated them as semitones, and written the three notes as c′, c′# and d′; in fact, the central note should probably be flatter than c′# by a small amount and the top one flatter than d′ by a bit more. It is also probable that the lowest interval in each of the diatonic tetrachords was slightly less than a tempered semitone.

Athenaios does not use the whole of the two-octave scale; the two lowest notes are not used in any of the three sections, nor are the two highest, so the total span of the composition is an octave and a fourth, from e flat to a′ flat. This brings us back to the problem of the range of male voices, which we have already examined briefly (p. 106). The traditional equivalents in modern notation were derived from the simple argument that the vocal notation system, which covers three octaves and a tone, reflected the total range of human voices from a fairly deep bass (F) to a fairly high treble (g″), which places the note M at the pitch of middle c. West[12] offers a different argument, based on the range of notes found in the surviving scores, which is considerably less; in a number of pieces which may be regarded as standard it is not much more than an octave, and only in a few, which we know to have been written for professional singers, does it extend to an octave and a fourth. If we take the traditional equivalents, the 'standard comfortable octave' runs from f to f′, which West regards as too high for a baritone, 'the commonest male voice in nature'.

Accordingly, in his transcriptions he lowers the traditionally accepted pitch by a minor third, and if this gives a score with an awkward key-signature he lowers it still further. As a result, his version of Limenios' composition is a whole fourth lower than all other versions. My own view, based on experience, is that to make things comfortable for baritones it is necessary to transpose both the Delphic *paians* down a fifth from the traditional pitch equivalents.

For the present purposes, however, it is convenient to stay with them.

Section 1

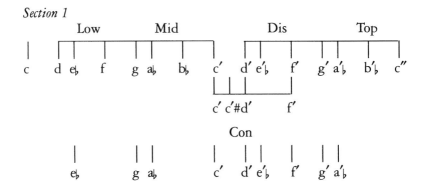

The notes in the bottom row are those used in section 1 of Athenaios' *paian*. Here Athenaios has almost completely ignored the conjunct tetrachord; he uses the note d′ flat only once (in bar A24) in anticipation of his extensive use of that tetrachord in the second section, just as in an old-fashioned piece of conventional music in C major one might introduce an accidental b flat a few bars before modulating to F major.

Here is a translation of the words of the first section. As West sensibly points out, there is nothing to be gained by printing them under the transliterated Greek, as the word order is very different, and the Greek and English words would not correspond.

> Hear us, ye who are assigned to dwell on Helikon where the trees grow tall, fair-armed daughters of Zeus the Lord of Thunder; come, that you may delight with songs your brother Phoibos (Apollo) with the golden hair – he who comes with the far-famed nymphs of Delphi over the twin peaks of this Parnassian cliff, to visit the ever-flowing Castalian springs, and to preside over the oracular rock on the Delphic headland.

> *Helikon*: a mountain in Boeotia, about 20 miles east of Delphi, and visible from the high points of the sanctuary.
> *Twin peaks*: the Phaidriades, either side of the ravine above the Castalian spring.
> *Delphic headland*: the spur jutting out towards the plain of Crisa, on which the modern village of Delphi stands.

Here is the score. As in all the transcriptions, words which are missing or illegible in the inscription, and have been restored by guesswork, are in square brackets; in this section, apart from the opening bar, they are all fairly certain.

Figure 10.2 Athenaios' *paian*, Section 1

It will be seen that the melody tends to meander around a small group of consecutive notes (a flat–c'–d'–e' flat) until bar 12, when it plunges to e flat, and reaches what sounds like a cadence there. It is very difficult for us to hear these notes with a totally innocent ear; the early bars give us a firm feeling of c minor, and most of the singers I have persuaded to perform the work for me have, quite understandably, regarded the e flat as the keynote of the relative major key, and sung it with firm emphasis. But in the Greek set-up e flat is a weak and unimportant note; the 'frame-note' of the scale ('lowest of the low') is d, which does not occur in the piece, while e flat is a 'movable' note a *diesis* above it, and has the nature of a passing-note or downwards-leading note.

Section 2

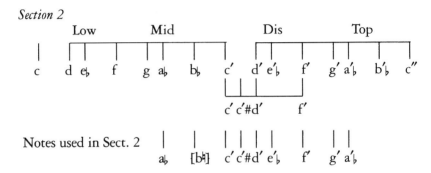

In this section the conjunct tetrachord is extensively used, but the melody does not go below a flat, so the compass is reduced to an octave. Otherwise the notes are the same, with two important exceptions. The note next to the top of the tetrachord 'Mid' (which would normally be b flat, a tone below *mesē*), is missing in section 1, and in this section is replaced by b natural (O in the Greek notation). This may perhaps explain the absence of b flat elsewhere; if the kithara-player tuned his fourth string to b natural, he would not have a spare string which could be tuned to b flat. Taken together with the assumption that he played in unison with the singers, this makes sense; Athenaios, himself a singer, avoids asking his colleagues to intone a note which the accompanist could not play for them.

But the b natural is a most peculiar feature. It does not fit into any of the scale structures approved by Aristoxenos, who specifically rules out any scale which has more than two small intervals in succession. This is precisely the feature which is exploited by the composer here; he takes a delight in wandering up and down the sequence b–c'–c'#–d', and though the interval b–c' was probably a full semitone[13] the two higher intervals might have been smaller.

The other anomaly in this section is the note on the last syllable of bar B9 – written as B(eta) in the Greek notation. It occurs only once in the whole piece, which makes one rather suspect a 'misprint', but the epigraphists all agree in reading it as B(eta). If correct, it signals a note one *diesis* above f'; as it occurs only once, it should perhaps be regarded as a 'momentary wobble' on the note f' (which, incidentally, reflects the word accent) – a decorative device, not a note in the scale structure.

The translation is as follows:

> Behold, Attica with its great city (Athens) is at prayer, dwellers on the unconquered land of the armed Tritonian goddess (Athena); and on the holy altars Hephaistos (i.e. fire) consumes the thighs of bull-calves; and together with the smoke, Arabian incense rises to the heavens. And the shrill, blaring aulos weaves a melody with fluttering notes, and the golden, sweet-voiced kithara blends with the song of praise.

aulos: the Greek has *lotos*, the wood from which the instrument was made (p. 33).
kithara: the archaic spelling *kitharis* is used.

231

Figure 10.3 Athenaios' *paian*, Section 2

(We have now reached the more mutilated part of the inscription, and the restorations are less reliable.)

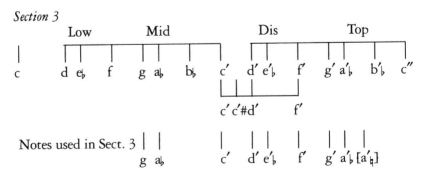

Section 3

Though it dips momentarily as far as g, the melody is mostly in the upper reach of the scale, including the highest note of the first three sections, a' flat. Once more, the note below *mesē* is missing, and its substitute b natural perhaps occurs once, but this is doubtful.[14] The small intervals of the conjunct tetrachord are not used, so the whole effect is strictly diatonic, with a range of just over an octave. There are some 'octave leaps' and the tone is bright and clear. The translation goes as follows:

> And the entire crowd of musicians, dwellers in Attica, sing in your honour beside this snow-capped mountain, son of great Zeus, renowned [kithara-player]; you who reveal to all mankind prophecies that never fail and are always true, now that you have captured the prophetic tripod [that the hostile serpent guarded] when [with your arrows] you wounded the dappled, squirming [beast, until the monster], uttering many a defiant hiss, [breathed his last].

crowd: in Greek, 'swarm', as of bees. The same expression is used by Limenios.

Musicians: the *technitai* of Dionysos (see p. 220) who were performing this work – a little bit of self-advertisement!

Snow-capped mountain: Mt Parnassos (8,200 ft, 2,500 m), immediately to the north of Delphi.

Tripod (an embarrassing word!): a hemispherical bowl with three long legs, often shown in vase-paintings. It was a powerful symbol of the control of the oracle, and Apollo is sometimes shown fighting for it.[15] The priestess who actually delivered the oracles sat on or near it.

Serpent: another reference to the Python, who guarded the shrine before Apollo seized it from the goddess Earth.

ho de techni-   tō-ōn propas   hes-   mos At-   thida lakhōn

ton kithar-   i- sei   kluton   pai- da mega- loo Dios hymn-

Figure 10.4 Athenaios' *paian*, Section 3

We do not know how much more Athenaios composed; the remainder of the inscription is lost apart from some small fragments which cannot be restored with any credibility. There is, however, one small glimpse of a feature which is both verbally and musically interesting. At the start of the fourth section (i.e. the tail-end of column 2 in the inscription) is the phrase 'and as the aggression of the Galatai' with a hitherto unused note, ✱ (vocal sign no. 48). So far, the highest note has been one *diesis* above the lowest note of the top tetrachord; this is one *diesis* higher again, and forms a 'clutch' of three notes (*pyknon*) similar to that in the conjunct tetrachord a fifth lower. The intonation of the intervals was probably the same – the intervals smaller and the notes flatter than those represented in our notation by $g'–g'_{\sharp}–a'$.

That is the musically interesting point; verbally, the mention of the *Galatai* is important. In Limenios' work they are called more vaguely *Barbaroi*, but the same word *Ares* is used for their 'aggression', and on that same motif the musical setting rises to its highest point in both compositions. This can hardly be a coincidence.

This is a convenient moment to examine the musical setting. Perhaps the most striking feature is the way in which it mirrors the rises and falls of the pitch-accents on the Greek words; this would almost certainly have given the work an old-fashioned sound, since the innovators of the late fifth century seem to have paid scant attention to the 'speech-melody', as Aristoxenos called it.[16] Here, apart from a few quite unimportant exceptions, the following principles seem to apply (for a more general account see Chapter 4):

(1) A syllable bearing the acute accent is on the highest pitch that occurs during the word; others may be on the same pitch, but none higher.
(2) If a syllable bearing the circumflex accent is divided between two notes (reflected in the text by the repetition of the letters) the second note is lower than the first – i.e. the circumflex is a 'falling' pitch-accent.[17]
(3) If the final syllable of a word has a grave accent (which replaces the acute in that position unless it is followed by a pause) the first syllable of the next word should be on the same pitch or higher, but not lower.

Not only the form of the words, but also the content is reflected in the music. The first section is calm and undramatic, invoking the Muses and reflecting the awesome beauty of the setting. It has even been argued that on the words 'twin-peaked rock of Parnassos' the notes $g'–a'_{\flat}–g'–e'_{\flat}–g'$ imitate the dip in the horizon; I am not sure about this. The second section starts with a dramatic flourish, using fewer consecutive notes and more interval-jumps until bar B9, when the description of the sacrifice scene takes on an exotic and mysterious quality, with the close-packed small intervals. Then in bar B16 the melody seems to 'leap into the air' along with the Arabian incense. (Incidentally, most of the singers who have performed the work for me have found this phrase difficult, not because the notes are difficult to intone, but because the progression is unfamiliar and unexpected.) It then returns to the droning sound of the aulos and the brighter tone of the kithara. The composer seems particularly fond of the cadence b–c–c♯–c–b (*anakidnatai* in bar B18–19 and *anamelpetai* in bar B28–9). The third section is bolder, starting with an octave leap, and keeping generally to the higher end of the scale. In bar C22 it leaps down an octave and immediately up again, a device used sparingly by Athenaios, but more freely by Limenios.

There is one other consideration regarding the practical side of playing the kithara accompaniment, which I take to have been almost entirely in unison with the voices, apart from a few ornamental phrases between sections or at pauses in the words. There are fourteen notes used altogether, if we assume that the *paramesos* (d′) was not exactly the same pitch as the note two *dieses* above c′. They could all be played on a kithara with eleven strings, tuned as shown in the following diagram, with the use of *dialēpsis* (octave harmonics).

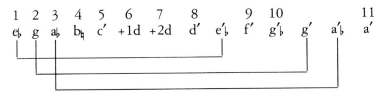

As we saw earlier, Timotheus is supposed to have increased the number of strings on his kithara to eleven at the end of the fifth century, long before this piece was written, and there are illustrations of lyres with perhaps as many as ten strings from the second century at the latest.

The second Delphic *paian*

This composition is in a different key, and explores the various sections of the two-octave scale in a different way; there are also some shifts which are best interpreted as key-changes.

The following diagram shows the basic scale for the first section, and the selection of notes used. The 'keynote' (*mese*) is d′, a tone higher than that of Athenaios' work, so it is in what the Greeks called the 'Lydian *tonos*'. But because Limenios goes no further than the top note of the 'disjunct', i.e. a fifth above the keynote, his highest note is virtually the same as Athenaios' – a′ natural.[18]

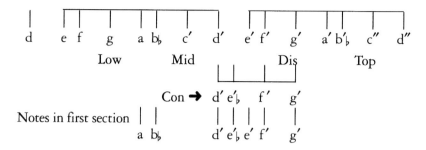

The range of notes in the first section (bars A1–31) is very limited, consisting mainly of the conjunct tetrachord with *paramesos* included, occasionally going down to the next 'standing-note' (a) and the note one *diesis* above it which, to avoid awkwardness in the notation, I have written as b flat. Nor is this limited range of notes exploited in a very imaginative way; the composer seems content to 'moon around' rather aimlessly.

The words are strongly reminiscent of Athenaios' opening section:

> Come ye to this twin-peaked slope of Parnassos with distant views, [where dancers are welcome], and [lead me in my songs], Pierian Goddesses who dwell on the snow-swept crags of Helikon. Sing in honour of Pythian Phoebus, golden-haired, skilled archer and musician, whom blessed Leto bore beside the celebrated marsh, grasping with her hands a sturdy branch of the grey-green olive tree in her time of travail.

Pieria: a region of north Greece, east of Mt Olympos, alternative home of the Muses.
skilled archer: literally, 'he who shoots from afar', a shortened form of Homer's stock epithet for Apollo.
celebrated marsh: a mysterious feature on the island of Delos, known as the 'wheel-shaped' marsh; Herodotus (II, 170) mentions a stone replica of it in Egypt.
olive tree: in other versions of the story, she has to prop herself against a mountain on Delos called Kynthos, and her travail lasts for nine days.

Figure 10.5 shows the score of Section 1.

Figure 10.5 Limenios' *paian*, Section 1

The range of notes in Section 2 expands upwards to a′ and downwards to e. There are several different ways of analysing the scale, but the simplest way is to assume that the key has changed from Lydian, with *mesē* on d′, to Hypolydian, a fourth lower. The tetrachords then run from e to a ('mid'), b to e′ ('dis') and e′ to a′ ('top'). 'Mid' has only its standing-notes, 'dis' is a complete tetrachord, and 'top' has one note missing. One result of this set-up is that the lowest note has to be approached by a considerable fall in pitch, quite commonly an octave.

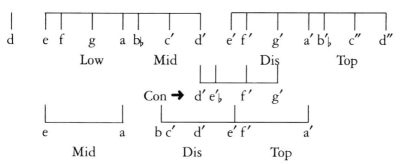

And the whole vault of heaven rejoiced, [cloudless and bright] and the air subdued to calmness the swift rushing of winds, and the [mighty] deep-thunderous swell of Nereus subsided, and great Okeanos who surrounds and embraces the earth with his waters. Then, leaving the island where Mount Kynthos stands, the god crossed over to the famed land of Attica where the first crops were grown, landing on the earth-peaked headland of the Tritonian goddess (Athena).

Nereus: a sea-god, rather less prestigious than Poseidon (whose name does not fit the rhythm)
Okeanos ('Ocean'): pictured as a river flowing continually around the circumference of the earth.
first crops: the legend was that Triptolemos was sent out from Eleusis (not very far from Athens) to teach mankind how to grow cereals.
headland: presumably the Acropolis of Athens, sacred to Athena.

Figure 10.6 shows the score for Section 2.

Figure 10.6 Limenios' *paian*, Section 2

In Section 3 the notes used are basically the same, with some additions.
The top part of the scale (above d′) is restored exactly as in Section 1. The
bottom half keeps all the notes from Section 2 and adds two more, each of
them a *diesis* above a standing-note; this gives a complete 'con' tetrachord
(a–b flat–c′–d′) and a complete 'dis' (b–c′–d′–e′), with all but the top note
of 'top' and all the notes of 'mid' except g, which in fact appears in the next
section.

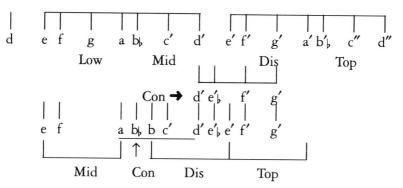

And the Libyan aulos, pouring forth a honey-sweet sound, sings
forth, mingling its delightful voice with the trilling melodies [of
the kithara]; and Echo, who lives among the rocks, cries forth ['O
Paian, I-e Paian']. And he (Apollo) rejoiced, because he had
received into his mind and understood the immortal thoughts of
Zeus. And so, from that beginning we call on him as Healer
(Pai-on), all of us who have always lived in this land, and the
great, inspired holy crowd of the Artists of Dionysos, who dwell
in the city of Kekrops.

Libyan: an adjective often applied to the aulos, probably because
the wood (*lōtos*) from which it was sometimes made came from
North Africa.
O Paian etc.: This is Pöhlmann's conjecture; West marks a gap.
the immortal thoughts: i.e. he had the gift of prophecy.
Artists of Dionysos: another plug!
Kekrops: a very early king of Athens.

Figure 10.7 shows the score for Section 3

hes - mos hi - er - os   tekhni -   to - on en - oi -   ko - os pol - eï

Kekropi - 'a.

Figure 10.7 Limenios' *paian*, Section 3

In Section 4 we have the fullest range of notes. It is simplest to assume that the key has changed back to the Lydian, with *mesē* on d' and *paramesos* on e'. Their tetrachords ('con' and 'dis') each have one note (the same note, g') missing.[19] For the first time here, in the tetrachord 'mid', we have a *pyknon* – a cluster of three notes with small intervals between them. The Greek notation does not indicate whether they should be chromatic or enharmonic, but it is generally agreed that they are chromatic here. I have written them in our notation as a–b flat–b, but the intervals might have been slightly less than semitones. Finally, we have a full diatonic tetrachord 'low'.

> But you, O god who owns the oracular tripod, come to this ridge of Parnassos where the gods tread, and where divine possession is welcomed. Weave a crown of bay about your wine-dark hair, and drawing with your hand [. . .] you encountered the monstrous child of Earth.

(From this point the score is badly mutilated, and I have not transcribed any more until the start of Section 5.)

> But, O scion of Leto of the lovely eyelids, you slew the savage child of Earth with your arrows, [and in the same way Tityos, because he] lusted after your mother . . . (most of four bars missing here) . . . the beast you slew . . . hissing from its lair . . . (three bars missing here) . . . Then you guarded the shrine of Earth, beside the navel-stone, O master, when the aggression of the barbarians, looting the hidden treasures, with no reverence for your oracular shrine, was destroyed in the whirling snow.

243

Divine possession: this probably refers to the worship of Dionysos at Delphi.

Tityos: a notorious 'sinner' who assaulted Leto; after being shot (by Apollo in this version) he was punished for all eternity in Hades (Odyssey 11, 576–81).

The beast: the Python once more.

Navel stone (omphalos): a round stone at Delphi, thought to mark the centre of the earth.

Barbarians: the Galatai, see p. 223.

Figure 10.8 shows the score of the first 22 bars of Section 4.

All - a, khrayays - mo - don hos ek - hayays tripoda,

bain ' epi the - os - tib - e - a ta - an - de Parn - a - ass - i - an

deir - a - da phil - en - the - on.

Am - phi plok - a - [mon su d' oi -] nō - ō - pa daph - nas kla - don

plex - a - men - os ā - a[plet - oos them - eli - oos t']a - ambrotai

244

Figure 10.8 Limenios' *paian*, Section 4

The fifth section of this work is described in the heading of the inscription as a *prosodion*, or processional hymn. The rhythm changes at this point from the cretic or paionic of the earlier sections ($^5/_8$ time) to a metrical line called the Glykonic, which continues until the last line, which is a shortened form of the same line. The basic pattern is:

— — — ∪ ∪ — ∪ —

with the variant

— — — ∪ — ∪ ∪ —

and the option of making either or both the first two syllables short; the last line is the 'shortened' version

— — — ∪ ∪ — —

The notes used in this section are the same as those in the first, with the single addition of g, a tone below the 'mid' tetrachord. In fact this only appears once, when the composer seems to be working towards the final cadence.

> But, O Phoebus, guard the city of Pallas Athena, founded by the gods, and its renowned people, and with him you, goddess Artemis, mistress of the Cretan bow and hounds, and glorious Leto: and at the same time watch over the folk who live in Delphi, their children and their livelihood. And come with kindly intent to the servants of Dionysos who have won holy victories; and may

the Roman dominion, crowned with mighty force of arms, be ever increased, vigorous and ageless in glorious victory.

(Octave lower than written)

[All' Ō Phoibe] sō - sde theo -   ktiston   Pallados [as - tu kai]

[la - on klei - non, syn] te the - a   tox - on des -pot - i Kray - si - on

[kun - on t'Art - em - is ay - de La -   to] ku - distā kai na - et - as

Del - phōn t[ay - mel - eit' ha - ma tek - nois sym] - biois, do - ma - sin a -

ptais - toos, Bak - hoo [t'hi - er - o - nī kai-sin   eu - men]eis mol - e - te

pros - pol - oi - si, tān te dor - i -   s[tepton kartei]   Rhō - mai - ōn

ark - hān aux - et' a - gay - ra - tō   thall - oo - san pher - e - ni - kan.

Figure 10.9 Limenios' *prosodion*

Opinions have long been divided as to the merits of these two compositions. Isobel Henderson[20] regarded them as rather poor stuff and Anderson, who dismisses them as Greco-Roman imitations of antiquity, does not deign to include them in his musical examples.[21] West gives a very full transcription and detailed comment on them – a much more sensible and useful exercise – and does not attempt to thrust upon the reader a series of judgements which are inevitably subjective, and may be quite misguided. I have spent a lot of time on them, simply because they seem to me to offer more of interest to the musically-minded reader than any of the other surviving scores. I must also admit that after having studied them for many years, I have taken quite a liking to them.

The Orestes fragment

We now travel back in time over almost three centuries, and from two substantial scores to a very brief and incomplete one. It would hardly be worth mentioning but for two considerations: first, because it is one of only two fragments surviving from known fifth-century tragedies, and second, because it might have been composed by Euripides.

It contains part of one stanza of a *choros* song from his *Orestes*, a play produced in 408 BC. That play may have been one of the last which Euripides himself saw staged in Athens before going into voluntary exile at the court of Archelaos the king of Macedonia, where he died two years later. We have the complete text of the play in the manuscripts of Euripides' work, but without any musical notation.

The play belongs to a group of his plays which deal with some very grim tragic themes (in this case Orestes' murder of his mother Clytemnestra) in a melodramatic and slightly satirical fashion. The plots involve hair's-breadth escapes from disaster and (more or less) happy endings for the heroes and heroines, usually brought about by that notorious device, the 'God from the Machine' – an actor playing a deity who was hoisted up on a crane from which he could harangue the other characters and arbitrarily sort out the problems. Most of these plays were written late in Euripides' life, when the grim realities of the Peloponnesian War made harrowing tragedies less acceptable to his audience.

The play begins with a prologue spoken by Orestes' sister Electra, explaining the background of the story over several generations and in great detail, ending with Clytemnestra's murder of her husband Agamemnon on his triumphal return from the Trojan War. (As a sample of the spirit of the play, Electra says, 'It would be unseemly for me, an unmarried girl, to speak of her reasons for doing so, and I leave it vague for you to think out' – Clytemnestra had of course taken a lover during her husband's absence.) Orestes consulted the oracle at Delphi, and was told by Apollo to punish his mother with death, a command expressly condemned by Electra, and described as an 'injustice'. Orestes obeyed it, and because he had killed someone related to himself by the closest possible tie of blood, he was pursued, hounded and driven mad by the Furies (*Erinyes*). Though they do not appear on the stage (as they did in Aeschylus' version of the story) they are constantly mentioned.

Throughout the prologue speech, and the dialogue with Helen which follows, Orestes is lying on the stage asleep, during one of his rare spells of remission from frenzy; and when the *choros* make their first entrance, they are concerned to keep very quiet so as not to wake him. Their first song is in the form of a musical dialogue with Electra, and this brings us to the first musical reference.

Dionysios of Halikarnassos[22] was a Greek literary critic who lived in Rome at the end of the first century BC, and was the leader of a literary circle there. In his book *On the Composition of Words* he speaks of the way in which poets have tinkered with the quantities of syllables to make them fit particular rhythmic patterns, and have set them to music in a way which does not always reflect the rises and falls indicated by the pitch-accents. As an example, he quotes lines 140–2 of this song, alleging (wrongly, in fact) that Euripides has not followed the 'rules' which required the musical setting to follow the rise and fall of pitch-accents.

Does this prove that he had a score of the music? There has been much argument over this. Most scholars have strong doubts about it. West argues that if he had, he would have used the notation symbols to illustrate his points, rather than the cumbersome verbal descriptions which he does use. West adds, however, 'if he . . . had been able to count on his readers' understanding it'. It seems to me likely that he would wish to be read by more than the very limited circle of unusually erudite Roman literati to whom this would apply. And if he did not have a score, how did he know what the musical setting was? West suggests that he had heard the play in performance (surely not in Rome, but during his early years in Halikarnassos). If so, then surely the musical director of the performance there must have had a score, as I have already argued on p. 219. We have evidence that the play was revived in Athens in 340 BC, almost 70 years after the original performance; but it is difficult to see how an oral tradition could have preserved all the music over a period of nearly three centuries beyond that.[23]

This sung dialogue between Electra and the *choros* is followed by a scene between her and Orestes, who now wakes up, and describes his torments and hallucinations. Then follows the first 'stationary song' by the *choros*; it has only one pair of stanzas (*strophē* and *antistrophē*), and the papyrus fragment gives some of the notes of the *antistrophē*. It was found in Egypt in 1890, and has been commented upon, edited and analysed by almost every student of ancient Greek music. What is offered here is a very brief, simplified and selective account.

The first stanza of the song begins with a prayer to the *Erinyes* to release Orestes from his bouts of madness. It was unlucky to mention them by that name, so they are euphemistically called the 'Eumenides', or 'kindly ones', which is the title of Aeschylus' play on the subject. Then the *choros* sympathize with Orestes for having to obey the command of Apollo.

The second stanza (*antistrophē*), as it has come down in the manuscript tradition, runs roughly as follows:

O Zeus, how pitiable, how murderous is the ordeal that comes upon you, hounding you, poor man, and adding tears to former tears, bringing into the house of the Avengers [another name for the Furies] *the blood of your mother which you shed, and which drives you to frenzy. Great prosperity is not permanent for mortals – I lament, I lament – [it vanishes] just as when some divine power rips aloft the sail of a swift yacht, and swamps it in dreadful toils as in the greedy, destructive waves of the sea.* What house should I honour more than that descended from a divine marriage, that of Tantalos?

rips aloft: this has a very specific meaning, which would be immediately obvious to the audience. The boat described is a small sailing boat with a square sail, and two ropes called 'sheets' which ran from the steersman's hand to its bottom corners. If they broke, or if he let them go, the sail would fly up in the air, and he would lose all control of the boat. (This is the origin of our phrase 'three sheets in the wind', though it has acquired rather different significance when applied to sailors.)

The papyrus fragment[24] contains the words between the asterisks, arranged in seven lines; the letters at the beginnings and ends of most lines are missing but can, of course, be filled in from the manuscript tradition. There is one significant difference between it and the papyrus text, but it is not uncommon to find such differences. The reason is that the texts of the manuscript tradition were worked on and edited by the Alexandrian scholars, who corrected mistakes and rejected variant versions which survived in inferior papyrus copies. The difference here is that the line 'I lament, I lament' comes before 'the blood of your mother . . . to frenzy'.[25] In addition, the first occurrence of the word 'I lament' has been lost. This affects the meaning, in that 'the blood of your mother' is now the object of the verb 'lament', instead of belonging with the previous sentence. There has been much scholarly argument as to whether the musical notation was also displaced, or whether the notes have been kept in their original order, and are now on the wrong words.

The metre of the lines is dochmiac (see p. 121), most of the lines being one of the standard modifications of the basic pattern:

Basic pattern ∪ — — ∪ —
Modification ∪ ∪∪ — ∪ —

Sometimes a long syllable is substituted for the first and/or the fourth (short) syllable, and attempts have been made to reconcile this exactly with the 'eight quavers' of the basic pattern (see p. 122). I have put crotchets for these long syllables, and evaded the problem they cause by not using bar-lines. I still have a suspicion that the *choros*-singers shortened them.

The notes of the vocal notation which occur in the score are as follows:

The range of pitch is quite small: the scale consists of a tetrachord a–d′, with a note one tone below a, similar to those found in Aristides' Dorian and Phrygian scales (see p. 104). There is a *pyknon* on a, indicated by the three consecutive letters ΠΡΣ; most scholars agree, in view of the tragedy context and other indications, that it was enharmonic, with two quarter-tone intervals. A tone above d′ is what looks like *paramesos* e′, and one more note a *diesis* (again a quarter-tone) above that. Of course we do not know whether there were other notes in the missing parts of the score. It might be argued, for instance, that the lowest note g is part of a diatonic tetrachord e–f–g–a.[26] If we regard d′ as the keynote (*mese*) it is in the 'Lydian tonos'.

Figure 10.10 shows the score, based on the information so far; once more, the words missing from the papyrus but replaced from the manuscripts are in square brackets and once again, to avoid awkward notation, the *pyknon* is treated as though it were chromatic, with semitone intervals.

In addition to the vocal notation symbols there are several other 'odd squiggles' on the score.[27] One occurs regularly between two dochmiacs when they are written on the same line, but not elsewhere (e.g. it does not appear on the fifth and sixth lines, where there is only one dochmiac; we do not know whether it appeared at the ends of the lines). It looks rather like a capital Z which has been 'straightened out' into right-angles, with a dot over the top bar. My own view is that this is nothing more than a colon mark, to indicate to the singer where one metrical unit ends and the next begins; it does not appear in the fifth or sixth lines because it is not needed there. The other view which has been put forward and accepted by a number of scholars[28] is that this is a symbol from the instrumental notation – no. 46, representing g′ and usually written as Z but changed in form here to distinguish it from the vocal symbol Z (no. 40) which stands for e′ and occurs several times in the singer's score. This seems to me intolerably clumsy and confusing. Among other considerations, we have to assume that the aulos-player and singer(s) used the same score, which is most unlikely. However, if this interpretation is correct, it would seem that the aulos-player played g′ at five places in the score (not a very

Figure 10.10 The Orestes fragment

challenging task!), perhaps 'droning on' through the following syllables.

As for the other group of three signs which intrudes twice, one may well feel inclined to give up in despair. It occurs after the first word in the fifth and sixth lines, which have clearly been spread out to make room for the insertions. The first sign is like a straggly fish-hook; the only sensible explanation I have found is that it is a 'division mark' (*diaeresis*) which indicates that we are changing from vocal to instrumental signs, and indeed the other two symbols are instrumental. But why is the 'hook' sign not used before the modified Z? The second and third signs are reversed gamma and reversed sigma, nos. 21 and 30, standing for notes two *dieses* above e and a respectively. If the intonation was enharmonic, as is generally agreed, this would mean f and b flat.[29] This also has been interpreted as an aulos *obbligato*, this time with the two pipes of the

251

instrument playing different notes. But the question of timing is very difficult, because if played at the points where the signs appear in the score, the intrusions seem to interrupt the flow of the words very dramatically; this is not acceptable unless we regard the words *deinon ponon* as being in some kind of parenthesis.

Is this a genuine composition by Euripides? The simple answer is that we cannot be sure that it is, but there is no proof that it is by anyone else, or indeed that it is not by Euripides. It has been accepted as genuine (though with some misgivings) by the great majority of scholars (including West, a fact which I regard as conclusive), and Anderson's arguments against it[30] seem to me to be based on the principle 'spurious until proved genuine', for which I can see no justification.

Some other fragments

Another papyrus fragment containing music which may have been composed by Euripides was identified in 1973 in the University Library, Leiden.[31] It is a little older than the Orestes fragment, dating from the third century BC, and has three snatches of melody from the setting of one of the *choros*-songs from Euripides' *Iphigeneia in Aulis*. This play was written in the last year of his life, and was not produced in Athens until 405 BC, a year after his death. It was produced by his son (of the same name) and it is possible that 'junior' composed the music; he must certainly have trained the *choros*. Unfortunately, this fragment is terribly scrappy, containing only three short separate phrases of a few notes (less than a quarter of the total) and it seems rather pointless to reproduce it here.[32]

One other score which has survived in an inscription is the so-called 'Epitaph of Seikilos'. It was carved on a tombstone in the form of a round pillar, which has had a chequered history. It was found by Sir William Ramsay in 1883 in Tralles, a small town in South Turkey near the modern Aidin. He spotted the musical notes over part of the text, and published a transcription. The pillar then disappeared for some time, to be 'rediscovered' near Smyrna (Izmir) in a private collection in 1922. It finally ended up in the National Museum in Copenhagen[33] in 1966. There is much doubt about its date, but the first century AD is the most probable guess.

The inscription begins with an elegiac couplet (the normal rhythm for inscriptions or dedications) without any musical notation signs; it reads 'I, the stone, am an image (*eikon*) and Seikilos places me here (to be) a long-lasting monument to immortal memory.' Then follows a very brief poem, with vocal notation signs above the words. It is often referred to as an 'epitaph', which in the literal sense it is, but its content is not as lugubrious as that word might suggest. It reads: 'As long as you live, let the world see you, and do not make yourself miserable; life is short, and Time demands his due.'

The scale of notes used is odd. Perhaps the simplest way to interpret it is to ask what the composer wanted, and then how he obtained it. He decided that he wanted a diatonic octave scale with the intervals in the order of the Phrygian species, namely (in tones) $1-\frac{1}{2}-1-1-1-\frac{1}{2}-1$. However, if he had pitched it in the Phrygian *tonos* (which naturally belongs with the Phrygian species) the range would have been f–f′. He thought that was a little too high, so he transposed it down a semitone to the Ionian *tonos*, with the 'keynote' b natural, and his composition running from e to e′. So the scale is:

$$e - f\sharp - g - a - b - c\sharp' - d' - e'$$

$$\underset{\text{mid}}{\rule{2.5cm}{0.4pt}} \qquad \underset{\text{dis}}{\rule{2.5cm}{0.4pt}}$$

The tetrachords 'mid' and 'dis' are marked below the notes. Now according to this set-up, the note *mesē* (b) should be the tonal centre of the piece; but it is not. In fact, it starts from, and revolves around a, and to our ears it sounds in the key of d major. The only explanation seems to be that it centres not on the '*mesē* by function' (see p. 96) which is b, but on the '*mesē* by position', i.e. the fourth note up from the lowest in the species, a. The rhythm is a very simple iambic (∪ —) which fits quite easily into bar-lines in $^6/_8$ time.

Here is the score (Figure 10.11).

Poor Seikilos has had a very bad press. Mrs Henderson was upset by the 'diatonic banality' of the melody, and Anderson claims that the text 'hardly rises above the level of doggerel'.[34] I leave it to the reader to decide whether these judgements are fair.

The next group of short pieces are almost the only ones which have been preserved in manuscript – that is, they were written down with notation from the start, and through a process of many copyings have come down to us. The oldest manuscripts which contain them date from the thirteenth century AD, and it is significant that not all of them include the musical notation. This shows that even when the musical score was available in a manuscript, it was not always copied.

Figure 10.11 Seikilos' 'epitaph'

The compositions are all attributed to Mesomedes in the manuscripts, though the first one may not be his. He was originally from Crete, but for some years he was attached to the court of Hadrian, Roman Emperor from AD 117 to 138. It would be entirely in keeping with Hadrian's character to have a 'chief musician' who was Greek; he was a passionate philhellene, interested in all branches of art and literature, and according to legend, himself a competent poet. The Greeks of his time were not slow to appreciate this; of the many honours which he received the one which he most enjoyed was being elected chief magistrate (*archon*) of Athens. Mesomedes' compositions are fairly conventional, in the manner of Greek 'hymns' from centuries before. They do not apparently have any topical or political (or Roman) significance.

The first composition in the collection is written in what looks like an Ionian dialect (unlike the rest), and the musical style is not quite the same, so it is probably not by Mesomedes. It is a short invocation to the Muse, asking for inspiration: 'Sing to me, dear Muse, lead me into my song; let a breeze from your sacred grove whirl about my mind.'

The notes used cover less than an octave, and can be fitted into a tetrachord structure:

$$g - a - a_\sharp - c' - d' - e' - f'$$
$$\underset{\text{mid}}{\lfloor\qquad\qquad\rfloor} \quad \underset{\text{dis}}{\lfloor\qquad\qquad\rfloor}$$

There is also an intrusive accidental $c'_\sharp$, a semitone below the keynote d', though there is some doubt about that note. If correct, it is not the same phenomenon as in Athenaios' *paian* (p. 230) as the accidental does not replace the 'right' note, c' natural – they are both there together. The piece is not really long enough to establish the tonal centre; for what it is worth, it begins and ends on a, the lowest note of the tetrachord 'mid'. The rhythm is once more iambic, made to fit nicely into $^6/_8$ time by the simple expedient of a false quantity on the first note of bars 3 and 5.

The next piece is probably by Mesomedes. It is possible to see from the

Figure 10.12 Invocation to a Muse

phonetic English that in the previous piece the feminine ending is spelt '-ay', while in this one it is spelt '-a', the 'Doric' dialect spelling. It is similar in content and spirit, being an appeal to the Muse Kalliope and to Apollo: 'Skilful Kalliope, leader of the delightful Muses, and you, skilful priest of our rites, son of Leto, Healer-god (*Paian*) of Delos, be at my side and be kindly to me.'

The scale on which it is based can be regarded as three tetrachords, 'low', 'mid' and 'dis', with the top two notes of the last missing.[35] So far as we can judge from so short a piece, the tonal centre is a.

$$e - f - g - a - a_{\sharp} - c' - d' - e' - f'$$

| low | mid | dis ... |

The rhythm is dactylic (like that of the epic hexameter) until the last three words, which are trochaic (— ∪ — ∪), in $^6/_8$ time.

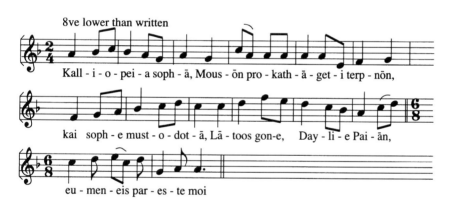

Figure 10.13 Invocation to Kalliope

We also have two longer pieces by Mesomedes – a hymn to the Sun, and a hymn to Nemesis, written in the elegant, if slightly florid, style which is typical of all the arts in the Hadrianic period. They are both in the same rhythm, which is basically anapaestic (∪ ∪ — | ∪ ∪ — etc.) with an interesting variation at the ends of the lines:

'normal' ∪ ∪ – | ∪ ∪ – | ∪ ∪ – | – | (∪ ∪ lost)
variant ∪ ∪ – | ∪ ∪ – | ∪ ∪ – | ∪ – | (∪ lost)

In the notation I have used $^2/_4$ time, but have shifted the bar-lines to make the rhythm more obvious. The *catalexis* (loss of the two short syllables) just before the end of the 'normal' line is represented by a rest

255

(not in the Greek notation) and the variant version has a syncopated beat in the fourth bar.

The scale of notes used in the Hymn to the Sun is closely similar to that used in the last piece.

Here is a translation:

Father of the Dawn with her snow-white eyelids, you who follow in your rose-pink chariot the track of your flying steeds, exulting in the gold of your hair, twining your darting rays across the boundless vault of sky, whirling around the whole earth the fount of your all-seeing beams, while flowing rivers of your deathless fire beget the lovely day. For you the peaceful chorus of stars dance their measure across Olympos their lord, forever singing their leisured song, rejoicing in the music of Apollo's lyre; and leading them the silvery-grey Moon marshals the months and seasons, drawn by her team of milk-white heifers. And your benevolent mind rejoices as it whirls around the manifold raiment of the universe.

Here is the score (Figure 10.14).

(One octave lower than written)

Khi - o - no - bleph - a - roo pat - er Ā - oos, // rhod - o -

essan hos an - tu - ga pō - lōn // ptā -

nois hup ' ik - ness - i di - ō - keis, // chrȳ -

seai - sin a - gall - om - en - os kom - ais // per - i

nō - ton a - peir - it - on oo - ran - oo // ak -

ti - na pol - y - stroph - on am - plek - ōn // ai -

ei - mon - a   kos - mon hel - iss-----   ōn.

Figure 10.14 Hymn to the Sun

The second longer piece by Mesomedes is a hymn to Nemesis, a rather puzzling figure among the Greek gods. As far as most Classical writers are concerned, she is a personification of Retribution, the punishment which eventually overtakes men who have offended against the gods, particularly by arrogant or presumptuous behaviour. Many of the traditional features of her image are mentioned here – she is a winged goddess who holds a pair of scales in her hands (a very distant ancestor of Justice on the Old Bailey!), who looms up on her victims unseen and overpowers them. At one point (in line 11) she seems to borrow an element from the image of the Fates, spinning the thread and 'measuring out' a quantity of life to men.

The last few lines present a problem. The music generally follows the rises and falls of the word-accents (as it does in the hymn to the Sun) but, as West points out,[36] the 'rule' is blatantly broken on the last word of the fifteenth line (where the pitch falls when it ought to rise). This may perhaps suggest that that was originally a cadence at the end of the piece. The remainder of the hymn is less interesting melodically, and may have been a separate composition.

The translation is as follows:

Winged goddess, Nemesis, who tilts the balance of our lives, dark-eyed goddess, daughter of Justice, who curbs with iron bit the foolish brayings of mortals, and who through hatred of man's destructive arrogance drives out black envy. Beneath your relentless and trackless wheel men's fortunes turn and twist; unseen you walk beside them, and bend low the proud man's neck. Beneath your arm you measure out his life-span, and stoop to gaze into the depths of his heart (?), your scales held firmly in your hand. Be benevolent to us, you who dispense justice, winged goddess Nemesis, who tilts the balance of our lives.

We sing in honour of Nemesis, immortal goddess, formidable Victory with wings outspread, joint counsellor with Justice who makes no mistakes, who punishes (*nemesōsa*) the arrogance of men, and bears it to the depths of Hades.

Here is the score (Figure 10.15).

(One octave lower than written)

Nem - e - si pter - o - ess - a bi - oo rhop - a, / / ky - an -

ō - pi the - ā, thyg - a - terr Di - kās, / / hā

koop - ha phry - ag - ma - ta thnā - tōn / / ep - ek -

heis ad - a - man - ti khal - i - nō / / ek -

thoos - a d'hyb - rin ol - o - ān brot-ōn / / melan -

a phton - on ek - tos e - laun - eis. / / hy - po

son trok - hon a - stat - on a - stib - ay / / khar - o -

pā mer - o - pōn strep - het - ai tuk - hā / / lay -

thoo - sa de par po - da bàīn - eis, / / gau -

roo - men - on auk - hen - a klin - eis.

259

Figure 10.15 Hymn to Nemesis

The next three fragments come from an ancient Greek treatise on music published by F. Bellermann in 1841; the authorship and date are unknown, and the work is therefore referred to as 'Bellermann's Anonymous'. They are short instrumental pieces, intended to illustrate certain rhythms, and because they have no words to indicate the long and short notes, the rhythm notation (*rhythmographia*; see p. 220) has to be used.

The basic rhythmic unit was the short syllable, indicated in the notation by a dot or point (*sēma* in Greek). It was equivalent to our quaver (or eighth-note) and the rhythms were labelled according to the number of 'points' per foot or bar. Thus 'six-point' means $^6/_8$ time, 'four-point' means $^2/_4$, and so on.

In the following examples I have added the Greek notation for notes and rhythm above the stave. Notes which are written plain or with a dot above them have the value of quavers. Those with a bar above the note-sign are crotchets (quarter-notes) and those with a ⌐ sign are dotted crotchets (the Greeks called them trisemes). Rests are also written, represented by the Greek letter Λ, which is the initial letter of the word for 'missing' (*leipei*). If the rest is plain, or has a dot above it, it is a quaver rest, and with a bar above it is a crotchet rest.

These three examples (Figure 10.16)[37] show the main features; they are instrumental exercises of little musical merit, faintly reminiscent of those Czerny studies of distant memory.

Figure 10.16 Studies for beginners

The final example (Figure 10.17) is a Christian hymn, copied on the back of an official papyrus document which was found at Oxyrhynchus in Egypt in 1922.[38] From the form of the writing it has been dated to the latter part of the third century AD, in the twilight of Greek civilization in Egypt. Egon Wellesz, the eminent historian of Byzantine music, regarded it as a transitional piece between the ancient Greek and Byzantine traditions, in which some influence from Syriac music could be detected.[39] West's view, however, is that almost every feature in it can be paralleled from Greek scores of a century or so before, making allowance for the fact that some trends in those documents had been carried further in the intervening years. One device is particularly obvious. For many years long syllables had been freely divided into two shorts on two different notes; now the process can be carried further, so that there are three notes over a single syllable, with a bar above them to show that they total one long (*diseme*, or crotchet). This might look like a triplet, and I have used that in the notation of Mesomedes' hymn to the Sun, but that is because there is no 'slur' on the notes. In this score a slur is placed between the second and third notes (and in one instance between the first and second) to show that they are semiquavers, and should be written as such.

As far as the content is concerned the opening lines, calling upon the forces of the universe to be silent while the poet sings, represent a well-used classical Greek convention.

There are five lines of text with notation. Most of the first line is illegible, and there is a nasty gap in the third line, but the gist of the words may have been as follows:

> [Let us sing to you, Father of worlds and ages, and with us the leading handmaidens of God.] . . . to the presiding Lord of all the stars; let . . . be silent, let the shining stars veil their light, [let the blast of the winds fall calm, and the currents] of foaming rivers, while we sing to the Father, the Son and the Holy Spirit, and let all the powers sing after us 'Amen, Amen'; let power and praise and glory be forever to God, who alone is the giver of all good gifts, Amen, Amen.

This piece of music is in a very real sense both an ending and a beginning. It is probably the latest in date of all the documents with Greek musical notation, and it is also the earliest preserved Christian hymn with a musical score. Perhaps this is an appropriate point at which to take our leave of the music of ancient Greece and Rome.

(One octave lower than written)

Figure 10.17 An early Christian hymn

APPENDIX 1

TECHNICAL ANALYSIS OF GREEK INTERVALS

For the discussion of Greek intervals in Chapter 5 the Aristoxenian method is used, by which they are represented as fractions or multiples of a tone. This has the advantage of being easily understandable, but is not scientifically accurate. The Pythagorean method, representing them as ratios, has the advantage of great accuracy, but the disadvantage that they cannot be added together or subtracted without cumbersome arithmetic. The system of logarithmic cents was designed to overcome this difficulty; any interval can be represented by a single number which, being a logarithm, can be added to or subtracted from another logarithm instead of being multiplied, thus giving us the best of both worlds – we can add and subtract intervals as easily as Aristoxenos, but be as accurate as Pythagoras.

The system of logarithmic cents was designed to deal with the tempered intervals of a modern keyboard instrument. The logarithmic number is adjusted so that the ratio 2:1 (the octave) is represented by 1,200 cents, the tempered fifth by 700, the tempered fourth by 500, the tone by 200 and the semitone by 100. The table opposite gives logarithmic cent values for all the Greek intervals mentioned in Chapter 5 and elsewhere in the book. For anyone who wishes to work out others, the procedure is given on p. 265.

The letters PDF in the second column stand for 'Pythagorean Discord Factor'; this is explained in Chapter 5 (p. 144). It gives a very approximate idea of the degree of discordancy between the two notes bounding the interval. The term 'Pythagorean' in column 5 indicates that these ratios for the intervals are found in any work based exclusively on the three basic concords (octave, fifth and fourth); this includes most of the Pythagoreans (but not Archytas), Plato (e.g. in his *Timaeus*) and those writers who base their calculations on the 'division of the monochord', including Euclid (p. 145).

Note the comparative degrees of discord in the Pythagorean and Archytan versions of the enharmonic tetrachord.

The intervals of Greek music in logarithmic cents

Ratio	PDF	Log. cents	Greek name	Context	Modern name
2:1	1	1,200	dia pason	general	octave
3:1	2	1,902		general	twelfth
3:2	3	702	dia pente	general	fifth (perfect)
4:3	5	498	dia tessarōn	general	fourth (perfect)
4:1	3	2,400	dis dia pasōn	general	double octave
5:4	7	386	ditonon	Archytas' enharmonic	major third
8:7	13	231	1+ $^1/_6$ tones	Archytas' diatonic	septimal tone
9:8	15	204	tonos	general	major tone
10:9	17	182		Ptolemy	minor tone
16:15	29	112	hemitonion	Archytas' enharmonic	major semitone
28:27	53	63	$^1/_3$ tone (diesis)	Archytas, all genera	none
36:35	69	49	diesis	Archytas' enharmonic	none
81:64	143	499	ditonon	Pythagorean	ditone
256:243	497	90	leimma	Pythagorean	semitone

Pythagorean |____?____|____?____|_____|
    < 256:243 [PDF 497] ><—— 81:64 [PDF 143]——>

Archytas |_____|_____|_____|
    < 28:27 >< 36:35 ><———— 5:4 [PDF 7]————>
    [PDF53] [PDF 69]
    < 16:15 [PDF 29] >

Should any reader wish to calculate the cents equivalent for a given ratio, it can be easily done on a pocket calculator, provided that it is a 'scientific' one with a logarithmic function – a key marked 'log 10^x'. The procedure is to divide the larger number of the ratio by the smaller, and take the logarithm of the resulting number. Then, in order to scale it so that an octave is represented by 1,200 cents, the fifth by 700 and so on, the result should be multiplied by a factor of 3,987. If the calculator has brackets, it can be done in a single operation, as follows:

(LN = larger number of ratio, SN = smaller number, ÷ = 'divided by')

[1] log 10^x [2] ([3] LN [4] ÷ [5] SN [6]) [7] × [8] 3,987 [9] = answer.

The answer should be rounded up or down to the nearest whole number. For example, take the 'Pythagorean ditone', in the ratio 81/64:

log. (81/64) = 0.1023, × 3,987 = 407.8902, rounded up to 408 cents.

Or the 'septimal tone' in Archytas' diatonic, ratio 8/7

log. (8/7) = 0.0580, × 3,987 = 231.2139, rounded down to 231 cents.

APPENDIX 2

THE CONSTRUCTION OF THE WATER-ORGAN (*HYDRAULIS*)

This device is described in detail in Book 1, Chapter 42 of the *Pneumatika* by Hero of Alexandria. He lived in the latter part of the first century AD in Alexandria, a century or more after the period of the Ptolemies, but apparently had access to the works of Ktesibios, who is generally believed to have been the original inventor.[1] A more detailed account of Hero's life and work is given in my *Engineering in the Ancient World*.[2]

The account may be paraphrased as follows: the structure is based on a 'small altar' (*bōmiskos*) which is hollow and made of bronze, normally cylindrical and about 3–4 ft (90–120 cm) high and 2ft (60 cm) in diameter. It is filled about half full of water, and a bronze bell is fixed inside, of about the same height but smaller diameter,[3] propped up from

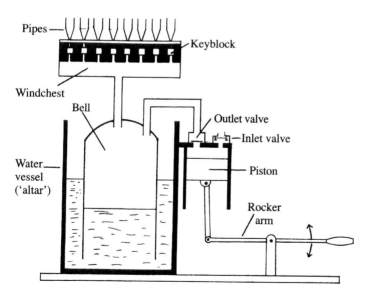

Appendix 2.1 Sectional diagram of the *hydraulis*

267

the base of the 'altar' so that the water can flow back and forth between them. From the top of the bell there are two pipes (made of bronze and soldered into the bell to make them airtight); one bends at right-angles over the top edge of the 'altar' and down into a cylinder; the other rises vertically to the wind-chest.

The cylinder is inverted (i.e. its 'base' is at the top) and inside it is a piston which makes an airtight fit; this was achieved by some skilful lathe-turning. On its lower surface the piston has two ridges with a pin passing through them and through the top end of the driving-rod (the equivalent of the 'little end' in a car engine) so that the rod can move laterally without putting the piston out of line with the cylinder. The lower end of the rod is attached to a rocker-arm which pivots on the top of a post rigidly mounted on the base. A hard-working organ-blower pumps the handle up and down.

On the top of the cylinder are two circular holes. On top of the one furthest from the 'altar' is mounted a round 'pillbox' (*pyxis*) with holes of the same size in its top and base. This forms the inlet valve; a disc, larger than the holes but of slightly smaller diameter than the 'pillbox' is held in position just clear of its upper hole by four pins with large heads. This valve is normally open, but when the piston rises it is closed by the air pressure and the air is forced into the bell.[4] There must also have been a non-return valve to stop the air coming back into the cylinder when the piston was lowered, but Hero does not describe it. This may be because he did not realize that there was one concealed inside another 'pillbox' on the other side of the 'cylinder head'. If it was there, it would have been the same as the other valve, except that the disc did not need to be held in place by pins – it would fall shut by gravity.

When the pump was operated the air in the top of the bell would be compressed, and the water level inside it would fall, while that of the water outside would rise. This would create a reservoir of compressed air, so that although both the supply from the pump and the demand from the organ would fluctuate, the pressure in the bell would stay reasonably constant. (If the organist stopped playing and the blower went on pumping, the air would simply bubble out from under the bell).

The wind-chest (made of wood) extended across the base of the main organ case. Above its 'roof' were a series of square 'pigeon-holes' with round holes in their top and bottom surfaces. The organ pipes, which were of the 'flue' type (see Figure 7.1, p. 167), were fitted into the upper holes, and the lower holes opened into the wind-chest. In each of the 'pigeon-holes' there was a square wooden plug, described as a 'stopper' (*pōma*) or a 'little brick' (*plinthidion*), tight enough to prevent air escaping, but able to slide in and out. Each plug had a vertical hole through it which, when the plug was pushed right into the pigeon-hole, lined up with those in the top and bottom surfaces, and allowed air to pass from the

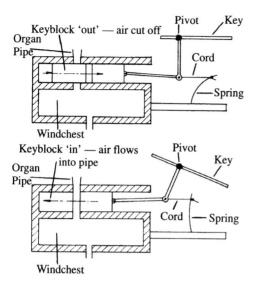

Appendix 2.2 Section through the key-mechanism

wind-chest into the pipe. The movements of the plugs were controlled by the key mechanism.

This consisted of a T-shaped 'key' which pivoted about its top centre, probably on a round metal rod fixed across the instrument at the appropriate height. The lower arm was attached to the near end of the plug with a double pivot, with rods of such a length that when the key was horizontal the plug was pulled out far enough to shut off the air from the pipe. When the key was pressed down it would push the plug in to the back of the pigeon-hole, and the holes would line up, allowing air through to the pipe. In order to stop the pipe sounding when the key was released, a spring, made from a curved strip of animal horn, was fixed in a plank which ran across the front of the wind-chest, and its tip was attached by a length of gut string to the lower end of the key. When the key was depressed, and the plug moved forward into the pigeon-hole, the spring was stretched (i.e. straightened), and drew the plug out again when the key was released. Hero notes that the string should still be taut even then. We do not know the size of the keys – the ancient authors vary between 'using the fingers' and 'using the hands' to press the keys down. Some of the illustrations appear to show instruments with something like 24 pipes across a case less than 3 ft (90 cm) wide; their keys could not have been much wider than those on a modern instrument. (At one point Hero makes a rather disturbing suggestion: '. . . if one *or all* of the keys are pressed. . . .')

Though Vitruvius was writing almost a century before Hero, he describes a slightly more complicated instrument. It has two pumping-cylinders, one either side of the water-vessel (the mosaic picture in Figure 8.15 shows this), and he adds the detail that the pistons should be 'covered with leather and wool' – presumably some kind of washer on the top surface to prevent leakage of air. He gives the measurements of the inlet vents as three *digiti* ($2^1/_6$ in., or 55 mm), which suggests that the diameter of the cylinders was at least 6 in. (15 cm), and probably quite a lot more. The inlet valve is called a 'cymbal', meaning a cone- or dome-shaped stopper which hangs inside the cylinder, held up against the inlet hole by a bronze dolphin which is weighted and pivoted so as to pull on a length of chain attached to the tip of the 'dome'. Like Hero, he fails to mention the non-return valves on the outlets of the cylinders.

Vitruvius seems also to be describing a system of stops, by which air is supplied to, or cut off from, four, six or eight 'ranks' (as we would call them) of pipes. The mechanism is that of a rotary tap, with an 'iron handle' on the end of a thick round rod with holes bored through it which may or may not line up with corresponding holes in the wind-chest. He then describes a key-mechanism similar to Hero's, except that the 'key-block' was apparently quite long (it ran from the front to the rear of the top surface of the wind-chest) and had a row of holes which controlled the air flow to several ranks simultaneously. The ranks were most probably pitched in different keys or octaves, and are likely to have been all of the same (flue) type.

APPENDIX 3

THE BRAURON AULOS

A number of auloi have survived from the ancient world, and have been studied for the information they offer on the construction, range and capabilities of the ancient instrument. Unfortunately, no two of them can confidently be treated as a pair, from which we could derive information on the technique of playing two instruments together. Many of them have appeared at various times on the market without any archaeological find-data from which they might have been dated, and the provenance of many of them is unknown. One very important exception to this is the Brauron aulos, which I was allowed to examine and publish in 1963.[1] It was found in a spring at the north-west corner of the ancient temple of Artemis at Brauron (nowadays called Vravrona) on the east coast of Attica, not very far south from Marathon. It was reliably dated to the late sixth or early fifth century BC, which means that it is one of the earliest surviving instruments, made on the old, simple pattern to play one of the old aulos scales – Lydian, Phrygian or Dorian. The surviving parts are the two lower sections, with fingerholes I, T, II, III, IV and the vent-hole, which can be clearly distinguished by its sharp-cut edge, as it came straight from the drill; the other holes have been hollowed out to fit the player's fingers (see p. 34).

In my initial examination of the instrument and the spacing of its fingerholes, I adopted a mathematical approach which has since been applied to other instruments by a number of scholars. The intervals between the notes can be roughly estimated by the following procedure. We start with the assumption that the interval between two of the holes (say I and II) was a fourth. We can then estimate the length of the portions that are lost – probably two *holmoi* and a short length of reed extrusion – by finding a length which, when added to the length between the top of the surviving part of the instrument and I, and that between the same point and II, will give two lengths which are in the ratio 4:3. Given this incremental distance, we can add it to the other resonant lengths and work out the intervals between them. If they form a pattern which is intelligible in terms of Greek scale-structures, then the initial assumption (that the

271

interval between I and II was a fourth) was probably correct.

This, however, I regarded as a starting-point, and believed that the next step was to make a facsimile of the instrument, and experiment with various reeds to see if in fact it did produce the notes as predicted by the arithmetic. Unfortunately, this process turned out to be something of a will-o'-the-wisp. The trouble is that it is very difficult to find a double reed which is exactly suited to a cylindrical bore of about 10 mm (0.3 in.). If an unsuitable reed (such as a bassoon reed) is used, the pitch of the note from each hole can be varied quite wildly in each direction; in fact, Aristoxenos was perfectly right when he said (see p. 208) that the positioning of the fingerholes does not determine the intervals between them – the manipulation of the fingers and the player's breath control and embouchure are much more important. It would be perfectly possible for an ancient player to achieve perfect intonation, *because he knew exactly what the pitch ought to be*, but without that knowledge we are wandering in the dark.

About ten years ago I began to explore another line of enquiry. It became clear to me that the 'instrumental' notation was closely related to the performance of an aulos. It is a fact that none of the surviving instruments and fragments have holes close enough to give intervals less than a tone; clearly, the smaller intervals (semitones and *dieses*) must have been produced by manipulation, using the fingers and breath control, and that is precisely the indication given by the 'triads' of symbols in three different positions in the 'instrumental' notation (see Chapter 9, p. 209). If so, then the notes from the open fingerholes must have been the 'naturals', which are either 'fixed' notes, which were the notes on which a *pyknon* could be based, and which were considered in later harmonic theory to be the notes bounding the tetrachords, or else what the theorists called *diatonoi*, notes one tone below the 'fixed' notes which were used in diatonic scales. As we have already noted, the older scales 'did not use all the notes', so we might expect to find pairs of fingerholes which would give notes a fourth apart with no intervening holes, but in fact we do not; so it is probable that when Olympos 'passed over the *diatonos*' in the *spondeion* scale (see p. 105) he was deliberately missing out a note which he could have played from an open hole if he had wanted to.

From the procedure which I evolved for examining the intervals it is also possible to assess the actual pitch of the notes from the open holes on surviving auloi. The cylindrical bore of the aulos and the fact that it is effectively closed at the top end (unlike a flute) makes it act as a 'quarter-wave resonator', in which there is maximum variation of the air pressure just inside the reed, and virtually no variation at the lower end. The distance from the reed to that point is therefore a quarter of the total wavelength of the sound, and the pitch of the note at which the pipe resonates can be found by dividing the speed of sound by the wavelength.

The speed of sound in air varies with the temperature of the air; but as this is air (plus some moisture) from the player's lungs, and as the player normally warms up the instrument to that temperature before playing, it can be taken as normally about 18° C (64° F). At that temperature, sound travels at about 34,228 cm (374 yards) per second.

If we then take the measurements of the Brauron aulos from the top of the higher surviving section down to each hole in turn, and add to them a fixed increment (arbitrarily chosen, but reasonable in view of the usual sizes of *holmoi*) of 15 cm (6 in.), we get the following interesting results:

Frequency calculated from resonant length of pipe

Hole	Distance (cm) from top		$^1/_4$ wave	Full wave length	Resonance frequency	Frequency of nearest note	
I	2	+15 =	17	68	504 Hz^2	c″	512 Hz
T	4.9	+15 =	19.9	79.6	430 Hz	a′	432 Hz
II	7.7	+15 =	22.7	90.8	377 Hz	g′	384 Hz
III	10.5	+15 =	25.5	102	335 Hz	f′	341 Hz
IV	13.9	+15 =	28.9	115.6	296 Hz	d′	288 Hz
Vent	18.2	+15 =	33.2	132.8	258 Hz	c′	256 Hz

The fixed increment of 15 cm was just a guess, and it should be remembered that these are purely theoretical figures for the pitches; in performance, the player could easily vary or correct them over a range of at least a semitone in either direction.

The possible implications for the notation are also interesting. It will be remembered that a *pyknon* (a cluster of three notes separated by two small intervals, called *dieses* in Greek) could be played from any of the fingerholes except the top one (I). If we keep to the traditional pitch equivalents, the notation signs for the notes in the table above would extend above the original range of the instrumental signs, which only went up as far as f′ (sign no. 43); but if we assume that a small aulos of this type transposed up an octave, the instrumental signs from no. 13 (c) to no. 34 (c′) could have been used. Each of the 'naturals' has an exact triad (normal position, second position and third position) except the highest (no. 34) which has slightly different signs for the second and third positions. As they would not be required for the Brauron aulos (or any other of that precise size) this may be significant. The table opposite shows the total range of notes potentially available from the instrument; this is of course a 'katapyknotic diagram' (see p. 210), showing a *pyknon* on every note except the highest, and does not represent the notes used for any actual piece of music (see p. 35).

Note raised by two *dieses*	+2d	+2d	+2d	+2d	+2d	
Note raised by one *diesis*	+1d	+1d	+1d	+1d	+1d	
'Natural' note	c′	d′	f′	g′	a′	c″
Fingerhole	Vent	IV	III	II	T	I

It might have been possible to play on this instrument some of the 'very ancient' scales described by Aristides Quintilianus, which he claims were the ones referred to by Plato in the famous passage in the *Republic* (see pp. 103–4). The first on his list is the Lydian (he does not specify which of various different forms). The intervals are in tones or fractions.

|¹/₄| 2 | 1 |¹/₄|¹/₄| 2 |¹/₄|

I have argued in Chapter 3 (p. 104) that this is a version which has been tinkered with by Eratokles in order to make it fit his 'cyclic' system. It seems very unlikely that a scale which had been in common use for many years before would have exhibited such an odd feature as the lone *diesis* at the top and bottom, or such a close resemblance to the 'species of the octave' scales which he devised. If we cancel this 'circulation' of the intervals, we are left with a scale of the form:

|¹/₄ |¹/₄| 2 | 1 | 1 |¹/₄ |¹/₄ | 2 | |

This gives the standard scale of later theory – two enharmonic tetrachords with a disjunctive tone between them. It could have been played on the Brauron aulos, as follows:

¹/₄	¹/₄	2	1	1	¹/₄	¹/₄	2	
c′ +1 +2		f′	g′ +1 +2		c″
Vent	III	II		I

(Holes IV and T might have been partially opened for the *dieses* above c′ and g′.)

The Phrygian scale, as given by Aristides, also covers an octave, and has the following pattern, which could also be played on the same instrument; the Greek notation is given in Figure Appendix 3.1 in the bottom line.

Is either of these scales to be preferred as the 'right' one? I believe so. By the normal perception of a Greek scale, f′ would have been regarded as the keynote (*mesē*) of the Lydian scale, and g′ that of the Phrygian. But in the almost unanimous opinion of the theorists, the Phrygian *tonos*, or key, was a tone lower than the Lydian (see p. 98). So if the Brauron aulos played the Lydian scale it would have been at the wrong pitch in relation to the Phrygian. There is one further telling piece of evidence. When speaking of

	1		¼	¼		2		1		¼	¼		1	
c'		d'	+1	+2		g'		a'	+1	+2			c''
Vent		IV				II		T					I
E		⊢	⊥	⊣		F		C	∪	∩			⌐

Appendix 3.1 The Phrygian *harmonia* played on the Brauron aulos

the confusion which surrounded the number of *tonoi* and their relative pitches, Aristoxenos mentions the arguments used by some musicologists which were based 'on examination of the fingerholes bored in an aulos'. I have already argued (pp. 97–8) that the claim that the keys were 'three *dieses* apart' was based on the aulos-player's view of the matter. Aristoxenos also says[3] that some authorities add below the keys he has just been listing one called the 'Hypophrygian aulos key'; this, by the normal interpretation should mean the key of g, a fourth lower than the Phrygian, whose keynote was c.

May I therefore suggest that the Brauron aulos was a 'Phrygian' aulos, which played in the Phrygian *harmonia* in the Hypophrygian aulos key of g, transposing an octave up from the notation.

NOTES AND SUGGESTED READING

For reasons which have been explained in the preface, a formal bibliography is not included in this volume. Instead, a small number of useful works, all of which are referred to in the text, are listed here. Then, at the head of the notes for each chapter, some works are suggested for follow-up reading.

General works on the subject

For a concise survey, see Winnington-Ingram's article on 'Music in Greece I (ancient)' in the *New Grove Dictionary of Music and Musicians*, Stanley Sadie (ed.) (Macmillan, London 1980).

The most useful and accessible general work on the subject is West, M.L. *Ancient Greek Music* (Clarendon paperbacks, Oxford 1994). It is referred to in the text simply as 'West'.

The references to source material and evidence are almost all to be found in Barker, Andrew, *Greek Musical Writings*, Cambridge University Press: Vol. 1 'The Musician and his Art' (1984) referred to as 'Barker I'; Vol. 2 'Harmonic and Acoustic Theory' (1989) referred to as 'Barker II'.

Another general work on the subject is Anderson, Warren D., *Music and Musicians in Ancient Greece* (Cornell University Press, Ithaca, NY and London 1994).

A useful reference work, which explains the technical terms of Greek music, is Michaelides, Solon, *The Music of Ancient Greece – an encyclopaedia* (Faber and Faber, London 1978).

There are two excellent collections of illustrations in two volumes of the series *Musikgeschichte in Bildern*, ed. H. Besseler and Max Schneider, published by DVfM (Leipzig). They are: Vol. II part 4, *Griechenland*, ed. Max Wegner (1963) referred to as 'Wegner MGB'; and Vol. II part 5, *Etrurien und Rom*, ed. Günter Fleischhauer (1966), referred to as 'Fleischhauer MGB'. They contain excellent reproductions of many illustrations, with introduction and comments (in German).

1 MUSIC IN GREEK LIFE, POETRY AND DRAMA

Suggested reading: Pickard-Cambridge, A.W., *Dithyramb, Tragedy and Comedy*, originally published 1937. 2nd edn, revised by T.B.L. Webster 1962, and again by John Gould and D.M. Lewis (Oxford University Press 1968). This is also called the '2nd edition', which has caused some confusion in libraries.

There is a vast literature on Greek tragedy and comedy; some of the more recent works are marred by various obsessions (notably structuralism and feminism). Two will suffice here, the first being concerned with the theatrical, staging and acting aspects of Greek tragedy: Taplin, Oliver, *Greek Tragedy in Action* (Methuen, London 1978) and on comedy, and Dover, Kenneth, *Aristophanic Comedy* (London 1972).

1   E.g. Berlin black-figure amphora, cat. 1686, and on the Parthenon north frieze. The slab showing the four aulos-players and two of the kithara-players was lost in the explosion of 1687, but the numbers are known from Carrey's drawings; they are referred to as Slab VII figures 20–25. The lower end of the front aulos-player's pipes, and parts of his hands, overlap on to Slab VI (which is in Athens) and badly-damaged parts of the last two kithara-players are on Slab VIII.

2   The Athenian calendar was not properly adapted to the solar year, and required a correction every so often, so that the same date by their reckoning could be some days behind or ahead of ours.

3   Athenaeus, *Deipnosophistae* 617b–e; Barker I pp. 273–274.

4   E.g. the *Thargelia*, a crop-fertility rite in honour of Apollo, and festivals in honour of the craftsmen's deities, Prometheus and Hephaestos.

5   Pausanias X, 7.

6   *Pythian* 1, 1–4.

7   Isthmian 7, 3–4, fr. 61, 6–8.

8   *Olympian* 6, 87–8. There has been some argument recently about the mode of performance; it has been suggested that there was a solo singer and a dancing *choros*. The following articles are relevant: Lefkowitz, Mary R., 'Who sang Pindar's victory odes?' *A.J. Phil.* 109 (1988): 1–11; Heath, Malcolm, 'Receiving the komos – the context and performance of epinician', *A.J. Phil.* 109 (1988): 180–195; Carey, Christopher, 'The victory ode in performance; the case for the chorus', *Classical Philology* 86 (1991): 192–200.

9   E.g. *Pythian* 2, 67–8.

10   *Symp.* 176E.

11   In the Greek text lines 1122–1264; in the Penguin Classics translation by David Barrett, pp. 80–85.

12   Lines 1351–76. The song by Simonides which the son is asked to sing may have been a 'victory ode', but this is no kind of evidence for the normal performance of such a piece.

13   E.g. in Euripides' *Phoenissae* 791, the Argive army is (paradoxically) called 'a band of revellers without an aulos' and in Sophocles' *Oedipus at Colonus* (line 1223) Death is described as 'without lyre or *choros*'.

14   E.g. on the François Vase: see John Boardman, *Athenian Black-Figure Vases* (Thames and Hudson, London 1974) pl. 46 (the neck frieze).

15   Bacchylides fr. 13; when he speaks of its 'song' he is being ironical!

16   Athenaeus 12, 535d.

17   Boardman lists it under the Brygos painter (*Athenian Red-Figure Vases – the Archaic Period*, Thames and Hudson, London 1975) but says on p. 136 'a very late work, if his at all'.

18   See D.L. Page, *Alkman, the Partheneion* (O.U.P., Oxford 1951), esp. pp. 44–69.

19   See Claude Calame, *Les Choeurs de jeunes filles en Grèce archaique* (Rome 1977).

20   D.A. Campbell, *JHS* 84 (1964): pp. 63ff.

21   For example, Euripides' *Andromache* 103–116.

22   Kephisophon, in *Frogs* 1451, and elsewhere.

23   *Poetics* 1449a 10–11.

24   Oxyrhynchus Papyrus 2256, fr. 3.1b. For sensible accounts of the early

stages of drama, see D.W. Lucas, *The Greek Tragic Poets* (2nd edn), Cohen and West, London 1959 or H.D.F. Kitto, *Greek Tragedy* (3rd edn), Barnes and Noble inc., New York 1961.

25 *Poetics* 1449a 18.

26 This is a very common problem in modern productions even when the musical accompaniment is tape-recorded and the volume can be controlled.

27 *Frogs* 939–944.

28 Xenophon (*Symposion* 6,3) speaks of an actor reciting lines in this rhythm to an aulos accompaniment; but he may be talking about something unusual.

2(a) THE AULOS

Kathleen Schlesinger's massive work, *The Greek Aulos* (Methuen, London 1939) is *not* recommended. It contains a vast amount of information (some of it now out of date) on woodwind instruments, but her study of the Greek aulos is vitiated by faulty method.

Baines, Anthony, *Woodwind Instruments and their History* (W.W. Norton, New York 1957) is old-fashioned but very readable and informative.

1 They included Sir John Beazley. He described a vase-painting of an unclothed male aulos-player as 'nude youth fluting'. I have used this memorable phrase as the caption for Figure 2c.2, where it is entirely accurate.

2 The practice seemed to be dying out in the 1980s, but it was saddening to find it back again in *Looking at Greek Vases*, ed. T. Rasmussen and N.J. Spivey, C.U.P., 1991; it makes a nonsense of Mary Beard's interpretation of the symbol on p. 29 of *Looking at Greek Vases* – the lady is not a crypto-shepherdess!

3 In the National Museum, Athens.

4 In the Heraklion Museum, cat. 396. Illustrated in Martin Robertson, *Greek Painting* (Macmillan, London 1978), pp. 26–30.

5 Bk 10, 13 and Bk 18, 495.

6 In Hero's description of the organ (see Appendix 2, Figure Appendix 2.2) the socket into which the key-block slid was called *glottokomeion*.

7 K. Schlesinger, in her formidable work *The Greek Aulos* (Methuen, London 1939, reprinted Groningen 1970) argued that they were replaced by a single reed in the late fifth century, and some other authors who accepted her modal theories (notably N.B. Bodley) have supported this view; but it is not justified by the evidence.

8 The main reed-beds in Southern France were almost destroyed in the Second World War, but have re-grown, and other sources have been found in the U.S.A. and Australia.

9 The Greek word in the MS which I have interpreted as 'the early technique' is not intelligible; some editors think it means 'for purposes of accom‒paniment' (see note 10).

10 I am sure that Barker (I, p. 188 n. 9) is right in interpreting *kataspasmata* in this way. The verb *ischein* need not, as Schlesinger thought, mean 'curb' – it can just mean 'have'.

11 For a detailed discussion, see Barker I, pp. 186–189.

12 Aristoxenos II, 42 (Barker II, p. 158); Plutarch, *Moralia* 948b and 1096a.

13 801b, Barker II, p. 103 and 804a, ibid. p. 108.

14 Porphyrios' commentary on Ptolemy, p. 20 1–2 Düring.

15 *Historia Animalium* (Zoological Researches) 565a23.

16 The top end of the Reading aulos has a flare which could have served this purpose, though it is rather small.

17 See my article, 'A newly-discovered aulos', in the *Annual of the British School at Athens* 63 (1968): 231–238.

18 See my article 'Fragments of auloi found in the Athenian Agora' in *Hesperia* 33: 392–400.

19 The Louvre auloi show signs of shaping, particularly around the thumbholes; this suggests that they did not have keywork, and must therefore have been 'single-pipes' (*monauloi*).

20 Pausanias 9, 12, 5 and Athenaeus 631e; see also ibid., 184d (Barker I, p. 271).

21 The best surviving example of this mechanism is described and illustrated in N.B. Bodley, 'The auloi of Meroe', in *Amer. Journal of Archaeology* 50 (1946): 217–239; it appears in Plates VII and VIII, numbered fragment 14.

22 Simonides fragment 56 (*Poetae Melici Graeci* 947); Plato, *Republic* 399C.

23 Bk 1, ch. 20–1, Barker II, p. 139–140.

24 Plutarch, *Moralia* 1096a, in an essay entitled 'It is not possible to live happily by Epicurus' precepts'.

25 *Harvard Studies in Classical Philology* IV (1893): 1–60.

26 See the article quoted in note 18, Figure 1 A, p. 393, and fragment A in Plate 70.

27 1138a, Barker I, p. 226.

28 Plutarch (?), *Moralia* 853E, in an essay called 'A comparison of Aristophanes and Menander'.

29 The view was first set out by Andrew Barker in a collection of essays (in Italian) – *La Musica in Grecia*, ed. B. Gentili and R. Pretagostini (Laterza, Rome 1988), pp. 96–107. It had been arrived at independently by West (pp. 72–73).

30 I am not able to agree with Annie Bélis in her opinion that the Louvre auloi are a pair (I have argued in note 19 that they are 'single-pipes'). The Elgin auloi may have been a pair, but they have become so badly distorted that measurements are unreliable.

31 Black-figure hydria, British Museum cat. B 300.

32 There is a much-discussed passage in Plato's *Laws* (812 d–e) in which he speaks with disapproval of lyre accompaniments which do not follow exactly the melody and rhythm of the words; but this is probably a matter of ornamentation, not true polyphony.

33 *Histories* I, 17.

2(b) KITHARA AND LYRE

There is an excellent account of these instruments, with copious illustrations, in Maas, Martha and Snyder, Jane M., *Stringed Instruments of Ancient Greece* (Yale University Press, New Haven 1989).

1 In the Heraklion Museum, cat. 396. Illustrated in Martin Robertson, *Greek Painting* (Macmillan, London 1978), pp. 26–30.

2 Max Wegner uses the term 'cradle-kithara' (*Wiegenkithara*), apparently seeing it as a lateral cross-section through the cradle, without baby.

3 Dr Helen Roberts emphasises this in her account of the reconstruction of the lyre (*World Archaeology* 12/3 (1981): 303–312).

4 This question is examined by R.A. Higgins and R.P. Winnington-Ingram, 'Lute-players in Greek Art', *Journal of Hellenic Studies* LXXXV (1965): 69.

5 Book 21, 406–409.
6 Under *kollops* in the Etymologicum Magnum, Scholiast on Aristophanes' *Wasps* 572, etc.
7 852b 11–21.
8 Plato Comicus fr.186K, Eubulus fr.11K and Eustathius s.v.
9 *World Archaeology* 12/3 (1981): 305–308.
10 Scholiast on Aristophanes, *Frogs* 510 and elsewhere.
11 British Museum cat. B 300 – the same vase from which Figure 2a.14 is derived.
12 See the discussion of the *strobilos* on p. 59.
13 Curt Sachs, in his *History of Musical Instruments* (Dent, London 1942) mistakenly thought that *para* could mean 'opposite' in this context (which it does not), and rearranged the strings so as to conform to those on an Egyptian instrument – the perils of comparative musicology!
14 I find it rather hard to accept West's suggestion (p. 68) that dancers might use a lyre or kithara more or less as a percussion instrument of indeterminate pitch.
15 The text in line 1263 reads 'someone plays a *diaulion*'.
16 Lines 1296–7; literally, 'a song to be sung while winding up a bucket from a well'.
17 (Aristophanes, *Clouds* 316–318.) For a discussion of the problems, see E.K. Borthwick, *Classical Quarterly* 9 (1959): 23–29.
18 E.g. *Laws* 812 d–e.
19 *Zeitschrift für Musikwissenschaft* 6 (1924): 289–301.
20 'The pentatonic tuning of the Greek lyre – a theory examined', *Classical Quarterly* N.S. VI (1956): 169–186.
21 *Tonarten und Stimmungen der antiken Musik*, Copenhagen 1939.
22 'Studies in Musical Terminology in fifth-century literature', *Eranos* 43 (1945): 192ff.
23 Ar. *Frogs* 1327 and Scholiast. There was a prostitute called Kyrene who offered her clients a choice of twelve positions; for those inclined to pursue the innuendo further, *harmonia* could mean, or at least suggest, copulation, and the 'five strings' could be a kind of bed.
24 *Imago Musicae* 1 (1984).
25 Aristophanes, *Clouds* 964–965.
26 See Helen Roberts in *World Archaeology* 12/3 (1981) Plate 72 (between pages 242 and 243).
27 Brussels A 1020, Corpus Vasorum Antiquorum Belgium 1, Plate 2 no. 4. The right-hand figure is in West's Plate 23.
28 Fragment 51, quoted by Hippolytus, IX, 9, 1.
29 Fragment 36 Pearson, = 33 N. Compare also Aristophanes, *Frogs* 229–34.

2(c) OTHER INSTRUMENTS

1 *Rep.* 399d7.
2 *Iphigeneia in Aulis* 1036 ff. On the François Vase it is very difficult to see the instrument except in a large-scale reproduction; it is on one of the two friezes immediately below the neck.
3 The question is discussed in detail by M.L. West, 'When is a harp a pan-pipe?' in *Classical Quarterly* 47/1 (1997): 48–55.
4 *Idyll* I,129.
5 E.g. West, p. 93 and Barker II, p. 103 n.17; Anderson rightly disagrees (p. 184).

6　These pipes, from the Castellani Collection and of uncertain provenance, are not generally on display. They are, I believe, a pair of ordinary auloi with bronze outer casings which have been wrongly restored, one with a closed upper end. The miniature maenad busts with holes through them which slant downwards, are in fact fingerholes (II), and not intended for the insertion of a reed. It is obvious at a glance that it would be quite impossible to play either of them transversely, as the fingerholes are in line with the supposed reed-socket, and would be over the player's shoulder. West, on p. 93, falls into this error, which had been castigated by Bodley some years before (*American Journal of Archaeology* 50 (1946): 231 and note 18a).

7　J. van Leeuwen, in his 1901 edition of the play, comment on line 863.

8　In German textbooks, esp. Wegner, it is called 'flat-iron harp' (Bugelhärfe).

9　Compare the volute-krater by the Sisyphus Painter, Munich 3268 (Wegner, *Das Musikleben der Griechen*, pl. 22) and bell-krater Naples 80084, West, Plate 17.

10　A. Barker in Gentili and Pretagostini, pp. 96–107. West (pp. 72–73), *La Musica in Grecia*, agrees.

11　Book 8, ch. 6.

12　See my article 'Ship-shape and Sambuca-fashion', in *Journal of Hellenic Studies* vol. LXXXVI (1966) in which I took into account nautical and military considerations as well as the organological. See also Chapter 2(b) p. 74 and note 27.

13　The painting is reproduced in a number of books on Pompeii; a particularly good specimen is in *Great Treasures of Pompeii and Herculaneum*, ed. T.H. Feder, Abbeville Press (New York 1978), p. 43.

14　'Lute-players in Greek Art', *Journal of Hellenic Studies* 85 (1965): 62–71.

15　Ps.-Aristotle on *Acoustics* 803a (Barker II, p. 106). See also Sophocles, *Electra* 711 (starting a chariot-race), Aeschylus *Eumenides* 566–9 (summoning an assembly) and many other contexts.

16　In a satirical passage in Aristophanes' *Clouds* a 'research assistant' in Socrates' Institute points out that the bore of the trumpet is small until it reaches the bell, at which point it suddenly expands to a much larger diameter, and that this is the point at which the sound is generated (this idea was widely held by acoustical scientists (see p. 139)). He goes on to say that a mosquito's intestine is similarly narrow, with a sudden expansion at its rear end – hence its characteristic noise. A very serious piece of research!

17　In the Eleusis Museum, cat. 907.

18　See Annie Bélis, 'Un nouveau document musical', *Bulletin de Correspondence Hellénique* CVIII (1984): 99–109. See also Barker II, pp. 479–482.

19　*Iliad* 18, 219.

20　*Frogs* 1304–7.

21　See B.M. cat F156, illustrated in Dyfri Williams, *Greek Vases in the British Museum* (B.M. publications 1985) plate 65d, p. 59.

22　E.g. Euripides, *Bacchae* 124–5. It is described as a 'leather-stretching circle'.

23　See Wegner, MGB illustration 33, p. 61.

24　1 Corinthians 13.1.

25　*Das Musikleben der Griechen*, De Gruyter, Berlin 1949.

3 SCALES, INTERVALS AND TUNING

The 'classic' work on this subject was Winnington-Ingram's *Mode in Ancient Greek Music* (Cambridge University Press 1936, reprinted Hakkert, Amsterdam

1968). It still remains valuable, and has not been superseded. There is also a lot of discussion of the scales and intonations in Barker II, particularly in his commentaries on Aristoxenos and Aristides Quintilianus.

1 The 'classic' edition of this work was by H.S. Macran (Oxford 1902) with introduction, Greek text, translation and commentary which is still valuable. For today's readers, however, it is effectively superseded by Andrew Barker's translation with explanatory notes in 'Barker II' (pp. 119–189). Some editors of Aristoxenos have had doubts about the unity of the work, and considered that it may be an amalgamation of two versions, but Annie Bélis argues effectively against this (*Aristoxène de Tarente et Aristote: Le Traité d'harmonique*, Klincksieck, Paris 1986).

2 Bk I ch. 8; Barker II pp. 132–3.

3 Bk I ch. 20; Barker II pp. 139ff.

4 Bk I ch. 20; Barker II p. 139.

5 Ps.-Plutarch *De Musica* 1137b; Barker I, p. 223.

6 For the technically-minded, it is 90 cents, in the ratio 256/243.

7 Bk.1 ch. 23, Barker II pp. 141–142.

8 'Aristoxenos and the intervals of Greek Music', *Classical Quarterly* 26 (1932): 195–208.

9 Barker does not give a full translation of this work – justifiably, since the few significant points in it are discussed elsewhere in his vol. II.

10 *Mode in Ancient Greek Music*, Cambridge U.P., Cambridge 1936.

11 Ps.-Arist. *Probl.* XIX, 20; Barker I p. 195 and XIX, 36; ibid. p. 199.

12 West has an admirably lucid account of the question on pp. 220–224.

13 *Harm.* 2 ch. 37; Barker II p. 153–154. On p. 154 n.33 he has a different explanation.

14 397a–401b, Barker I pp. 130–133.

15 Ps.-Plutarch *De Musica* ch. 16, 1136c, Barker I p. 221.

16 For a review of the list, see West, pp. 177–184.

17 Lines 55–61, 83–87, 126–9, 152–165, etc.

18 Preface to his Teubner edition of 1963.

19 Winnington-Ingram's Teubner text pp. 15–19, Barker II pp. 417–420.

20 Taking Plato's order as 1–6, they appear as 4-5-6-3-1-2.

21 1137b, Barker I pp. 216–218, 223–224.

22 The most detailed examination of the *spondeion* scale is in Winnington-Ingram's article in *Classical Quarterly* 22 (1928): 83. See also Barker I Appendix B pp 255–257.

23 Fr.165K.

24 Bk I, ch. 5, Barker II p. 129.

25 Bk I, ch. 6, Barker II p. 130.

26 The word used is *schema*, but it clearly means the same as *eidos* in the later writers.

27 Bk II ch. 36, Barker II p. 153.

4 MUSIC, WORDS AND RHYTHM

Most of the books on this subject are inclined to be very technical, and date from a time when it was possible to assume a knowledge of Greek on the part of the reader. The best recent introduction to the subject is Laetitia Parker's article 'Metre, Greek' in the new (3rd) edition of the Oxford Classical Dictionary. Martin West's account of the subject is available in three 'packages': (a) Chapter 5 of his *Ancient Greek Music* (pp. 129–159); (b) *Introduction to Greek Metre* (Oxford

1987); or, for those who prefer the 'whole works', (c) *Greek Metre* (Oxford 1982). All of these have full bibliographies.
1   One of the best short accounts is the article 'Greek Dance' by J.W. Fitton, in *Classical Quarterly* 23/2 (1973): 254–274.
2   The invention of the scheme of accents is usually attributed to Aristophanes of Byzantium, one of the eminent scholars who worked in the Museum at Alexandria (see Chapter 7).
3   This is clearly implied in Aristides Quintilianus I,13 (Barker II, p. 434).
4   E.g. West, p. 134.
5   It is known in the technical jargon as 'dactylo-epitrite'.
6   Stelios Psaroudakis composed a 'trireme tune' in this rhythm for the visit of the Greek Navy trireme 'Olympias' to the Thames in 1994, but unfortunately it was not found possible to test its efficacy..
7   R.C.H. Witt, in his Ph.D. thesis *Ethos, rhythm and responsion in the Cantica of Greek Tragedy* (University of Reading, 1973) concluded that 'the tragic ode's passions and rhythms are so implicated in the dramatic fabric as to resist any rigorous theory of associations'.
8   *Frogs* 302–4.

5 MUSIC AND ACOUSTICAL SCIENCE

There is no full-length work devoted to this subject, but there are many useful comments in Barker II, especially pp. 85–109. On the 'scientific' views of the Pythagoreans, see: Guthrie, W.K.C., *A History of Greek Philosophy* Vol. I (Cambridge University Press 1968) and Burkert, W. (trans. E.L. Minar) *Lore and Science in Ancient Pythagoreanism* (Cambridge, Mass. 1972).
1   The most explicit statement of this concept – that numbers can be assigned to pitches – is in the *Division of the Monochord* attributed to Euclid. This is discussed on p. 145.
2   *Harmonics* Bk I ch. 8, Barker II pp. 291–293.
3   E.g. Bk I, ch. 15, Barker II pp. 306–311.
4   *Harmonics* Bk 2, ch 12, Barker II pp. 340–342.
5   *Harmonics* Bk 2, ch. 2, Barker II pp. 319–322.
6   This is established geometrically in Euclid.
7   It was preserved by Porphyrios (late 3rd century AD) in his commentary on Ptolemy's *Harmonics* (pp. 56.5–57.27 Düring, Barker II pp. 39–42).
8   The most cogent arguments in his favour were set out by H.B. Gottschalk in an article 'The De Audibilibus and Peripatetic acoustics', in *Hermes* 96 (1968): 435–60. Barker (II pp. 98–99) feels that the case for Strato is not proven, nor is the case against Aristotle's authorship.
9   See M.R. Cohen and I.E. Drabkin, *A Sourcebook in Greek Science* (McGraw-Hill, London/New York 1948).
10 There is a very good example of this in the *Pneumatica* of Hero of Alexandria; he shows, by means of a carefully devised experiment, that one theory of how a siphon works must be wrong, but later repeats the disproved theory. I have chosen this example because Strato is believed to have devised the excellent experiment (discussed in my *Engineering in the Ancient World* (Constable, London 1997), pp. 192–194), and he may be the author of our present text.
11 This is explained in the introduction to Hero's *Pneumatica*, and put to practical use in the experimental pneumatic catapult; see my *Engineering in the Ancient World* (Constable, London 1997), pp. 128–130.
12 800b, Barker II pp. 100–101.

13 801a, Barker II p. 101 med.
14 See my *Engineering in the Ancient World* ch. 5.
15 *Paraneneurismenon* (Düring's emendation, p. 76). Barker II p. 108 translates 'badly plaited' – not quite the right word.
16 Barker II p. 106 med.
17 801b, Barker II pp. 102–103; Düring p. 71.
18 In the technical language, the reed would be badly mismatched with the acoustical impedance of the resonator.
19 Barker, presumably in answer to this problem, interprets the passage as referring to two different kinds of reed (II p. 103 n.17).
20 *De Audib.* 803b, Barker II p. 107 med.
21 803b2, Barker II p. 106 para. 4.
22 Barker (II p. 107 n.40) takes the speed to be that of transmission through the air, assuming that the author is still maintaining his theory that higher-pitched sounds travel faster. But this seems to me to be inconsistent with the statement that 'the last of the sounds (of the higher note) coincides with that from the slower', since if the higher-pitched sounds travel faster, the gaps between their impacts (what we would call their wavelength) will be longer. In fact, if the speed differential is *pro rata*, and the impacts from a note an octave higher travel twice as fast, the wavelengths of all sounds would be the same, and all their impacts would coincide. Nor is it quite true to say that 'there is *nothing* to suggest that height of pitch is caused or constituted by greater frequency of impact', especially as Barker admits that higher frequency is an inevitable 'secondary effect' of rapid movement. I am inclined rather to agree with Gottschalk (note 8).
23 If, as I believe, this is the correct interpretation, it invalidates some of Ptolemy's criticisms of the theory (14.6 ff., Barker II p. 288 lines 2 ff.).
24 Commentary on Ptolemy's *Harmonics*, Düring p.107.15ff., Barker II pp. 34–35.
25 For a discussion, see Barker II pp. 190–191.
26 It is closely paralleled in Archimedes' treatise on hydrostatics, which starts with 'axioms' about the nature of liquid substances.
27 The early philosopher Anaximenes believed that air was the single physical element from which all the others were created by 'compression' and 'rarefaction'. See Kirk, G.S. and Raven, J.E., *The Pre-Socratic Philosophers* (Cambridge University Press, 1957); 2nd edn revised M. Schofield 1983, p. 144.
28 Barker II p. 197.
29 The proof is that the tone is an 'epimorial' interval, in the ratio $9/8$. To find a mean proportional between 9 and 8 involves dividing the 'monad' or unit by which they are measured, and this is not allowed.

6 MUSIC AND MYTH

A useful and sensible introduction to the subject is: Kirk, G.S., *The Nature of Greek Myths* (Penguin Books, Harmondsworth 1974).

For information on mythical persons and events, Betty Radice's *Who's Who in the Ancient World* (Penguin Books, Harmondsworth 1971) is useful and culturally more wide-ranging than most; see also Grant, Michael and Hazel, John, *Who's Who in Classical Mythology* (Routledge, London 1994).

1 A clear and sensible account can be found in G.S. Kirk, *The Nature of Greek Myths* (Penguin Books, Harmondsworth 1974).

2 The best source for this story is Pindar *Olympian* 7, 45–51.
3 The oldest surviving version of his story is in Homer, *Iliad* VI, 130–140.
4 It covered a large area, part of which is now a frontier province of Greece still called Thrace, together with the portion of modern Turkey to the west of the Dardanelles, and part of Bulgaria.
5 *Georgics* IV, 453–527.
6 Compare the opening passage of Theokritos' *Idyll* 2.
7 Kirk, op.cit. p. 171.
8 Illustrated in a number of books, e.g. J. Boardman, *Greek Art* (London, Thames and Hudson, revised 1973) Plate 5 p.15.
9 Compare Sophocles, *Antigone*, 955–965.
10 N. 24, p. 140.
11 The earliest source for this story is Homer, *Iliad* II, 594–600.
12 Ovid, *Metamorphoses* 10, 78–85.
13 Ps. Plutarch, *De Mus.* 1133f.; Barker I p. 212; Dioscorides, late 3rd c. BC, *Anthologia Palatina* IX, 340.
14 Pausanias X, 30, 8–9.
15 *Symposion* 215 B-C.
16 Quoted in Athenaeus 624b; Barker I p. 281.
17 Barker (I p. 57 n. 10) takes it to refer to the multiplicity of notes it could play – the *polychordia* (see p. 38). This seems to me to be less important in this context.
18 For the details, see the introduction to E.R. Dodds's edition of Euripides *Bacchae* (OUP 1944) pp. xxii–xxxiii.
19 *Moralia* 456B-C; compare also Apollodoros 1, 4, 2, Melanippides fr. 2B; Telestes fr. 2B, and others.
20 Fragment of tragedy by unknown author, Nauck TGF p. 911.
21 Pausanias 1, 24, 1; Telestes in Athenaeus 616f; Barker I p. 273.
22 This relief sculpture is in the National Museum, Athens, cat. Nos 215/6.
23 *Bibliotheca* I, iv, 2, most easily found in the Loeb text vol.1, pp. 29ff.
24 There are a number of representations of Apollo holding his kithara reversed (i.e. back view) – see Higgins and Winnington-Ingram, 'Lute-players in Greek Art', *Journal of Hellenic Studies* LXXXV (1965): 69–70. But I cannot see how this could have any bearing on Marsyas' instrument.
25 Herodotus VII, 26; Plato, *Euthydemus* 285C, etc. Ovid (*Met.* 6, 382–400) goes into gruesome detail, and has Marsyas transformed into a river of that name.
26 Pausanias II, 7, 9.
27 Ovid, *Met.* 11, 1–66.
28 *Rep.* 399E.
29 Pausanias II, 22, 8.
30 *Deipnosophists* 616f.
31 In Aristophanes' *Knights* (985–996) the *choros* relate that Kleon, a turbulent demagogue, when a schoolboy, had always tuned his lyre to the Dorian *harmonia* which is described elsewhere as 'the one our forefathers handed down'. This is probably quite accurate, even though it is introduced for the sake of a terrible pun which follows: the music-teacher expelled him, because he changed over from the 'Greek-Doristian' (*Doristi*) *harmonia* to the 'Grease-my-fistian' (*Dorodokisti*).
32 It has been suggested that the text should read *choroktypos*, which would mean 'causing the *choros* to stamp their feet': see Barker I p. 273 n. 58.
33 Chapter 2, para.1–6: the Greek words are *philoneikon* and *philoproton*.

34 J.Boardman, *Journal of Hellenic Studies* 76 (1956): 18–20.
35 I, 689–712.
36 *De Rerum Natura* V, 1382–1383.

7 THE YEARS BETWEEN – ALEXANDRIA AND SOUTHERN ITALY

Chapters 7 and 8 are very wide-ranging, and there are no books which cover the whole range of either. Perhaps the most useful suggestion would be to consult the Oxford Classical Dictionary under the following entries (among others): Alexandria; Alexandrian Poetry; Theocritus; Comedy, Greek (New); Etruscans; Drama, Roman; Plautus; Terence; Lyric poetry, Latin; Horace; and (needless to say) Nero.

1 E.g. in Plutarch, *Moralia* 56E ('How to tell a Flatterer from a Friend').
2 See Liddell–Scott–Jones, *Greek-English Lexicon*, under 'byblos'.
3 The earliest firm statements that the library or a bookstore was burnt come from Plutarch (late first century AD) in his *Life of Julius Caesar* ch. 49 and Dio Cassius (early third century ad) in Bk 42 ch. 38 of his *History*. Seneca (mid-first century AD) puts in a bid at 400,000, though his nephew Lucan seems not to have known that the fire destroyed any books, and the top bids of 700,000 come from Aulus Gellius (second century AD) and Ammianus Marcellinus (fourth century AD).
4 Theocritus, *Idyll* I, California 3–6.
5 See my *Engineering in the Ancient World* (Constable, London 1997).
6 For examples, see N.B. Bodley, 'The auloi of Meroë', *American Journal of Archaeology* 50 (1946): 217–240, and Annie Bélis, 'Auloi Grecs du Louvre', in *Bulletin de Correspondence Hellénique* CVIII (1984): 111–122.
7 Bodley's suggestion of a single beating reed, like those in the drones of Scottish bagpipes, was based on his acceptance of Schlesinger's theories. She believed that that type of reed (her interpretation of the word *syrinx*) replaced the double reed in the late fifth century, because it was better suited to the modal scales which she favoured. But her whole theory was based on inadequate evidence (and some misinterpretation of it), and cannot be accepted.
8 Barker (I, p. 259) suggests that the *monaulos* may have been the same as the 'reedless aulos', a primitive end-blown flute with a plaintive tone; it is usually mentioned in pastoral contexts, and the speaker in Athenaeus' party, a sophisticated city-dweller, may have despised it as 'rustic'.
9 'Lute-players in Greek Art', *Journal of Hellenic Studies* LXXXV (1965): 69.
10 There is a surprising mistake in footnote 51 of the article just quoted. It is stated that 'the function of the bridge is to keep the strings from contact with the soundbox. If the yoke is brought forward, a bridge is no longer necessary; and it would seem that the former bridge now takes on the function of a tailpiece.' The bridge is always necessary; its function is not to keep the strings from beating against the soundbox, but to convert the variations in their tension into a much amplified movement perpendicular to the sounding-board, and cause a large area of it to vibrate and send out sound-waves. For this to happen there must be a bridge and a tailpiece, and they must be at least an inch or two (2.5–5 cm) apart.
11 *Olympian* 1, 8–17.
12 The quotation is from Letter 7, 326b, which may not have been written by Plato himself, but certainly reflects his feelings.

13 E.g. Aristotle, *Poetics* ch. 3, 1448a29–b3. See D.W. Lucas, *The Greek Tragic Poets* (Cohen and West, London 1959) ch. 2.
14 This is Chapter 7, 'Farce and Tragedy' in *Looking at Greek Vases*, ed. Rasmussen and Spivey (C.U.P. 1991). The vase is illustrated in pl. 66, p.163.

8 THE ROMAN MUSICAL EXPERIENCE

1 Georgics II, 193.
2 Bk 9 ch. 30.
3 Ovid, *Fasti* VI, 654 ff.
4 Ibid., 689–90 . . . *ne forte notentur/contra collegae iussa redisse sui* 'so they should not have their names taken for returning to work without the order from the Union'.
5 The clearest evidence is in Herodotus I, 96.
6 The best example is on the large plate of the 'Mildenhall Collection' in the British Museum.
7 See Fleischhauer MGB pl. 12.
8 In the Tomba dei Relievi in Caere.
9 *Aeneid* VII, 511–515; see my article 'A Hellish Note', *Classical Quarterly* N.S. IX (1958): 219–220.
10 Fleischhauer MGB pl. 15, p. 41.
11 Fleischhauer MGB figs. 41, 43.
12 *Institutio Oratoriae* Bk 10, para. 1–131.
13 There was a story in antiquity that when Livius Andronicus, one of the earliest poets, was getting old, his singing voice failed, and he got a young man to sing for him while he mimed the appropriate actions. But he wrote in other *genres* besides tragedy, and we do not know what kind of work was involved in this episode.
14 *Poetics* 1456 a 29.
15 See E.W. Handley's edition of the play (Methuen, London 1965), pp. 283–5.
16 *Menander and Plautus: a study in comparison* (Lewis, London 1968).
17 Act 1 scene 2, lines 96–157.
18 In Herodotus' account of the emigration of the Etruscans from Asia Minor, he says that they went 'to the territory of the *Ombrikoi*' who must surely be the Umbrians. The Etruscans eventually occupied the corresponding area to the west of the Apennines.
19 It is highly probable that the actors in Atellan plays, like those in the *Commedia dell'Arte*, had a one-page summary of the plot pinned to the scenery, by which they reminded themselves of the next scene as they came on stage. It is the origin of our word 'scenario'.
20 Horace, in *Epistles* II, 1, 170 ff. compares him to a 'Dossennus' – perhaps a hunchback villain – among his 'greedy parasites'. Plautus' middle name, Maccius, sounds suspiciously like Maccus, the buffoon character.
21 *Pro Murena* ch. 12 para. 26.
22 Naples, National Museum cat. 6687, Fleischhauer MGB Plate 52.
23 *De Re Rustica*, I, 2, para. 15–17.
24 For a concise and clear account of their views on science, and those of their rivals the Epicureans, see G.E.R. Lloyd, *Greek Science after Aristotle* ch. 3 (Chatto & Windus, London 1973).
25 Their opinions are preserved in Diogenes Laertius (Bk VII, 158) probably referring to Zeno (333–261 BC) or Chrysippus (282–206 BC), and in more

detail in Plutarch's *Placita Philosophorum* IV, 19, 4 (in Plutarch's text 902B–903A).

26 Barker II p. 99 n.3.

27 A detailed account of this system can be found in my article 'Assisted Resonance in Ancient Theatres', in *Greece and Rome* XIV (1967): 80–94.

28 See Elizabeth Rawson, *Intellectual Life in the Late Roman Republic* (Duckworth, London 1985), especially pp. 168–169. Andrew Wallace-Hadrill, in his review article, is equally dismissive. A.T. Hodge, in *Roman Aqueducts and Water Supply* (Duckworth, London 1992) is even more derogatory, comparing Vitruvius' work to a 'poor undergraduate essay' (p. 15) and seeming to castigate Frontinus for not having used decimals centuries before they were invented (p. 296). This is totally unjustifiable. Unfortunately, the most easily available Latin text of Vitruvius – in the Loeb Classical Library, edited by F. Granger – is not always accurate or reliable.

29 Bk V, ch. 5, § 7. He speaks of many wooden theatres being built in Rome without resonators; for stone theatres one has to look in 'the regions of Italy' (i.e. the Greek cities of the south) or in Greece itself.

30 Strange that Hodge (op. cit. p. 14) should say that Vitruvius never mentions money!

31 *Odes* III, 26.

32 *Odes* IV, 6, 33ff.

33 In conversation, the late Prof. Iain Fletcher told me that the same applied to Swinburne's 'reproductions' of Greek tragedy – *Atalanta in Calydon* and *Erechtheus*.

34 Compare Fleischhauer MGB plate 54, p. 99.

35 *Aeneid* IX, 617–20.

36 Ps.-Aristotle on audible sounds (see pp. 138–144) 800b, Barker II p. 100.

37 Quintilian has some sensible remarks on the subject, *Institutio Oratoriae* Bk 1, ch. 10, 1–33 and elsewhere.

38 Chapters 21–23.

39 Dio Cassius 61, 20, 2.

40 As Robert Graves did in his version (Penguin Books, Harmondsworth 1957).

41 They included the original performance of Aeschylus' *Eumenides* (*Furies*); the entrance of the *choros*, horribly attired, resulted (so the story runs) not merely in premature labour, but induced abortion.

9 NOTATION AND PITCH

For Chapters 9 and 10 I have relied heavily on a German work, Egert Pöhlmann's *Denkmäler altgriechischer Musik* (Hans Carl, Nuremberg 1970). It contains almost all the scores known in 1970, with the Greek notation accurately reproduced and a transcription in modern notation on the facing page. There is also a commentary (in German, of course) on each group of pieces, and notes on the text (*apparatus criticus*, as it is called). A few scores have come to light since then, and are included in West's chapter 10 (pp. 277–326). His transcriptions are based on his theory that the modern equivalents for the Greek signs should be at least a minor third lower than the traditionally accepted ones (which Pöhlmann adopts, and I have followed him), and sometimes even lower.

1 Plutarch, *Life of Nicias* ch. 29.

2 From Plutarch, 'On how to Listen to Poets', *Moralia* 46b.

3 p. 270.
4 I am leaving out of this account a different system of notation, which uses some of the same or similar symbols, which is given in Aristides Quintilianus I, 7 – see Barker II pp. 412–413 and notes. Alypios' scheme has enough problems and more.
5 See West, pp. 260–263.
6 *Philebus* 56a.
7 *Met.* N, 1093b 1–4, translated in Barker II p. 73.
8 The word *nētē* is inserted after 'highest' in some manuscripts of Aristotle's work, but was almost certainly put there by a copyist or editor who believed (wrongly) that Aristotle meant a scale.
9 Most scholars, including Winnington-Ingram and Barker, have taken '24' to be the semitones of a two-octave scale.
10 Bk I, 7; Barker II p. 131.
11 *Republic* 399d; Barker I p. 132.
12 This sign, which Alypios describes as 'O with a line below it' must be distinguished from the obsolete letter koppa (ϙ), which looks very similar, but was used mainly for the numeral 90 after the fifth century.
13 The problems were discussed by Winnington-Ingram in *Philologus* 122 (1978): 241–248.
14 The ratio for the lowest interval is 28/27, or 63 cents, and the central interval is 8/7, or 231 cents.
15 *Harm.* I, 13; Düring pp. 30–31. See the very detailed discussion in Barker II pp. 46–52.

10 SOME SURVIVING SCORES

1 For a discussion, see West pp. 269–273.
2 See Plutarch, *Lives of the Ten Orators* 851E. For a fuller account, see D.L. Page's edition of Euripides' *Medea* (OUP 1952) pp. xxxvii–xli.
3 See Pickard-Cambridge, *Dithyramb, Tragedy and Comedy*, rev. Gould and Lewis (Oxford 1968) pp. 279–321.
4 See Solon Michaelides, *The Music of Ancient Greece* (London, Faber & Faber 1978) pp. 321–323.
5 There is a clause in the Hippocratic Oath which commits the members of the 'medical guild' to share information and make lecture notes etc. available to apprenticed and sworn members, but to no other.
6 See E.G. Turner, *J.H.S.* 76: 95–98.
7 Dittenberger, *Sylloge Inscriptionum Graecarum* 698.
8 See Annie Bélis's article 'A proposito degli Inni Delphici ad Apollo' in *La Musica in Grecia*, ed. B.Gentili and R. Pretagostini (Laterza 1988), pp. 205–218, with photographs.
9 See J.U. Powell, *Collectanea Alexandrina* (OUP 1925), p.173.
10 This was the view taken by Powell, op.cit. and by Pöhlmann in *Denkmäler Altgriechischer Musik* (Nuremberg 1970).
11 See West p. 267.
12 Ibid. pp. 273–276.
13 O (standing for b natural) is also a 'natural' in the Greek notation scheme, and was probably tuned in the sequence of perfect fifths c–g–d–a–e–b.
14 It would be very easy for the stonemason to omit the small dot which distinguishes Θ from O (Athenaios may not have written it very clearly on the papyrus), and that note (Θ, = e′♭) would be acceptable in the context,

provided that the first note in the word (missing from the inscription) was on that pitch or higher.

15 See, for example, John Boardman, *Athenian Red-figure Vases – the Archaic Period* pl. 40.1 (Tarquinia, RC 6843) (Thames and Hudson, London 1975).

16 Aristoxenos, *Harm.* I, 18; Barker II p. 138.

17 The apparent exception in the word *thnatoi-ois* in bar C15 has led editors to amend the text to read a′♭ instead of d′♭.

18 It has already been mentioned that West transposes the score down by a minor third, and then by a further tone, so the highest pitch in his version is e′.

19 There is a difficult problem in bar 103. The note N (= f′)appears once only, in a 'jump' of a ninth from e. Elsewhere f′ is indicated by the symbol for a *diesis* above e′, but here the 'natural' is used, possibly to indicate a different intonation.

20 'Ancient Greek Music', in the *New Oxford History of Music* vol. I, ed. Egon Wellesz (London 1957).

21 I find it strange, therefore, that he includes the Orestes and Iphigeneia fragments, and spends some pages on them, though he argues with great force that they also are late Hellenistic imitations, and cannot be authentic compositions of Euripides.

22 A Greek city in south-west Turkey, now Bodrum.

23 West also mentions (p. 277) a scholium (note by an ancient commentator) on line 176 which asserts that that line was 'sung at a very high pitch'. This is in itself odd, as the *choros* are trying not to wake Orestes; but it does suggest that the ancient commentator (we do not know his name or his date) had a score.

24 Vienna Pap. G2315, Rainer inventory 8029.

25 In the numbering of modern editions, line 339 is before 338.

26 See Pöhlmann p. 81.

27 I have ignored the 'points' (small dots over some letters, which may have indicated *arsis* or *thesis*; see p. 114). They are the subject of much argument, most of which does not help in the re-creation of the music.

28 Including West and Anderson.

29 Pöhlmann reads f♯ and b natural as though it were chromatic.

30 Anderson, pp. 220–222.

31 Leiden Papyrus, inventory no. 510.

32 Several recordings of this fragment have been produced in the last ten years or so, and some of them do not make it absolutely clear that almost 80 per cent of the notes are conjecturally restored.

33 Inventory no. 14897.

34 M.I. Henderson, *New Oxford History of Music* (1957) vol. I p. 370; Anderson, p. 226.

35 I have followed Winnington-Ingram in regarding the note N in the fourth bar as an error for M (stands for c′).

36 p. 308.

37 They are nos. 104, 100 and 98 from Bellermann; nos. 7, 9 and 10 from Pöhlmann (pp. 36–37); and 28, 26 and 24 in West (p. 309).

38 Oxyrhynchus Papyrus 1786; in Pöhlmann pp. 106–109, and in West, p. 324–326.

39 E. Wellesz, 'The earliest example of Christian hymnody', in *Classical Quarterly* 39 (1945): 34–45.

APPENDIX 2: THE CONSTRUCTION OF THE WATER-ORGAN (*HYDRAULIS*)

1 His dates are uncertain, probably third century BC.
2 Constable, London 1997.
3 In order to get the maximum displacement of water, and thus the maximum amount of compressed air, the ratio of the diameters of the 'altar' and the bell should be about 1.4 : 1.
4 In Vitruvius' description (*De Architectura* Bk 10 ch. 8) of a slightly more complicated instrument the inlet valve is held shut by a weighted lever attached to the disc by a chain, and forced open by the air entering the cylinder when the piston is lowered.

APPENDIX 3: THE BRAURON AULOS

1 *Annual of the British School at Athens* 58 (1963): 116–119.
2 In older textbooks this was given in 'v.p.s.' (vibrations per second), and later as 'c/s' (cycles per second); nowadays, in Standard European Jargon it is Hz (Hertz).
3 Chapter 37.22; Barker II p. 153.

INDEX